CLEP-11 COLLEGE-LEVEL EXAMINATION
PROGRAM SERIES

This is your
PASSBOOK for...

College Composition

Test Preparation Study Guide
Questions & Answers

COPYRIGHT NOTICE

This book is SOLELY intended for, is sold ONLY to, and its use is RESTRICTED to individual, bona fide applicants or candidates who qualify by virtue of having seriously filed applications for appropriate license, certificate, professional and/or promotional advancement, higher school matriculation, scholarship, or other legitimate requirements of education and/or governmental authorities.

This book is NOT intended for use, class instruction, tutoring, training, duplication, copying, reprinting, excerption, or adaptation, etc., by:

1) Other publishers
2) Proprietors and/or Instructors of "Coaching" and/or Preparatory Courses
3) Personnel and/or Training Divisions of commercial, industrial, and governmental organizations
4) Schools, colleges, or universities and/or their departments and staffs, including teachers and other personnel
5) Testing Agencies or Bureaus
6) Study groups which seek by the purchase of a single volume to copy and/or duplicate and/or adapt this material for use by the group as a whole without having purchased individual volumes for each of the members of the group
7) Et al.

Such persons would be in violation of appropriate Federal and State statutes.

PROVISION OF LICENSING AGREEMENTS – Recognized educational, commercial, industrial, and governmental institutions and organizations, and others legitimately engaged in educational pursuits, including training, testing, and measurement activities, may address request for a licensing agreement to the copyright owners, who will determine whether, and under what conditions, including fees and charges, the materials in this book may be used them. In other words, a licensing facility exists for the legitimate use of the material in this book on other than an individual basis. However, it is asseverated and affirmed here that the material in this book CANNOT be used without the receipt of the express permission of such a licensing agreement from the Publishers. Inquiries re licensing should be addressed to the company, attention rights and permissions department.

All rights reserved, including the right of reproduction in whole or in part, in any form or by any means, electronic or mechanical, including photocopying, recording, or by any information storage and retrieval system, without permission in writing from the Publisher.

Copyright © 2025 by
National Learning Corporation

212 Michael Drive, Syosset, NY 11791
(516) 921-8888 • www.passbooks.com
E-mail: info@passbooks.com

PASSBOOK® SERIES

THE *PASSBOOK® SERIES* has been created to prepare applicants and candidates for the ultimate academic battlefield – the examination room.

At some time in our lives, each and every one of us may be required to take an examination – for validation, matriculation, admission, qualification, registration, certification, or licensure.

Based on the assumption that every applicant or candidate has met the basic formal educational standards, has taken the required number of courses, and read the necessary texts, the *PASSBOOK® SERIES* furnishes the one special preparation which may assure passing with confidence, instead of failing with insecurity. Examination questions – together with answers – are furnished as the basic vehicle for study so that the mysteries of the examination and its compounding difficulties may be eliminated or diminished by a sure method.

This book is meant to help you pass your examination provided that you qualify and are serious in your objective.

The entire field is reviewed through the huge store of content information which is succinctly presented through a provocative and challenging approach – the question-and-answer method.

A climate of success is established by furnishing the correct answers at the end of each test.

You soon learn to recognize types of questions, forms of questions, and patterns of questioning. You may even begin to anticipate expected outcomes.

You perceive that many questions are repeated or adapted so that you can gain acute insights, which may enable you to score many sure points.

You learn how to confront new questions, or types of questions, and to attack them confidently and work out the correct answers.

You note objectives and emphases, and recognize pitfalls and dangers, so that you may make positive educational adjustments.

Moreover, you are kept fully informed in relation to new concepts, methods, practices, and directions in the field.

You discover that you are actually taking the examination all the time: you are preparing for the examination by "taking" an examination, not by reading extraneous and/or supererogatory textbooks.

In short, this PASSBOOK®, used directedly, should be an important factor in helping you to pass your test.

NONTRADITIONAL EDUCATION

Students returning to school as adults bring more varied experience to their studies than do the teenagers who begin college shortly after graduating from high school. As a result, there are numerous programs for students with nontraditional learning curves. Hundreds of colleges and universities grant degrees to people who cannot attend classes at a regular campus or have already learned what the college is supposed to teach.

You can earn nontraditional education credits in many ways:
- Passing standardized exams
- Demonstrating knowledge gained through experience
- Completing campus-based coursework, and
- Taking courses off campus

Some methods of assessing learning for credit are objective, such as standardized tests. Others are more subjective, such as a review of life experiences.

With some help from four hypothetical characters – Alice, Vin, Lynette, and Jorge – this article describes nontraditional ways of earning educational credit. It begins by describing programs in which you can earn a high school diploma without spending 4 years in a classroom. The college picture is more complicated, so it is presented in two parts: one on gaining credit for what you know through course work or experience, and a second on college degree programs. The final section lists resources for locating more information.

Earning High School Credit

People who were prevented from finishing high school as teenagers have several options if they want to do so as adults. Some major cities have back-to-school programs that allow adults to attend high school classes with current students. But the more practical alternatives for most adults are to take the General Educational Development (GED) tests or to earn a high school diploma by demonstrating their skills or taking correspondence classes.

Of course, these options do not match the experience of staying in high school and graduating with one's friends. But they are viable alternatives for adult learners committed to meeting and, often, continuing their educational goals.

GED Program

Alice quit high school her sophomore year and took a job to help support herself, her younger brother, and their newly widowed mother. Now an adult, she wants to earn her high school diploma – and then go on to college. Because her job as head cook and her family responsibilities keep her busy during the day, she plans to get a high school equivalency diploma. She will study for, and take, the GED tests. Every year, about half a million adults earn their high school credentials this way. A GED diploma is accepted in lieu of a high school one by more than 90 percent of employers, colleges, and universities, so it is a good choice for someone like Alice.

The GED testing program is sponsored by the American Council on Education and State and local education departments. It consists of examinations in five subject areas: Writing, science, mathematics, social studies, and literature and the arts. The tests also measure skills such as analytical ability, problem solving, reading comprehension, and ability to understand and apply information. Most of the questions are multiple choice; the writing test includes an essay section on a topic of general interest.

Eligibility rules for taking the exams vary, but some states require that you must be at least 18. Tests are given in English, Spanish, and French. In addition to standard print, versions in large print, Braille, and audiocassette are also available. Total time allotted for the tests is 7 1/2 hours.

The GED tests are not easy. About one-fourth of those who complete the exams every year do not pass. Passing scores are established by administering the tests to a sample of graduating high school seniors. The minimum standard score is set so that about one-third of graduating seniors would not pass the tests if they took them.

Because of the difficulty of the tests, people need to prepare themselves to take them. Often, they start by taking the Official GED Practice Tests, usually available through a local adult education center. Centers are listed in your phone book's blue pages under "Adult Education," "Continuing Education," or "GED." Adult education centers also have information about GED preparation classes and self-study materials. Classes are generally arranged to accommodate adults' work schedules. National Learning Corporation publishes several study guides that aim to thoroughly prepare test-takers for the GED.

School districts, colleges, adult education centers, and community organizations have information about GED testing schedules and practice tests. For more information, contact them, your nearest GED testing center, or:

GED Testing Service
One Dupont Circle, NW, Suite 250
Washington, DC 20036-1163
1(800) 62-MY GED (626-9433)
(202) 939-9490

Skills Demonstration

Adults who have acquired high school level skills through experience might be eligible for the National External Diploma Program. This alternative to the GED does not involve any direct instruction. Instead, adults seeking a high school diploma must demonstrate mastery of 65 competencies in 8 general areas: Communication; computation; occupational preparedness; and self, social, consumer, scientific, and technological awareness.

Mastery is shown through the completion of the tasks. For example, a participant could prove competency in computation by measuring a room for carpeting, figuring out the amount of carpet needed, and computing the cost.

Before being accepted for the program, adults undergo an evaluation. Tests taken at one of the program's offices measure reading, writing, and mathematics abilities. A take-home segment includes a self-assessment of current skills, an individual skill evaluation, and an occupational interest and aptitude test.

Adults accepted for the program have weekly meetings with an assessor. At the meeting, the assessor reviews the participant's work from the previous week. If the task has not been completed properly, the assessor explains the mistake. Participants continue to correct their errors until they master each competency. A high school diploma is awarded upon proven mastery of all 65 competencies.

Fourteen States and the District of Columbia now offer the External Diploma Program. For more information, contact:
>
> External Diploma Program
> One Dupont Circle, NW, Suite 250
> Washington, DC 20036-1193
> (202) 939-9475

Correspondence and Distance Study

Vin dropped out of high school during his junior year because his family's frequent moves made it difficult for him to continue his studies. He promised himself at the time he dropped out that he would someday finish the courses needed for his diploma. For people like Vin, who prefer to earn a traditional diploma in a nontraditional way, there are about a dozen accredited courses of study for earning a high school diploma by correspondence, or distance study. The programs are either privately run, affiliated with a university, or administered by a State education department.

Distance study diploma programs have no residency requirements, allowing students to continue their studies from almost any location. Depending on the course of study, students need not be enrolled full time and usually have more flexible schedules for finishing their work. Selection of courses ranges from vo-tech to college prep, and some programs place different emphasis on the types of diplomas offered. University affiliated schools, for example, allow qualified students to take college courses along with their high school ones. Students can then apply the college credits toward a degree at that university or transfer them to another institution.

Taking courses by distance study is often more challenging and time consuming than attending classes, especially for adults who have other obligations. Success depends on each student's motivation. Students usually do reading assignments on their own. Written exercises, which they complete and send to an instructor for grading, supplement their reading material.

A list of some accredited high schools that offer diplomas by distance study is available free from the Distance Education and Training Council, formerly known as the National Home Study Council. Request the "DETC Directory of Accredited Institutions" from:

> The Distance Education and Training Council
> 1601 18th Street, NW.
> Washington, DC 20009-2529
> (202) 234-5100

Some publications profiling nontraditional college programs include addresses and descriptions of several high school correspondence ones. See the Resources section at the end of this article for more information.

Getting College Credit For What You Know

Adults can receive college credit for prior coursework, by passing examinations, and documenting experiential learning. With help from a college advisor, nontraditional students should assess their skills, establish their educational goals, and determine the number of college credits they might be eligible for.

Even before you meet with a college advisor, you should collect all your school and training records. Then, make a list of all knowledge and abilities acquired through experience, no matter how irrelevant they seem to your chosen field. Next, determine your educational goals: What specific field do you wish to study? What kind of a degree do you want? Finally, determine how your past work fits into the field of study. Later on, you will evaluate educational programs to find one that's right for you.

People who have complex educational or experiential learning histories might want to have their learning evaluated by the Regents Credit Bank. The Credit Bank, operated by Regents College of the University of the State of New York, allows people to consolidate credits earned through college, experience, or other methods. Special assessments are available for Regents College enrollees whose knowledge in a specific field cannot be adequately evaluated by standardized exams. For more information, contact the Regents Credit Bank at:

Regents College
7 Columbia Circle
Albany, NY 12203-5159
(518) 464-8500

Credit For Prior College Coursework

When Lynette was in college during the 1970s, she attended several different schools and took a variety of courses. She did well in some classes and poorly in others. Now that she is a successful business owner and has more focus, Lynette thinks she should forget about her previous coursework and start from scratch. Instead, she should start from where she is.

Lynette should have all her transcripts sent to the colleges or universities of her choice and let an admissions officer determine which classes are applicable toward a degree. A few credits here and there may not seem like much, but they add up. Even if the subjects do not seem relevant to any major, they might be counted as elective credits toward a degree. And comparing the cost of transcripts with the cost of college courses, it makes sense to spend a few dollars per transcript for a chance to save hundreds, and perhaps thousands, of dollars in books and tuition.

Rules for transferring credits apply to all prior coursework at accredited colleges and universities, whether done on campus or off. Courses completed off campus, often called extended learning, include those available to students through independent study and correspondence. Many schools have extended learning programs; Brigham Young University, for example, offers more than 300 courses through its Department of Independent Study. One type of extended learning is distance learning, a form of correspondence study by technological means such as television, video and audio, CD-ROM, electronic mail, and computer tutorials. See the Resources section at the end of this article for more information about publications available from the National University Continuing Education Association.

Any previously earned college credits should be considered for transfer, no matter what the subject or the grade received. Many schools do not accept the transfer of courses graded below a C or ones taken more than a designated number of years ago. Some colleges and universities also have limits on the number of credits that can be transferred and applied toward a degree. But not all do. For example, Thomas Edison State College, New Jersey's State college for adults, accepts the transfer of all 120 hours of credit required for a baccalaureate degree – provided all the credits are transferred from regionally accredited schools, no more than 80 are at the junior college level, and the student's grades overall and in the field of study average out to C.

To assign credit for prior coursework, most schools require original transcripts. This means you must complete a form or send a written, signed request to have your transcripts released directly to a college or university. Once you have chosen the schools you want to apply to, contact the schools you attended before. Find out how much each transcript costs, and ask them to send your transcripts to the ones you are applying to. Write a letter that includes your name (and names used during attendance, if different) and dates of attendance, along with the names and addresses of the schools to which your transcripts should be sent. Include payment and mail to the registrar at the schools you have attended. The registrar's office will process your request and send an official transcript of your coursework to the colleges or universities you have designated.

Credit For Noncollege Courses

Colleges and universities are not the only ones that offer classes. Volunteer organizations and employers often provide formal training worth college credit. The American Council on Education has two programs that assess thousands of specific courses and make recommendations on the amount of college credit they are worth. Colleges and universities accept the recommendations or use them as guidelines.

One program evaluates educational courses sponsored by government agencies, business and industry, labor unions, and professional and voluntary organizations. It is the Program on Noncollegiate Sponsored Instruction (PONSI). Some of the training seminars Alice has participated in covered topics such as food preparation, kitchen safety, and nutrition. Although she has not yet earned her GED, Alice can earn college credit because of her completion of these formal job-training seminars. The number of credits each seminar is worth does not hinge on Alice's current eligibility for college enrollment.

The other program evaluates courses offered by the Army, Navy, Air Force, Marines, Coast Guard, and Department of Defense. It is the Military Evaluations Program. Jorge has never attended college, but the engineering technology classes he completed as part of his military training are worth college credit. And as an Army veteran, Jorge is eligible for a service that takes the evaluations one step further. The Army/American Council on Education Registry Transcript System (AARTS) will provide Jorge with an individualized transcript of American Council on Education credit recommendations for all courses he completed, the military occupational specialties (MOS's) he held, and examinations he passed while in the Army. All Army and National Guard enlisted personnel and veterans who enlisted after October 1981 are eligible for the transcript. Similar services are being considered by the Navy and Marine Corps.

To obtain a free transcript, see your Army Education Center for a 5454R transcript request form. Include your name, Social Security number, basic active service date, and complete address where you want the transcript sent. Mail your request to:
AARTS Operations Center
415 McPherson Ave.
Fort Leavenworth, KS 66027-1373

Recommendations for PONSI are published in *The National Guide to Educational Credit for Training Programs;* military program recommendations are in *The Guide to the Evaluation of Educational Experiences in the Armed Forces*. See the Resources section at the end of this article for more information about these publications.

Former military personnel who took a foreign language course through the Defense Language Institute may request course transcripts by sending their name, Social Security number, course title, duration of the course, and graduation date to:

Commandant, Defense Language Institute
Attn: ATFL-DAA-AR
Transcripts
Presidio of Monterey
Monterey, CA 93944-5006

Not all of Jorge's and Alice's courses have been assessed by the American Council on Education. Training courses that have no Council credit recommendation should still be assessed by an advisor at the schools they want to attend. Course descriptions, class notes, test scores, and other documentation may be helpful for comparing training courses to their college equivalents. An oral examination or other demonstration of competency might also be required.

There is no guarantee you will receive all the credits you are seeking – but you certainly won't if you make no attempt.

Credit By Examination

Standardized tests are the best-known method of receiving college credit without taking courses. These exams are often taken by high school students seeking advanced placement for college, but they are also available to adult learners. Testing programs and colleges and universities offer exams in a number of subjects. Two U.S. Government institutes have foreign language exams for employees that also may be worth college credit.

It is important to understand that receiving a passing score on these exams does not mean you get college credit automatically. Each school determines which test results it will accept, minimum scores required, how scores are converted for credit, and the amount of credit, if any, to be assigned. Most colleges and universities accept the American Council on Education credit recommendations, published every other year in the 250-page *Guide to Educational Credit by Examination*. For more information, contact:

The American Council on Education
Credit by Examination Program
One Dupont Circle, Suite 250
Washington, DC 20036-1193
(202) 939-9434

Testing programs:

You might know some of the five national testing programs by their acronyms or initials: CLEP, ACT PEP: RCE, DANTES, AP, and NOCTI. (The meanings of these initialisms are explained below.) There is some overlap among programs; for example, four of them have introductory accounting exams. Since you will not be awarded credit more than once for a specific subject, you should carefully evaluate each program for the subject exams you wish to take. And before taking an exam, make sure you will be awarded credit by the college or university you plan to attend.

CLEP (College-Level Examination Program), administered by the College Board, is the most widely accepted of the national testing programs; more than 2,800 accredited schools award credit for passing exam scores. Each test covers material taught in basic

undergraduate courses. There are five general exams – English composition, humanities, college mathematics, natural sciences, and social sciences and history – and many subject exams. Most exams are entirely multiple-choice, but English composition exams may include an essay section. For more information, contact:
>CLEP
>P.O. Box 6600
>Princeton, NJ 08541-6600
>(609) 771-7865

ACT PEP: RCE (American College Testing Proficiency Exam Program: Regents College Examinations) tests are given in 38 subjects within arts and sciences, business, education, and nursing. Each exam is recommended for either lower- or upper-level credit. Exams contain either objective or extended response questions, and are graded according to a standard score, letter grade, or pass/fail. Fees vary, depending on the subject and type of exam. For more information or to request free study guides, contact:
>ACT PEP: Regents College Examinations
>P.O. Box 4014
>Iowa City, IA 52243
>(319) 337-1387
>(New York State residents must contact Regents College directly.)

DANTES (Defense Activity for Nontraditional Education Support) standardized tests are developed by the Educational Testing Service for the Department of Defense. Originally administered only to military personnel, the exams have been available to the public since 1983. About 50 subject tests cover business, mathematics, social science, physical science, humanities, foreign languages, and applied technology. Most of the tests consist entirely of multiple-choice questions. Schools determine their own administering fees and testing schedules. For more information or to request free study sheets, contact:
>DANTES Program Office
>Mail Stop 31-X
>Educational Testing Service
>Princeton, NJ 08541
>1(800) 257-9484

The AP (Advanced Placement) Program is a cooperative effort between secondary schools and colleges and universities. AP exams are developed each year by committees of college and high school faculty appointed by the College Board and assisted by consultants from the Educational Testing Service. Subjects include arts and languages, natural sciences, computer science, social sciences, history, and mathematics. Most tests are 2 or 3 hours long and include both multiple-choice and essay questions. AP courses are available to help students prepare for exams, which are offered in the spring. For more information about the Advanced Placement Program, contact:
>Advanced Placement Services
>P.O. Box 6671
>Princeton, NJ 08541-6671
>(609) 771-7300

NOCTI (National Occupational Competency Testing Institute) assessments are designed for people like Alice, who have vocational-technical skills that cannot be evaluated by other tests. NOCTI assesses competency at two levels: Student/job ready and teacher/experienced worker. Standardized evaluations are available for occupations such as auto-body repair, electronics, mechanical drafting, quantity food preparation, and upholstering. The tests consist of multiple-choice questions and a performance component. Other services include workshops, customized assessments, and pre-testing. For more information, contact:

NOCTI
500 N. Bronson Ave.
Ferris State University
Big Rapids, MI 49307
(616) 796-4699

Colleges and universities:

Many colleges and universities have credit-by-exam programs, through which students earn credit by passing a comprehensive exam for a course offered by the institution. Among the most widely recognized are the programs at Ohio University, the University of North Carolina, Thomas Edison State College, and New York University.

Ohio University offers about 150 examinations for credit. In addition, you may sometimes arrange to take special examinations in non-laboratory courses offered at Ohio University. To take a test for credit, you must enroll in the course. If you plan to transfer the credit earned, you also need written permission from an official at your school. Books and study materials are available, for a cost, through the university. Exams must be taken within 6 months of the enrollment date; most last 3 hours. You may arrange to take the exam off campus if you do not live near the university.

Ohio University is on the quarter-hour system; most courses are worth 4 quarter hours, the equivalent of 3 semester hours. For more information, contact:

Independent Study
Tupper Hall 302
Ohio University
Athens, OH 45701-2979
1(800) 444-2910
(614) 593-2910

The University of North Carolina offers a credit-by-examination option for 140 independent study (correspondence) courses in foreign languages, humanities, social sciences, mathematics, business administration, education, electrical and computer engineering, health administration, and natural sciences. To take an exam, you must request and receive approval from both the course instructor and the independent studies department. Exams must be taken within six months of enrollment, and you may register for no more than two at a time. If you are not near the University's Chapel Hill campus, you may take your exam under supervision at an accredited college, university, community college, or technical institute. For more information, contact:

Independent Studies
CB #1020, The Friday Center
UNC-Chapel Hill
Chapel Hill, NC 27599-1020
1(800) 862-5669 / (919) 962-1134

The Thomas Edison College Examination Program offers more than 50 exams in liberal arts, business, and professional areas. Thomas Edison State College administers tests twice a month in Trenton, New Jersey; however, students may arrange to take their tests with a proctor at any accredited American college or university or U.S. military base. Most of the tests are multiple choice; some also include short answer or essay questions. Time limits range from 90 minutes to 4 hours, depending on the exam. For more information, contact:

Thomas Edison State College
TECEP, Office of Testing and Assessment
101 W. State Street
Trenton, NJ 08608-1176
(609) 633-2844

New York University's Foreign Language Program offers proficiency exams in more than 40 languages, from Albanian to Yiddish. Two exams are available in each language: The 12-point test is equivalent to 4 undergraduate semesters, and the 16-point exam may lead to upper level credit. The tests are given at the university's Foreign Language Department throughout the year.

Proof of foreign language proficiency does not guarantee college credit. Some colleges and universities accept transcripts only for languages commonly taught, such as French and Spanish. Nontraditional programs are more likely than traditional ones to grant credit for proficiency in other languages.

For an informational brochure and registration form for NYU's foreign language proficiency exams, contact:

New York University
Foreign Language Department
48 Cooper Square, Room 107
New York, NY 10003
(212) 998-7030

Government institutes:

The Defense Language Institute and Foreign Service Institute administer foreign language proficiency exams for personnel stationed abroad. Usually, the tests are given at the end of intensive language courses or upon completion of service overseas. But some people – like Jorge, who knows Spanish – speak another language fluently and may be allowed to take a proficiency exam in that language before completing their tour of duty. Contact one of the offices listed below to obtain transcripts of those scores. Proof of proficiency does not guarantee college credit, however, as discussed above.

To request score reports from the Defense Language Institute for Defense Language Proficiency Tests, send your name, Social Security number, language for which you were tested, and, most importantly, when and where you took the exam to:

Commandant, Defense Language Institute
Attn: ATFL-ES-T
DLPT Score Report Request
Presidio of Monterey
Monterey, CA 93944-5006

To request transcripts of scores for Foreign Service Institute exams, send your name, Social Security number, language for which you were tested, and dates or year of exams to:

Foreign Service Institute
Arlington Hall
4020 Arlington Boulevard
Rosslyn, VA 22204-1500
Attn: Testing Office (Send your request to the attention of the testing office of the foreign language in which you were tested)

Credit For Experience

Experiential learning credit may be given for knowledge gained through job responsibilities, personal hobbies, volunteer opportunities, homemaking, and other experiences. Colleges and universities base credit awards on the knowledge you have attained, not for the experience alone. In addition, the knowledge must be college level; not just any learning will do. Throwing horseshoes as a hobby is not likely to be worth college credit. But if you've done research on how and where the sport originated, visited blacksmiths, organized tournaments, and written a column for a trade journal – well, that's a horseshoe of a different color.

Adults attempting to get credit for their experience should be forewarned: Having your experience evaluated for college credit is time-consuming, tedious work – not an easy shortcut for people who want quick-fix college credits. And not all experience, no matter how valuable, is the equivalent of college courses.

Requesting college credit for your experiential learning can be tricky. You should get assistance from a credit evaluations officer at the school you plan to attend, but you should also have a general idea of what your knowledge is worth. A common method for converting knowledge into credit is to use a college catalog. Find course titles and descriptions that match what you have learned through experience, and request the number of credits offered for those courses.

Once you know what credit to ask for, you must usually present your case in writing to officials at the college you plan to attend. The most common form of presenting experiential learning for credit is the portfolio. A portfolio is a written record of your knowledge along with a request for equivalent college credit. It includes an identification and description of the knowledge for which you are requesting credit, an explanatory essay of how the knowledge was gained and how it fits into your educational plans, documentation that you have acquired such knowledge, and a request for college credit. Required elements of a portfolio vary by schools but generally follow those guidelines.

In identifying knowledge you have gained, be specific about exactly what you have learned. For example, it is not enough for Lynette to say she runs a business. She must identify the knowledge she has gained from running it, such as personnel management, tax law, marketing strategy, and inventory review. She must also include brief descriptions about her knowledge of each to support her claims of having those skills.

The essay gives you a chance to relay something about who you are. It should address your educational goals, include relevant autobiographical details, and be well organized, neat, and convey confidence. In his essay, Jorge might first state his goal of becoming an engineer. Then he would explain why he joined the Army, where he got hands-on training and experience in developing and servicing electronic equipment.

This, he would say, led to his hobby of creating remote-controlled model cars, of which he has built 20. His conclusion would highlight his accomplishments and tie them to his desire to become an electronic engineer.

Documentation is evidence that you've learned what you claim to have learned. You can show proof of knowledge in a variety of ways, including audio or video recordings, letters from current or former employers describing your specific duties and job performance, blueprints, photographs or artwork, and transcripts of certifying exams for professional licenses and certification – such as Alice's certification from the American Culinary Federation. Although documentation can take many forms, written proof alone is not always enough. If it is impossible to document your knowledge in writing, find out if your experiential learning can be assessed through supplemental oral exams by a faculty expert.

Earning a College Degree

Nontraditional students often have work, family, and financial obligations that prevent them from quitting their jobs to attend school full time. Can they still meet their educational goals? Yes.

More than 150 accredited colleges and universities have nontraditional bachelor's degree programs that require students to spend little or no time on campus; over 300 others have nontraditional campus-based degree programs. Some of those schools, as well as most junior and community colleges, offer associate's degrees nontraditionally. Each school with a nontraditional course of study determines its own rules for awarding credit for prior coursework, exams, or experience, as discussed previously. Most have charges on top of tuition for providing these special services.

Several publications profile nontraditional degree programs; see the Resources section at the end of this article for more information. To determine which school best fits your academic profile and educational goals, first list your criteria. Then, evaluate nontraditional programs based on their accreditation, features, residency requirements, and expenses. Once you have chosen several schools to explore further, write to them for more information. Detailed explanations of school policies should help you decide which ones you want to apply to.

Get beyond the printed word – especially the glowing words each school writes about itself. Check out the schools you are considering with higher education authorities, alumni, employers, family members, and friends. If possible, visit the campus to talk to students and instructors and sit in on a few classes, even if you will be completing most or all of your work off campus. Ask school officials questions about such things as enrollment numbers, graduation rate, faculty qualifications, and confusing details about the application process or academic policies. After you have thoroughly investigated each prospective college or university, you can make an informed decision about which is right for you.

Accreditation

Accreditation is a process colleges and universities submit to voluntarily for getting their credentials. An accredited school has been investigated and visited by teams of observers and has periodic inspections by a private accrediting agency. The initial review can take two years or more.

Regional agencies accredit entire schools, and professional agencies accredit either specialized schools or departments within schools. Although there are no national accrediting standards, not just any accreditation will do. Countless "accreditation associations" have been invented by schools, many of which have no academic programs and sell phony degrees, to accredit themselves. But 6 regional and about 80 professional accrediting associations in the United States are recognized by the U.S. Department of Education or the Commission on Recognition of Postsecondary Accreditation. When checking accreditation, these are the names to look for. For more information about accreditation and accrediting agencies, contact:

    Institutional Participation Oversight Service Accreditation and State Liaison Division
    U.S. Department of Education
    ROB 3, Room 3915
    600 Independence Ave., SW
    Washington, DC 20202-5244
    (202) 708-7417

Because accreditation is not mandatory, lack of accreditation does not necessarily mean a school or program is bad. Some schools choose not to apply for accreditation, are in the process of applying, or have educational methods too unconventional for an accrediting association's standards. For the nontraditional student, however, earning a degree from a college or university with recognized accreditation is an especially important consideration. Although nontraditional education is becoming more widely accepted, it is not yet mainstream. Employers skeptical of a degree earned in a nontraditional manner are likely to be even less accepting of one from an unaccredited school.

Program Features

Because nontraditional students have diverse educational objectives, nontraditional schools are diverse in what they offer. Some programs are geared toward helping students organize their scattered educational credits to get a degree as quickly as possible. Others cater to those who may have specific credits or experience but need assistance in completing requirements. Whatever your educational profile, you should look for a program that works with you in obtaining your educational goals.

A few nontraditional programs have special admissions policies for adult learners like Alice, who plan to earn their GEDs but want to enroll in college in the meantime. Other features of nontraditional programs include individualized learning agreements, intensive academic counseling, cooperative learning and internship placement, and waiver of some prerequisites or other requirements – as well as college credit for prior coursework, examinations, and experiential learning, all discussed previously.

Lynette, whose primary goal is to finish her degree, wants to earn maximum credits for her business experience. She will look for programs that do not limit the number of credits awarded for equivalency exams and experiential learning. And since well-documented proof of knowledge is essential for earning experiential learning credits, Lynette should make sure the program she chooses provides assistance to students submitting a portfolio.

Jorge, on the other hand, has more credits than he needs in certain areas and is willing to forego some. To become an engineer, he must have a bachelor's degree; but because he is accustomed to hands-on learning, Jorge is interested in getting experience as he gains more technical skills. He will concentrate on finding schools with strong cooperative education, supervised fieldwork, or internship programs.

Residency Requirements

Programs are sometimes deemed nontraditional because of their residency requirements. Many people think of residency for colleges and universities in terms of tuition, with in-state students paying less than out-of-state ones. Residency also may refer to where a student lives, either on or off campus, while attending school.

But in nontraditional education, residency usually refers to how much time students must spend on campus, regardless of whether they attend classes there. In some nontraditional programs, students need not ever step foot on campus. Others require only a very short residency, such as one day or a few weeks. Many schools have standard residency requirements of several semesters but schedule classes for evenings or weekends to accommodate working adults.

Lynette, who previously took courses by independent study, prefers to earn credits by distance study. She will focus on schools that have no residency requirement. Several colleges and universities have nonresident degree completion programs for adults with some college credit. Under the direction of a faculty advisor, students devise a plan for earning their remaining credits. Methods for earning credits include independent study, distance learning, seminars, supervised fieldwork, and group study at arranged sites. Students may have to earn a certain number of credits through the degree-granting institution. But many programs allow students to take courses at accredited schools of their choice for transfer toward their degree.

Alice wants to attend lectures but has an unpredictable schedule. Her best course of action will be to seek out short residency programs that require students to attend seminars once or twice a semester. She can take courses that are televised and videotape them to watch when her schedule permits, with the seminars helping to ensure that she properly completes her coursework. Many colleges and universities with short residency requirements also permit students to earn some credits elsewhere, by whatever means the student chooses.

Some fields of study require classroom instruction. As Jorge will discover, few colleges and universities allow students to earn a bachelor's degree in engineering entirely through independent study. Nontraditional residency programs are designed to accommodate adults' daytime work schedules. Jorge should look for programs offering evening, weekend, summer, and accelerated courses.

Tuition and Other Expenses

The final decisions about which schools Alice, Jorge, and Lynette attend may hinge in large part on a single issue: Cost. And rising tuition is only part of the equation. Beginning with application fees and continuing through graduation fees, college expenses add up.

Traditional and nontraditional students have some expenses in common, such as the cost of books and other materials. Tuition might even be the same for some courses, especially for colleges and universities offering standard ones at unusual times. But for nontraditional programs, students may also pay fees for services such as credit or transcript review, evaluation, advisement, and portfolio assessment.

Students are also responsible for postage and handling or setup expenses for independent study courses, as well as for all examination and transcript fees for transferring credits. Usually, the more nontraditional the program, the more detailed the fees. Some schools charge a yearly enrollment fee rather than tuition for degree completion candidates who want their files to remain active.

Although tuition and fees might seem expensive, most educators tell you not to let money come between you and your educational goals. Talk to someone in the financial aid department of the school you plan to attend or check your library for publications about financial aid sources. The U.S. Department of Education publishes a guide to Federal aid programs such as Pell Grants, student loans, and work-study. To order the free 74-page booklet, *The Student Guide: Financial Aid from the U.S. Department of Education,* contact:

> Federal Student Aid Information Center
> P.O. Box 84
> Washington, DC 20044
> 1 (800) 4FED-AID (433-3243)

Resources

Information on how to earn a high school diploma or college degree without following the usual routes is available from several organizations and in numerous publications. Information on nontraditional graduate degree programs, available for master's through doctoral level, though not discussed in this article, can usually be obtained from the same resources that detail bachelor's degree programs.

National Learning Corporation publishes study guides for all of these exams, for both general examinations and tests in specific subject areas. To order study guides, or to browse their catalog featuring more than 5,000 titles, visit NLC online at www.passbooks.com, or contact them by phone at (800) 632-8888.

Organizations

Adult learners should always contact their local school system, community college, or university to learn about programs that are readily available. The following national organizations can also supply information:

> American Council on Education
> One Dupont Circle
> Washington, DC 20036-1193
> (202) 939-9300

Within the American Council on Education, the Center for Adult Learning and Educational Credentials administers the National External Diploma Program, the GED Program, the Program on Noncollegiate Sponsored Instruction, the Credit by Examination Program, and the Military Evaluations Program.

College-Level Examination Program (CLEP)

1. WHAT IS CLEP?

CLEP stands for the College-Level Examination Program, sponsored by the College Board. It is a national program of credit-by-examination that offers you the opportunity to obtain recognition for college-level achievement. No matter when, where, or how you have learned – by means of formal or informal study – you can take CLEP tests. If the results are acceptable to your college, you can receive credit.

You may not realize it, but you probably know more than your academic record reveals. Each day you, like most people, have an opportunity to learn. In private industry and business, as well as at all levels of government, learning opportunities continually occur. If you read widely or intensively in a particular field, think about what you read, discuss it with your family and friends, you are learning. Or you may be learning on a more formal basis by taking a correspondence course, a television or radio course, a course recorded on tape or cassettes, a course assembled into programmed tests, or a course taught in your community adult school or high school.

No matter how, where, or when you gained your knowledge, you may have the opportunity to receive academic credit for your achievement that can be counted toward an undergraduate degree. The College-Level Examination Program (CLEP) enables colleges to evaluate your achievement and give you credit. A wide range of college-level examinations are offered by CLEP to anyone who wishes to take them. Scores on the tests are reported to you and, if you wish, to a college, employer, or individual.

2. WHAT ARE THE PURPOSES OF THE COLLEGE-LEVEL EXAMINATION PROGRAM?

The basic purpose of the College-Level Examination Program is to enable individuals who have acquired their education in nontraditional ways to demonstrate their academic achievement. It is also intended for use by those in higher education, business, industry, government, and other fields who need a reliable method of assessing a person's educational level.

Recognizing that the real issue is not how a person has acquired his education but what education he has, the College Level Examination Program has been designed to serve a variety of purposes. The basic purpose, as listed above, is to enable those who have reached the college level of education in nontraditional ways to assess the level of their achievement and to use the test results in seeking college credit or placement.

In addition, scores on the tests can be used to validate educational experience obtained at a nonaccredited institution or through noncredit college courses.

Some colleges and universities may use the tests to measure the level of educational achievement of their students, and for various institutional research purposes.

Other colleges and universities may wish to use the tests in the admission, placement, and guidance of students who wish to transfer from one institution to another.

Businesses, industries, governmental agencies, and professional groups now accept the results of these tests as a basis for advancement, eligibility for further training, or professional or semi-professional certification.

Many people are interested in the examination simply to assess their own educational progress and attainment.

The college, university, business, industry, or government agency that adopts the tests in the College-Level Examination Program makes its own decision about how it will use and interpret the test scores. The College Board will provide the tests, score them, and report the results either to the individuals who took the tests or the college or agency that administered them. It does NOT, and cannot, award college credit, certify college equivalency, or make recommendations regarding the standards these institutions should establish for the use of the test results.

Therefore, if you are taking the tests to secure credit from an institution, you should FIRST ascertain whether the college or agency involved will accept the scores. Each institution determines which CLEP tests it will accept for credit and the amount of credit it will award. If you want to take tests for college credit, first call, write, or visit the college you wish to attend to inquire about its policy on CLEP scores, as well as its other admission requirements.

The services of the program are also available to people who have been requested to take the tests by an employer, a professional licensing agency, a certifying agency, or by other groups that recognize college equivalency on the basis of satisfactory CLEP scores. You may, of course, take the tests SOLELY for your own information. If you do, your scores will be reported only to you.

While neither CLEP nor the College Board can evaluate previous credentials or award college credit, you will receive, with your scores, basic information to help you interpret your performance on the tests you have taken.

3. WHAT ARE THE COLLEGE-LEVEL EXAMINATIONS?

In order to meet different kinds of curricular organization and testing needs at colleges and universities, the College-Level Examination Program offers 35 different subject tests falling under five separate general categories: Composition and Literature, Foreign Languages, History and Social Sciences, Science and Mathematics, and Business.

4. WHAT ARE THE SUBJECT EXAMINATIONS?

The 35 CLEP tests offered by the College Board are listed below:

COMPOSITION AND LITERATURE:
- American Literature
- Analyzing and Interpreting Literature
- English Composition
- English Composition with Essay
- English Literature
- Freshman College Composition
- Humanities

FOREIGN LANGUAGES
- French
- German
- Spanish

HISTORY AND SOCIAL SCIENCES
- American Government
- Introduction to Educational Psychology
- History of the United States I: Early Colonization to 1877
- History of the United States II: 1865 to the Present
- Human Growth and Development
- Principles of Macroeconomics
- Principles of Microeconomics
- Introductory Psychology
- Social Sciences and History
- Introductory Sociology
- Western Civilization I: Ancient Near East to 1648
- Western Civilization II: 1648 to the Present

SCIENCE AND MATHEMATICS
- College Algebra
- College Algebra-Trigonometry
- Biology
- Calculus
- Chemistry
- College Mathematics
- Natural Sciences
- Trigonometry
- Precalculus

BUSINESS
- Financial Accounting
- Introductory Business Law
- Information Systems and Computer Applications
- Principles of Management
- Principles of Marketing

CLEP Examinations cover material taught in courses that most students take as requirements in the first two years of college. A college usually grants the same amount of credit to students earning satisfactory scores on the CLEP examination as it grants to students successfully completing the equivalent course.

Many examinations are designed to correspond to one-semester courses; some, however, correspond to full-year or two-year courses.

Each exam is 90 minutes long and, except for English Composition with Essay, is made up primarily of multiple-choice questions. Some tests have several other types of questions besides multiple choice. To see a more detailed description of a particular CLEP exam, visit www.collegeboard.com/clep.

The English Composition with Essay exam is the only exam that includes a required essay. This essay is scored by college English faculty designated by CLEP and does not require an additional fee. However, other Composition and Literature tests offer optional essays, which some college and universities require and some do not. These essays are graded by faculty at the individual institutions that require them and require an additional $10 fee. Contact the particular institution to ask about essay requirements, and check with your test center for further details.

All 35 CLEP examinations are administered on computer. If you are unfamiliar with taking a test on a computer, consult the CLEP Sampler online at www.collegeboard.com/clep. The Sampler contains the same tutorials as the actual exams and helps familiarize you with navigation and how to answer different types of questions.

Points are not deducted for wrong or skipped answers – you receive one point for every correct answer. Therefore it is best that an answer is supplied for each exam question, whether it is a guess or not. The number of correct answers is then converted to a formula score. This formula, or "scaled," score is determined by a statistical process called *equating*, which adjusts for slight differences in difficulty between test forms and ensures that your score does not depend on the specific test form you took or how well others did on the same form. The scaled scores range from 20 to 80 – this is the number that will appear on your score report.

To ensure that you complete all questions in the time allotted, you would probably be wise to skip the more difficult or perplexing questions and return to them later. Although the multiple-choice items in these tests are carefully designed so as not to be tricky, misleading, or ambiguous, on the other hand, they are not all direct questions of factual information. They attempt, in their way, to elicit a response that indicates your knowledge or lack of knowledge of the material in question or your ability or inability to use or interpret a fact or idea. Thus, you should concentrate on answering the questions as they appear to be without attempting to out-guess the testmakers.

5. WHAT ARE THE FEES?

The fee for all CLEP examinations is $55. Optional essays required by some institutions are an additional $10.

6. WHEN ARE THE TESTS GIVEN?

CLEP tests are administered year-round. Consult the CLEP website (www.collegeboard.com/clep) and individual test centers for specific information.

7. WHERE ARE THE TESTS GIVEN?

More than 1,300 test centers are located on college and university campuses throughout the country, and additional centers are being established to meet increased needs. Any accredited collegiate institution with an explicit and publicly available policy of credit by examination can become a CLEP test center. To obtain a list of these centers, visit the CLEP website at www.collegeboard.com/clep.

8. HOW DO I REGISTER FOR THE COLLEGE-LEVEL EXAMINATION PROGRAM?

Contact an individual test center for information regarding registration, scheduling and fees. Registration/admission forms can also be obtained on the CLEP website.

9. MAY I REPEAT THE COLLEGE-LEVEL EXAMINATIONS?

You may repeat any examination providing at least six months have passed since you were last administered this test. If you repeat a test within a period of time less than six months, your scores will be cancelled and your fees forfeited. To repeat a test, check the appropriate space on the registration form.

10. WHEN MAY I EXPECT MY SCORE REPORTS?

With the exception of the English Composition with Essay exam, you should receive your score report instantly once the test is complete.

11. HOW SHOULD I PREPARE FOR THE COLLEGE-LEVEL EXAMINATIONS?

This book has been specifically designed to prepare candidates for these examinations. It will help you to consider, study, and review important content, principles, practices, procedures, problems, and techniques in the form of varied and concrete applications.

12. QUESTIONS AND ANSWERS APPEARING IN THIS PUBLICATION

The College-Level Examinations are offered by the College Board. Since copies of past examinations have not been made available, we have used equivalent materials, including questions and answers, which are highly recommended by us as an appropriate means of preparing for these examinations.

If you need additional information about CLEP Examinations, visit www.collegeboard.com/clep.

THE COLLEGE-LEVEL EXAMINATION PROGRAM

How The Program Works

CLEP examinations are administered at many colleges and universities across the country, and most institutions award college credit to those who do well on them. The examinations provide people who have acquired knowledge outside the usual educational settings the opportunity to show that they have learned college-level material without taking certain college courses.

The CLEP examinations cover material that is taught in introductory-level courses at many colleges and universities. Faculties at individual colleges review the tests to ensure that they cover the important material taught in their courses. Colleges differ in the examinations they accept; some colleges accept only two or three of the examinations while others accept nearly all of them.

Although CLEP is sponsored by the College Board and the examinations are scored by Educational Testing Service (ETS), neither of these organizations can award college credit. Only accredited colleges may grant credit toward a degree. When you take a CLEP examination, you may request that a copy of your score report be sent to the college you are attending or plan to attend. After evaluating your scores, the college will decide whether or not to award you credit for a certain course or courses, or to exempt you from them. If the college gives you credit, it will record the number of credits on your permanent record, thereby indicating that you have completed work equivalent to a course in that subject. If the college decides to grant exemption without giving you credit for a course, you will be permitted to omit a course that would normally be required of you and to take a course of your choice instead.

What the Examinations Are Like

The examinations consist mostly of multiple-choice questions to be answered within a 90-minute time limit. Additional information about each CLEP examination is given in the examination guide and on the CLEP website.

Where To Take the Examinations

CLEP examinations are administered throughout the year at the test centers of approximately 1,300 colleges and universities. On the CLEP website, you will find a list of institutions that award credit for satisfactory scores on CLEP examinations. Some colleges administer CLEP examinations to their own students only. Other institutions administer the tests to anyone who registers to take them. If your college does not administer the tests, contact the test centers in your area for information about its testing schedule.

Once you have been tested, your score report will be available instantly. CLEP scores are kept on file at ETS for 20 years; and during this period, for a small fee, you may have your transcript sent to another college or to anyone else you specify. (Your scores will never be sent to anyone without your approval.)

APPROACHING A COLLEGE ABOUT CLEP

The following sections provide a step-by-step approach to learning about the CLEP policy at a particular college or university. The person or office that can best assist students desiring CLEP credit may have a different title at each institution, but the following guidelines will lead you to information about CLEP at any institution.

Adults returning to college often benefit from special assistance when they approach a college. Opportunities for adults to return to formal learning in the classroom are now widespread, and colleges and universities have worked hard to make this a smooth process for older students. Many colleges have established special service offices that are staffed with trained professionals who understand the kinds of problems facing adults returning to college. If you think you might benefit from such assistance, be sure to find out whether these services are available at your college.

How to Apply for College Credit

STEP 1. Obtain the General Information Catalog and a copy of the CLEP policy from the colleges you are considering. If you have not yet applied for admission, ask for an admissions application form too.

Information about admissions and CLEP policies can be obtained by contacting college admissions offices or finding admissions information on the school websites. Tell the admissions officer that you are a prospective student and that you are interested in applying for admission and CLEP credit. Ask for a copy of the publication in which the college's complete CLEP policy is explained. Also get the name and the telephone number of the person to contact in case you have further questions about CLEP.

At this step, you may wish to obtain information from external degree colleges. Many adults find that such colleges suit their needs exceptionally well.

STEP 2. If you have not already been admitted to the college you are considering, look at its admission requirements for undergraduate students to see if you can qualify.

This is an important step because if you can't get into college, you can't get college credit for CLEP. Nearly all colleges require students to be admitted and to enroll in one or more courses before granting the students CLEP credit.

Virtually all public community colleges and a number of four-year state colleges have open admission policies for in-state students. This usually means that they admit anyone who has graduated from high school or has earned a high school equivalency diploma.

If you think you do not meet the admission requirements, contact the admissions office for an interview with a counselor. Colleges do sometimes make exceptions, particularly for adult applicants. State why you want the interview and ask what documents you should bring with you or send in advance. (These materials may include a high school transcript, transcript of previous college work, completed application for admission, etc.) Make an extra effort to have all the information requested in time for the interview.

During the interview, relax and be yourself. Be prepared to state honestly why you think you are ready and able to do college work. If you have already taken CLEP examinations and scored high enough to earn credit, you have shown that you are able to do college work. Mention this achievement to the admissions counselor because it may increase your chances of being accepted. If you have not taken a CLEP examination, you can still improve your chances of being accepted by describing how your job training or independent study has helped prepare you for college-level work. Tell the counselor what you have learned from your work and personal experiences.

STEP 3. Evaluate the college's CLEP policy.

Typically, a college lists all its academic policies, including CLEP policies, in its general catalog. You will probably find the CLEP policy statement under a heading such as Credit-by-Examination, Advanced Standing, Advanced Placement, or External Degree Program. These sections can usually be found in the front of the catalog.

Many colleges publish their credit-by-examination policies in a separate brochure, which is distributed through the campus testing office, counseling center, admissions office, or registrar's office. If you find a very general policy statement in the college catalog, seek clarification from one of these offices.

Review the material in the section of this guide entitled Questions to Ask About a College's CLEP Policy. Use these guidelines to evaluate the college's CLEP policy. If you have not yet taken a CLEP examination, this evaluation will help you decide which examinations to take and whether or not to take the free-response or essay portion. Because individual colleges have different CLEP policies, a review of several policies may help you decide which college to attend.

STEP 4. If you have not yet applied for admission, do so early.

Most colleges expect you to apply for admission several months before you enroll, and it is essential that you meet the published application deadlines. It takes time to process your application for admission; and if you have yet to take a CLEP examination, it will be some time before the college receives and reviews your score report. You will probably want to take some, if not all, of the CLEP examinations you are interested in before you enroll so you know which courses you need not register for. In fact, some colleges require that all CLEP scores be submitted before a student registers.

Complete all forms and include all documents requested with your application(s) for admission. Normally, an admissions decision cannot be reached until all documents have been submitted and evaluated. Unless told to do so, do not send your CLEP scores until you have been officially admitted.

STEP 5. Arrange to take CLEP examination(s) or to submit your CLEP score(s).

You may want to wait to take your CLEP examinations until you know definitely which college you will be attending. Then you can make sure you are taking tests your college will accept for credit. You will also be able to request that your scores be sent to the college, free of charge, when you take the tests.

If you have already taken CLEP examinations, but did not have a copy of your score report sent to your college, you may request the College Board to send an official transcript at any time for a small fee. Use the Transcript Request Form that was sent to you with your score report. If you do not have the form, you may find it online at www.collegeboard.com/clep.

Your CLEP scores will be evaluated, probably by someone in the admissions office, and sent to the registrar's office to be posted on your permanent record once you are enrolled. Procedures vary from college to college, but the process usually begins in the admissions office.

STEP 6. Ask to receive a written notice of the credit you receive for your CLEP score(s).

A written notice may save you problems later, when you submit your degree plan or file for graduation. In the event that there is a question about whether or not you earned CLEP credit, you will have an official record of what credit was awarded. You may also need this verification of course credit if you go for academic counseling before the credit is posted on your permanent record.

STEP 7. Before you register for courses, seek academic counseling.

A discussion with your academic advisor can prevent you from taking unnecessary courses and can tell you specifically what your CLEP credit will mean to you. This step may be accomplished at the time you enroll. Most colleges have orientation sessions for new students prior to each enrollment period. During orientation, students are usually assigned an academic advisor who then gives them individual help in developing long-range plans and a course schedule for the next semester. In conjunction with this counseling, you may be asked to take some additional tests so that you can be placed at the proper course level.

External Degree Programs

If you have acquired a considerable amount of college-level knowledge through job experience, reading, or noncredit courses, if you have accumulated college credits at a variety of colleges over a period of years, or if you prefer studying on your own rather than in a classroom setting, you may want to investigate the possibility of enrolling in an external degree program. Many colleges offer external degree programs that allow you to earn a degree by passing examinations (including CLEP), transferring credit from other colleges, and demonstrating in other ways that you have satisfied the educational requirements. No classroom attendance is required, and the programs are open to out-of-state candidates as well as residents. Thomas A. Edison State College in New Jersey and Charter Oaks College in Connecticut are fully accredited independent state colleges; the New York program is part of the state university system and is also fully accredited. If you are interested in exploring an external degree, you can write for more information to:

Charter Oak College
The Exchange, Suite 171
270 Farmington Avenue
Farmington, CT 06032-1909

Regents External Degree Program
Cultural Education Center
Empire State Plaza
Albany, New York 12230

Thomas A. Edison State College
101 West State Street
Trenton, New Jersey 08608

Many other colleges also have external degree or weekend programs. While they often require that a number of courses be taken on campus, the external degree programs tend to be more flexible in transferring credit, granting credit-by-examination, and allowing independent study than other traditional programs. When applying to a college, you may wish to ask whether it has an external degree or weekend program.

Questions to Ask About a College's CLEP Policy

Before taking CLEP examinations for the purpose of earning college credit, try to find the answers to these questions:

1. Which CLEP examinations are accepted by this college?

A college may accept some CLEP examinations for credit and not others - possibly not the one you are considering. The English faculty may decide to grant college English credit based on the CLEP English Composition examination, but not on the Freshman College Composition examination. Or, the mathematics faculty may decide to grant credit based on the College Mathematics to non-mathematics majors only, requiring majors to take an examination in algebra, trigonometry, or calculus to earn credit. For these reasons, it is important that you know the specific CLEP tests for which you can receive credit.

2. Does the college require the optional free-response (essay) section as well as the objective portion of the CLEP examination you are considering?

Knowing the answer to this question ahead of time will permit you to schedule the optional essay examination when you register to take your CLEP examination.

3. Is credit granted for specific courses? If so, which ones?

You are likely to find that credit will be granted for specific courses and the course titles will be designated in the college's CLEP policy. It is not necessary, however, that credit be granted for a specific course in order for you to benefit from your CLEP credit. For instance, at many liberal arts colleges, all students must take certain types of courses; these courses may be labeled the core curriculum, general education requirements, distribution requirements, or liberal arts requirements. The requirements are often expressed in terms of credit hours. For example, all students may be required to take at least six hours of humanities, six hours of English, three hours of mathematics, six hours of natural science, and six hours of social science, with no particular courses in these disciplines specified. In these instances, CLEP credit may be given as 6 hrs. English credit or 3 hrs. Math credit without specifying for which English or mathematics courses credit has been awarded. In order to avoid possible disappointment, you should know before taking a CLEP examination what type of credit you can receive and whether you will only be exempted from a required course but receive no credit.

4. How much credit is granted for each examination you are considering, and does the college place a limit on the total amount of CLEP credit you can earn toward your degree?

Not all colleges that grant CLEP credit award the same amount for individual tests. Furthermore, some colleges place a limit on the total amount of credit you can earn through CLEP or other examinations. Other colleges may grant you exemption but no credit toward your degree. Knowing several colleges' policies concerning these issues may help you decide which college you will attend. If you think you are capable of passing a number of CLEP examinations, you may want to attend a college that will allow you to earn credit for all or most of them. For example, the state external degree programs grant credit for most CLEP examinations (and other tests as well).

5. What is the required score for earning CLEP credit for each test you are considering?

Most colleges publish the required scores or percentile ranks for earning CLEP credit in their general catalog or in a brochure. The required score may vary from test to test, so find out the required score for each test you are considering.

6. What is the college's policy regarding prior course work in the subject in which you are considering taking a CLEP test?

Some colleges will not grant credit for a CLEP test if the student has already attempted a college-level course closely aligned with that test. For example, if you successfully completed English 101 or a comparable course on another campus, you will probably not be permitted to receive CLEP credit in that subject, too. Some colleges will not permit you to earn CLEP credit for a course that you failed.

7. Does the college make additional stipulations before credit will be granted?

It is common practice for colleges to award CLEP credit only to their enrolled students. There are other stipulations, however, that vary from college to college. For example, does the college require you to formally apply for or accept CLEP credit by completing and signing a form? Or does the college require you to validate your CLEP score by successfully completing a more advanced course in the subject? Answers to these and other questions will help to smooth the process of earning college credit through CLEP.

The above questions and the discussions that follow them indicate some of the ways in which colleges' CLEP policies can vary. Find out as much as possible about the CLEP policies at the colleges you are interested in so you can choose a college with a policy that is compatible with your educational goals. Once you have selected the college you will attend, you can find out which CLEP examinations your college recognizes and the requirements for earning CLEP credit.

DECIDING WHICH EXAMINATIONS TO TAKE

If You're Taking the Examinations for College Credit or Career Advancement:

Most people who take CLEP examinations do so in order to earn credit for college courses. Others take the examinations in order to qualify for job promotions or for professional certification or licensing. It is vital to most candidates who are taking the tests for any of these reasons that they be well prepared for the tests they are taking so that they can advance as rapidly as possible toward their educational or career goals.

It is usually advisable that those who have limited knowledge in the subjects covered by the tests they are considering enroll in the college courses in which that material is taught. Those who are uncertain about whether or not they know enough about a subject to do well on a particular CLEP test will find the following guidelines helpful.

There is no way to predict if you will pass a particular CLEP examination, but answers to the questions under the seven headings below should give you an indication of whether or not you are likely to succeed.

1. Test Descriptions

Read the description of the test provided. Are you familiar with most of the topics and terminology in the outline?

2. Textbooks

Examine the suggested textbooks and other resource materials following the test descriptions in this guide. Have you recently read one or more of these books, or have you read similar college-level books on this subject? If you have not, read through one or more of the textbooks listed, or through the textbook used for this course at your college. Are you familiar with most of the topics and terminology in the book?

3. Sample Questions

The sample questions provided are intended to be typical of the content and difficulty of the questions on the test. Although they are not an exact miniature of the test, the proportion of the sample questions you can answer correctly should be a rough estimate of the proportion of questions you will be able to answer correctly on the test.

Answer as many of the sample questions for this test as you can. Check your answers against the correct answers. Did you answer more than half the questions correctly?

Because of variations in course content at different institutions, and because questions on CLEP tests vary from easy to difficult - with most being of moderate difficulty - the average student who passes a course in a subject can usually answer correctly about half the questions on the corresponding CLEP examination. Most colleges set their passing scores near this level, but some set them higher. If your college has set its required score above the level required by most colleges, you may need to answer a larger proportion of questions on the test correctly.

4. Previous Study

Have you taken noncredit courses in this subject offered by an adult school or a private school, through correspondence, or in connection with your job? Did you do exceptionally well in this subject in high school, or did you take an honors course in this subject?

5. Experience

Have you learned or used the knowledge or skills included in this test in your job or life experience? For example, if you lived in a Spanish-speaking country and spoke the language for a year or more, you might consider taking the Spanish examination. Or, if you have worked at a job in which you used accounting and finance skills, Principles of Accounting would be a likely test for you to take. Or, if you have read a considerable amount of literature and attended many art exhibits, concerts, and plays, you might expect to do well on the Humanities exam.

6. Other Examinations

Have you done well on other standardized tests in subjects related to the one you want to take? For example, did you score well above average on a portion of a college entrance examination covering similar skills, or did you obtain an exceptionally high score on a high school equivalency test or a licensing examination in this subject? Although such tests do not cover exactly the same material as the CLEP examinations and may be easier, persons who do well on these tests often do well on CLEP examinations, too.

7. Advice

Has a college counselor, professor, or some other professional person familiar with your ability advised you to take a CLEP examination?

If your answer was yes to questions under several of the above headings, you probably have a good chance of passing the CLEP examination you are considering. It is unlikely that you would have acquired sufficient background from experience alone. Learning gained through reading and study is essential, and you will probably find some additional study helpful before taking a CLEP examination.

If You're Taking the Examinations to Prepare for College

Many people entering college, particularly adults returning to college after several years away from formal education, are uncertain about their ability to compete with other college students. They wonder whether they have sufficient background for college study, and those who have been away from formal study for some time wonder whether they have forgotten how to study, how to take tests, and how to write papers. Such people may wish to improve their test-taking and study skills prior to enrolling in courses.

One way to assess your ability to perform at the college level and to improve your test-taking and study skills at the same time is to prepare for and take one or more CLEP examinations. You need not be enrolled in a college to take a CLEP examination, and you may have your scores sent only to yourself and later request that a transcript be sent to a college if you then decide to apply for credit. By reviewing the test descriptions and sample questions, you may find one or several subject areas in which you think you have substantial knowledge. Select one examination, or more if you like, and carefully read at least one of the textbooks listed in the bibliography for the test. By doing this, you will get a better idea of how much you know of what is usually taught in a college-level course in that subject. Study as much material as you can, until you think you have a good grasp of the subject matter. Then take the test at a college in your area. It will be several weeks before you receive your results, and you may wish to begin reviewing for another test in the meantime.

To find out if you are eligible for credit for your CLEP score, you must compare your score with the score required by the college you plan to attend. If you are not yet sure which college you will attend, or whether you will enroll in college at all, you should begin to follow the steps outlined. It is best that you do this before taking a CLEP test, but if you are taking the test only for the experience and to familiarize yourself with college-level material and requirements, you might take the test before you approach a college. Even if the college you decide to attend does not accept the test you took, the experience of taking such a test will enable you to meet with greater confidence the requirements of courses you will take.

You will find information about how to interpret your scores in WHAT YOUR SCORES MEAN, which you will receive with your score report, and which can also be found online at the CLEP website. Many colleges follow the recommendations of the American Council on Education (ACE) for setting their required scores, so you can use this information as a guide in determining how well you did. The ACE recommendations are included in the booklet.

If you do not do well enough on the test to earn college credit, don't be discouraged. Usually, it is the best college students who are exempted from courses or receive credit-by-examination. The fact that you cannot get credit for your score means that you should probably enroll in a college course to learn the material. However, if your score was close to the required score, or if you feel you could do better on a second try or after some additional study, you may retake the test after six months. Do not take it sooner or your score will not be reported and your fee will be forfeited.

If you do earn the score required to earn credit, you will have demonstrated that you already have some college-level knowledge. You will also have a better idea whether you should take additional CLEP examinations. And, what is most important, you can enroll in college with confidence, knowing that you do have the ability to succeed.

PREPARING TO TAKE CLEP EXAMINATIONS

Having made the decision to take one or more CLEP examinations, most people then want to know if it is worthwhile to prepare for them - how much, how long, when, and how should they go about it? The precise answers to these questions vary greatly from individual to individual. However, most candidates find that some type of test preparation is helpful.

Most people who take CLEP examinations do so to show that they have already learned the important material that is taught in a college course. Many of them need only a quick review to assure themselves that they have not forgotten some of what they once studied, and to fill in some of the gaps in their knowledge of the subject. Others feel that they need a thorough review and spend several weeks studying for a test. A few wish to take a CLEP examination as a kind of final examination for independent study of a subject instead of the college course. This last group requires significantly more study than those who only need to review, and they may need some guidance from professors of the subjects they are studying.

The key to how you prepare for CLEP examinations often lies in locating those skills and areas of prior learning in which you are strong and deciding where to focus your energies. Some people may know a great deal about a certain subject area, but may not test well. These individuals would probably be just as concerned about strengthening their test-taking skills as they are about studying for a specific test. Many mental and physical skills are used in preparing for a test. It is important not only to review or study for the examinations, but to make certain that you are alert, relatively free of anxiety, and aware of how to approach standardized tests. Suggestions on developing test-taking skills and preparing psychologically and physically for a test are given. The following section suggests ways of assessing your knowledge of the content of a test and then reviewing and studying the material.

Using This Study Guide

Begin by carefully reading the test description and outline of knowledge and skills required for the examination, if given. As you read through the topics listed there, ask yourself how much you know about each one. Also note the terms, names, and symbols that are mentioned, and ask yourself whether you are familiar with them. This will give you a quick overview of how much you know about the subject. If you are familiar with nearly all the material, you will probably need a minimum of review; however, if less than half of it is familiar, you will probably require substantial study to do well on the test.

If, after reviewing the test description, you find that you need extensive review, delay answering the sample question until you have done some reading in the subject. If you complete them before reviewing the material, you will probably look for the answers as you study, and then they will not be a good assessment of your ability at a later date.

If you think you are familiar with most of the test material, try to answer the sample questions.

Apply the test-taking strategies given. Keeping within the time limit suggested will give you a rough idea of how quickly you should work in order to complete the actual test.

Check your answers against the answer key. If you answered nearly all the questions correctly, you probably do not need to study the subject extensively. If you got about half the questions correct, you ought o review at least one textbook or other suggested materials on the subject. If you answered less than half the questions correctly, you will probably benefit from more extensive reading in the subject and thorough study of one or more textbooks. The textbooks listed are used at many colleges but they are not the only good texts. You will find helpful almost any standard text available to you., such as the textbook used at your college, or earlier editions of texts listed. For some examinations, topic outlines and textbooks may not be available. Take the sample tests in this book and check your answers at the end of each test. Check wrong answers.

Suggestions for Studying

The following suggestions have been gathered from people who have prepared for CLEP examinations or other college-level tests.

1. Define your goals and locate study materials

First, determine your study goals. Set aside a block of time to review the material provided in this book, and then decide which test(s) you will take. Using the suggestions, locate suitable resource materials. If a preparation course is offered by an adult school or college in your area, you might find it helpful to enroll.

2. Find a good place to study

To determine what kind of place you need for studying, ask yourself questions such as: Do I need a quiet place? Does the telephone distract me? Do objects I see in this place remind me of things I should do? Is it too warm? Is it well lit? Am I too comfortable here? Do I have space to spread out my materials? You may find the library more conducive to studying than your home. If you decide to study at home, you might prevent interruptions by other household members by putting a sign on the door of your study room to indicate when you will be available.

3. Schedule time to study

To help you determine where studying best fits into your schedule, try this exercise: Make a list of your daily activities (for example, sleeping, working, and eating) and estimate how many hours per day you spend on each activity. Now, rate all the activities on your list in order of their importance and evaluate your use of time. Often people are astonished at how an average day appears from this perspective. They may discover that they were unaware how large portions of time are spent, or they learn their time can be scheduled in alternative ways. For example, they can remove the least important activities from their day and devote that time to studying or another important activity.

4. Establish a study routine and a set of goals

In order to study effectively, you should establish specific goals and a schedule for accomplishing them. Some people find it helpful to write out a weekly schedule and cross out each study period when it is completed. Others maintain their concentration better by writing down the time when they expect to complete a study task. Most people find short periods of intense study more productive than long stretches of time. For example, they may follow a regular schedule of several 20- or 30-minute study periods with short breaks between them. Some people like to allow themselves rewards as they complete each study goal. It is not essential that you accomplish every goal exactly within your schedule; the point is to be committed to your task.

5. Learn how to take an active role in studying.

If you have not done much studying for some time, you may find it difficult to concentrate at first. Try a method of studying, such as the one outlined below, that will help you concentrate on and remember what you read.

    a. First, read the chapter summary and the introduction. Then you will know what to look for in your reading.

    b. Next, convert the section or paragraph headlines into questions. For example, if you are reading a section entitled, The Causes of the American Revolution, ask yourself: *What were the causes of the American Revolution?* Compose the answer as you read the paragraph. Reading and answering questions aloud will help you understand and remember the material.

c. Take notes on key ideas or concepts as you read. Writing will also help you fix concepts more firmly in your mind. Underlining key ideas or writing notes in your book can be helpful and will be useful for review. Underline only important points. If you underline more than a third of each paragraph, you are probably underlining too much.

d. If there are questions or problems at the end of a chapter, answer or solve them on paper as if you were asked to do them for homework. Mathematics textbooks (and some other books) sometimes include answers to some or all of the exercises. If you have such a book, write your answers before looking at the ones given. When problem-solving is involved, work enough problems to master the required methods and concepts. If you have difficulty with problems, review any sample problems or explanations in the chapter.

e. To retain knowledge, most people have to review the material periodically. If you are preparing for a test over an extended period of time, review key concepts and notes each week or so. Do not wait for weeks to review the material or you will need to relearn much of it.

Psychological and Physical Preparation

Most people feel at least some nervousness before taking a test. Adults who are returning to college may not have taken a test in many years or they may have had little experience with standardized tests. Some younger students, as well, are uncomfortable with testing situations. People who received their education in countries outside the United States may find that many tests given in this country are quite different from the ones they are accustomed to taking.

Not only might candidates find the types of tests and the kinds of questions on them unfamiliar, but other aspects of the testing environment may be strange as well. The physical and mental stress that results from meeting this new experience can hinder a candidate's ability to demonstrate his or her true degree of knowledge in the subject area being tested. For this reason, it is important to go to the test center well prepared, both mentally and physically, for taking the test. You may find the following suggestions helpful.

1. Familiarize yourself, as much as possible, with the test and the test situation before the day of the examination. It will be helpful for you to know ahead of time:

a. How much time will be allowed for the test and whether there are timed subsections.

b. What types of questions and directions appear on the examination.

c. How your test score will be computed.

d. How to properly answer the questions on the computer (See the CLEP Sample on the CLEP website)

e. In which building and room the examination will be administered. If you don't know where the building is, locate it or get directions ahead of time.

f. The time of the test administration. You might wish to confirm this information a day or two before the examination and find out what time the building and room will be open so that you can plan to arrive early.

g. Where to park your car or, if you wish to take public transportation, which bus or train to take and the location of the nearest stop.

h. Whether smoking will be permitted during the test.

i. Whether there will be a break between examinations (if you will be taking more than one on the same day), and whether there is a place nearby where you can get something to eat or drink.

2. Go to the test situation relaxed and alert. In order to prepare for the test:

a. Get a good night's sleep. Last minute cramming, particularly late the night before, is usually counterproductive.

b. Eat normally. It is usually not wise to skip breakfast or lunch on the day of the test or to eat a big meal just before the test.

c. Avoid tranquilizers and stimulants. If you follow the other directions in this book, you won't need artificial aids. It's better to be a little tense than to be drowsy, but stimulants such as coffee and cola can make you nervous and interfere with your concentration.

d. Don't drink a lot of liquids before the test. Having to leave the room during the test will disturb your concentration and take valuable time away from the test.

e. If you are inclined to be nervous or tense, learn some relaxation exercises and use them before and perhaps during the test.

3. Arrive for the test early and prepared. Be sure to:

a. Arrive early enough so that you can find a parking place, locate the test center, and get settled comfortably before testing begins. Allow some extra time in case you are delayed unexpectedly.

b. Take the following with you:

- Your completed Registration/Admission Form
- Two forms of identification – one being a government-issued photo ID with signature, such as a driver's license or passport
- Non-mechanical pencil
- A watch so that you can time your progress (digital watches are prohibited)
- Your glasses if you need them for reading or seeing the chalkboard or wall clock

c. Leave all books, papers, and notes outside the test center. You will not be permitted to use your own scratch paper; it will be provided. Also prohibited are calculators, cell phones, beepers, pagers, photo/copy devices, radios, headphones, food, beverages, and several other items.

d. Be prepared for any temperature in the testing room. Wear layers of clothing that can be removed if the room is too hot but will keep you warm if it is too cold.

4. When you enter the test room:

a. Sit in a seat that provides a maximum of comfort and freedom from distraction.

b. Read directions carefully, and listen to all instructions given by the test administrator. If you don't understand the directions, ask for help before test timing begins. If you must ask a question after the test has begun, raise your hand and a proctor will assist you. The proctor can answer certain kinds of questions but cannot help you with the test.

c. Know your rights as a test taker. You can expect to be given the full working time allowed for the test(s) and a reasonably quiet and comfortable place in which to work. If a poor test situation is preventing you from doing your best, ask if the situation can be remedied. If bad test conditions cannot be remedied, ask the person in charge to report the problem in the Irregularity Report that will be sent to ETS with the answer sheets. You may also wish to contact CLEP. Describe the exact circumstances as completely as you can. Be sure to include the test date and name(s) of the test(s) you took. ETS will investigate the problem to make sure it does not happen again, and, if the problem is serious enough, may arrange for you to retake the test without charge.

TAKING THE EXAMINATIONS

A person may know a great deal about the subject being tested, but not do as well as he or she is capable of on the test. Knowing how to approach a test is an important part of the testing process. While a command of test-taking skills cannot substitute for knowledge of the subject matter, it can be a significant factor in successful testing.

Test-taking skills enable a person to use all available information to earn a score that truly reflects his or her ability. There are different strategies for approaching different kinds of test questions. For example, free-response questions require a very different tack than do multiple-choice questions. Other factors, such as how the test will be graded, may also influence your approach to the test and your use of test time. Thus, your preparation for a test should include finding out all you can about the test so that you can use the most effective test-taking strategies.

Before taking a test, you should know approximately how many questions are on the test, how much time you will be allowed, how the test will be scored or graded, what types of questions and directions are on the test, and how you will be required to record your answers.

Taking Multiple-Choice Tests

1. Listen carefully to the instructions given by the test administrator and read carefully all directions before you begin to answer the questions.

2. Note the time that the test administrator starts timing the test. As you proceed, make sure that you are not working too slowly. You should have answered at least half the questions in a section when half the time for that section has passed. If you have not reached that point in the section, speed up your pace on the remaining questions.

3. Before answering a question, read the entire question, including all the answer choices. Don't think that because the first or second answer choice looks good to you, it isn't necessary to read the remaining options. Instructions usually tell you to select the best answer. Sometimes one answer choice is partially correct, but another option is better; therefore, it is usually a good idea to read all the answers before you choose one.

4. Read and consider every question. Questions that look complicated at first glance may not actually be so difficult once you have read them carefully.

5. Do not puzzle too long over any one question. If you don't know the answer after you've considered it briefly, go on to the next question. Make sure you return to the question later.

6. Make sure you record your response properly.

7. In trying to determine the correct answer, you may find it helpful to cross out those options that you know are incorrect, and to make marks next to those you think might be correct. If you decide to skip the question and come back to it later, you will save yourself the time of reconsidering all the options.

8. Watch for the following key words in test questions:

all	generally	never	perhaps
always	however	none	rarely
but	may	not	seldom
except	must	often	sometimes
every	necessary	only	usually

When a question or answer option contains words such as always, every, only, never, and none, there can be no exceptions to the answer you choose. Use of words such as often, rarely, sometimes, and generally indicates that there may be some exceptions to the answer.

9. Do not waste your time looking for clues to right answers based on flaws in question wording or patterns in correct answers. Professionals at the College Board and ETS put

a great deal of effort into developing valid, reliable, fair tests. CLEP test development committees are composed of college faculty who are experts in the subject covered by the test and are appointed by the College Board to write test questions and to scrutinize each question that is included on a CLEP test. Committee members make every effort to ensure that the questions are not ambiguous, that they have only one correct answer, and that they cover college-level topics. These committees do not intentionally include trick questions. If you think a question is flawed, ask the test administrator to report it, or contact CLEP immediately.

Taking Free-Response or Essay Tests

If your college requires the optional free-response or essay portion of a CLEP Composition and Literature exams, you should do some additional preparation for your CLEP test. Taking an essay test is very different from taking a multiple-choice test, so you will need to use some other strategies.

The essay written as part of the English Composition and Essay exam is graded by English professors from a variety of colleges and universities. A process called holistic scoring is used to rate your writing ability.

The optional free-response essays, on the other hand, are graded by the faculty of the college you designate as a score recipient. Guidelines and criteria for grading essays are not specified by the College Board or ETS. You may find it helpful, therefore, to talk with someone at your college to find out what criteria will be used to determine whether you will get credit. If the test requires essay responses, ask how much emphasis will be placed on your writing ability and your ability to organize your thoughts as opposed to your knowledge of subject matter. Find out how much weight will be given to your multiple-choice test score in comparison with your free-response grade in determining whether you will get credit. This will give you an idea where you should expend the greatest effort in preparing for and taking the test.

Here are some strategies you will find useful in taking any essay test:

1. Before you begin to write, read all questions carefully and take a few minutes to jot down some ideas you might include in each answer.

2. If you are given a choice of questions to answer, choose the questions you think you can answer most clearly and knowledgeably.

3. Determine in what order you will answer the questions. Answer those you find the easiest first so that any extra time can be spent on the more difficult questions.

4. When you know which questions you will answer and in what order, determine how much testing time remains and estimate how many minutes you will devote to each question. Unless suggested times are given for the questions or one question appears to require more or less time than the others, allot an equal amount of time to each question.

5. Before answering each question, indicate the number of the question as it is given in the test book. You need not copy the entire question from the question sheet, but it will be helpful to you and to the person grading your test if you indicate briefly the topic you are addressing – particularly if you are not answering the questions in the order in which they appear on the test.

6. Before answering each question, read it again carefully to make sure you are interpreting it correctly. Underline key words, such as those listed below, that often appear in free-response questions. Be sure you know the exact meaning of these words before taking the test.

analyze	demonstrate	enumerate	list
apply	derive	explain	outline
assess	describe	generalize	prove
compare	determine	illustrate	rank
contrast	discuss	interpret	show
define	distinguish	justify	summarize

If a question asks you to outline, define, or summarize, do not write a detailed explanation; if a question asks you to analyze, explain, illustrate, interpret, or show, you must do more than briefly describe the topic.

For a current listing of CLEP Colleges

where you can get credit and be tested, write:

CLEP, P.O. Box 6600, Princeton, NJ 08541-6600

Or e-mail: clep@ets.org, or call: (609) 771-7865

COLLEGE COMPOSITION MODULAR

CLEP introduced two new exams — College Composition and College Composition Modular. These exams replaced three current exams, which have been discontinued:

- English Composition has been replaced by College Composition Modular.
- English Composition with Essay has been replaced by College Composition.
- Freshman College Composition has been replaced by College Composition Modular.

Each college decides its own policy for the new exams, so check with your admissions office, test center, or academic adviser before taking a test.

Description of the Examination

The CLEP College Composition examinations assess writing skills taught in most first-year college composition courses. Those skills include analysis, argumentation, synthesis, usage, ability to recognize logical development and research. The exams cannot cover every skill (such as keeping a journal or peer editing) required in many first-year college writing courses. Candidates will, however, be expected to apply the principles and conventions used in longer writing projects to two timed writing assignments and to apply the rules of standard written English.

College Composition Modular contains a multiple-choice section that is supplemented with an essay section that is either provided and scored by the college or provided by CLEP and scored by the college. College Composition Modular is available for colleges that want a valid, reliable multiple-choice assessment and greater local control over the direct writing assessment. College Composition Modular contains approximately 90 questions to be answered in 90 minutes and, if the essay section provided by CLEP is chosen, two essays to be written in 70 minutes. Some colleges may opt to provide their own locally scored writing assessment or some other assessment or evaluation.

The exam includes some pretest multiple-choice questions that will not be counted toward the candidate's score.

Colleges set their own credit-granting policies and therefore differ with regard to their acceptance of the College Composition examinations. Most colleges will grant course credit for a first-year composition or English course that emphasizes expository writing; others will grant credit toward satisfying a liberal arts or distribution requirement in English.

The American Council on Education's College Credit Recommendation Service (ACE CREDIT) recommends the awarding of three credit hours or the equivalent for a score of 50 on the 90 minute multiple-choice College Composition Modular exam. If colleges elect to supplement the Modular version of the examination with an essay available from CLEP or with a writing assessment of their own, the credit recommendation is six credit hours, or the equivalent, for a score of 50.

Knowledge and Skills Required

The exam measures candidates' knowledge of the fundamental principles of rhetoric and composition and their ability to apply the principles of standard written English. In addition, the exam requires familiarity with research and reference skills. In one of the essays, candidates must develop a position by building an argument in which they synthesize information from two provided sources, which they must cite. The requirement that candidates cite the sources they use reflects the recognition of source attribution as an essential skill in college writing courses.

College Composition Modular

College Composition Modular allows institutions to administer and/or score test takers' essays themselves. The knowledge and skills assessed are the same as those measured by College Composition, but the format and timing allow a more extended indirect assessment of test-takers' knowledge and skills. The percentages of exam questions on each topic are the same in both exams:

    10%   Conventions of Standard Written English

    40%   Revision Skills, Including Sentence-Level Skills

    25%   Ability to Use Source Materials

    25%   Rhetorical Analysis

After completing the multiple-choice section, candidates take the direct writing assessment module based on the policy established by their college. Options include:

- An essay section developed and provided by CLEP that requires candidates to respond to two essay prompts designed to assess the same skills measured in the College Composition essay section. Copies of the handwritten essays are sent to the college designated by the candidate, along with the CLEP Optional Essay Scoring Guidelines

- An essay/writing assessment developed, administered and scored by the college.

- Colleges can also choose to associate the College Composition Modular score with another assessment or evaluation determined by the college.

HOW TO TAKE A TEST

You have studied long, hard and conscientiously.

With your official admission card in hand, and your heart pounding, you have been admitted to the examination room.

You note that there are several hundred other applicants in the examination room waiting to take the same test.

They all appear to be equally well prepared.

You know that nothing but your best effort will suffice. The "moment of truth" is at hand: you now have to demonstrate objectively, in writing, your knowledge of content and your understanding of subject matter.

You are fighting the most important battle of your life—to pass and/or score high on an examination which will determine your career and provide the economic basis for your livelihood.

What extra, special things should you know and should you do in taking the examination?

I. YOU MUST PASS AN EXAMINATION

A. WHAT EVERY CANDIDATE SHOULD KNOW
Examination applicants often ask us for help in preparing for the written test. What can I study in advance? What kinds of questions will be asked? How will the test be given? How will the papers be graded?

B. HOW ARE EXAMS DEVELOPED?
Examinations are carefully written by trained technicians who are specialists in the field known as "psychological measurement," in consultation with recognized authorities in the field of work that the test will cover. These experts recommend the subject matter areas or skills to be tested; only those knowledges or skills important to your success on the job are included. The most reliable books and source materials available are used as references. Together, the experts and technicians judge the difficulty level of the questions.
Test technicians know how to phrase questions so that the problem is clearly stated. Their ethics do not permit "trick" or "catch" questions. Questions may have been tried out on sample groups, or subjected to statistical analysis, to determine their usefulness.
Written tests are often used in combination with performance tests, ratings of training and experience, and oral interviews. All of these measures combine to form the best-known means of finding the right person for the right job.

II. HOW TO PASS THE WRITTEN TEST

A. BASIC STEPS

1) Study the announcement

How, then, can you know what subjects to study? Our best answer is: "Learn as much as possible about the class of positions for which you've applied." The exam will test the knowledge, skills and abilities needed to do the work.

Your most valuable source of information about the position you want is the official exam announcement. This announcement lists the training and experience qualifications. Check these standards and apply only if you come reasonably close to meeting them. Many jurisdictions preview the written test in the exam announcement by including a section called "Knowledge and Abilities Required," "Scope of the Examination," or some similar heading. Here you will find out specifically what fields will be tested.

2) Choose appropriate study materials

If the position for which you are applying is technical or advanced, you will read more advanced, specialized material. If you are already familiar with the basic principles of your field, elementary textbooks would waste your time. Concentrate on advanced textbooks and technical periodicals. Think through the concepts and review difficult problems in your field.

These are all general sources. You can get more ideas on your own initiative, following these leads. For example, training manuals and publications of the government agency which employs workers in your field can be useful, particularly for technical and professional positions. A letter or visit to the government department involved may result in more specific study suggestions, and certainly will provide you with a more definite idea of the exact nature of the position you are seeking.

3) Study this book!

III. KINDS OF TESTS

Tests are used for purposes other than measuring knowledge and ability to perform specified duties. For some positions, it is equally important to test ability to make adjustments to new situations or to profit from training. In others, basic mental abilities not dependent on information are essential. Questions which test these things may not appear as pertinent to the duties of the position as those which test for knowledge and information. Yet they are often highly important parts of a fair examination. For very general questions, it is almost impossible to help you direct your study efforts. What we can do is to point out some of the more common of these general abilities needed in public service positions and describe some typical questions.

1) General information

Broad, general information has been found useful for predicting job success in some kinds of work. This is tested in a variety of ways, from vocabulary lists to questions about current events. Basic background in some field of work, such as sociology or economics, may be sampled in a group of questions. Often these are principles which have become familiar to most persons through exposure rather than through formal training. It is difficult to advise you how to study for these questions; being alert to the world around you is our best suggestion.

2) Verbal ability

An example of an ability needed in many positions is verbal or language ability. Verbal ability is, in brief, the ability to use and understand words. Vocabulary and grammar tests are typical measures of this ability. Reading comprehension or paragraph interpretation questions are common in many kinds of civil service tests. You are given a paragraph of written material and asked to find its central meaning.

IV. KINDS OF QUESTIONS

1. Multiple-choice Questions

Most popular of the short-answer questions is the "multiple choice" or "best answer" question. It can be used, for example, to test for factual knowledge, ability to solve problems or judgment in meeting situations found at work.

A multiple-choice question is normally one of three types:
- It can begin with an incomplete statement followed by several possible endings. You are to find the one ending which best completes the statement, although some of the others may not be entirely wrong.
- It can also be a complete statement in the form of a question which is answered by choosing one of the statements listed.
- It can be in the form of a problem – again you select the best answer.

Here is an example of a multiple-choice question with a discussion which should give you some clues as to the method for choosing the right answer:

When an employee has a complaint about his assignment, the action which will best help him overcome his difficulty is to
    A. discuss his difficulty with his coworkers
    B. take the problem to the head of the organization
    C. take the problem to the person who gave him the assignment
    D. say nothing to anyone about his complaint

In answering this question, you should study each of the choices to find which is best. Consider choice "A" – Certainly an employee may discuss his complaint with fellow employees, but no change or improvement can result, and the complaint remains unresolved. Choice "B" is a poor choice since the head of the organization probably does not know what assignment you have been given, and taking your problem to him is known as "going over the head" of the supervisor. The supervisor, or person who made the assignment, is the person who can clarify it or correct any injustice. Choice "C" is, therefore, correct. To say nothing, as in choice "D," is unwise. Supervisors have and interest in knowing the problems employees are facing, and the employee is seeking a solution to his problem.

2. True/False

3. Matching Questions

Matching an answer from a column of choices within another column.

V. RECORDING YOUR ANSWERS

Computer terminals are used more and more today for many different kinds of exams.

For an examination with very few applicants, you may be told to record your answers in the test booklet itself. Separate answer sheets are much more common. If this separate answer sheet is to be scored by machine – and this is often the case – it is highly important that you mark your answers correctly in order to get credit.

VI. BEFORE THE TEST

YOUR PHYSICAL CONDITION IS IMPORTANT

If you are not well, you can't do your best work on tests. If you are half asleep, you can't do your best either. Here are some tips:

1) Get about the same amount of sleep you usually get. Don't stay up all night before the test, either partying or worrying—DON'T DO IT!
2) If you wear glasses, be sure to wear them when you go to take the test. This goes for hearing aids, too.
3) If you have any physical problems that may keep you from doing your best, be sure to tell the person giving the test. If you are sick or in poor health, you relay cannot do your best on any test. You can always come back and take the test some other time.

Common sense will help you find procedures to follow to get ready for an examination. Too many of us, however, overlook these sensible measures. Indeed, nervousness and fatigue have been found to be the most serious reasons why applicants fail to do their best on civil service tests. Here is a list of reminders:

- Begin your preparation early – Don't wait until the last minute to go scurrying around for books and materials or to find out what the position is all about.
- Prepare continuously – An hour a night for a week is better than an all-night cram session. This has been definitely established. What is more, a night a week for a month will return better dividends than crowding your study into a shorter period of time.
- Locate the place of the exam – You have been sent a notice telling you when and where to report for the examination. If the location is in a different town or otherwise unfamiliar to you, it would be well to inquire the best route and learn something about the building.
- Relax the night before the test – Allow your mind to rest. Do not study at all that night. Plan some mild recreation or diversion; then go to bed early and get a good night's sleep.
- Get up early enough to make a leisurely trip to the place for the test – This way unforeseen events, traffic snarls, unfamiliar buildings, etc. will not upset you.
- Dress comfortably – A written test is not a fashion show. You will be known by number and not by name, so wear something comfortable.
- Leave excess paraphernalia at home – Shopping bags and odd bundles will get in your way. You need bring only the items mentioned in the official notice you received; usually everything you need is provided. Do not bring reference books to the exam. They will only confuse those last minutes and be taken away from you when in the test room.

- Arrive somewhat ahead of time – If because of transportation schedules you must get there very early, bring a newspaper or magazine to take your mind off yourself while waiting.
- Locate the examination room – When you have found the proper room, you will be directed to the seat or part of the room where you will sit. Sometimes you are given a sheet of instructions to read while you are waiting. Do not fill out any forms until you are told to do so; just read them and be prepared.
- Relax and prepare to listen to the instructions
- If you have any physical problem that may keep you from doing your best, be sure to tell the test administrator. If you are sick or in poor health, you really cannot do your best on the exam. You can come back and take the test some other time.

VII. AT THE TEST

The day of the test is here and you have the test booklet in your hand. The temptation to get going is very strong. Caution! There is more to success than knowing the right answers. You must know how to identify your papers and understand variations in the type of short-answer question used in this particular examination. Follow these suggestions for maximum results from your efforts:

1) Cooperate with the monitor

The test administrator has a duty to create a situation in which you can be as much at ease as possible. He will give instructions, tell you when to begin, check to see that you are marking your answer sheet correctly, and so on. He is not there to guard you, although he will see that your competitors do not take unfair advantage. He wants to help you do your best.

2) Listen to all instructions

Don't jump the gun! Wait until you understand all directions. In most civil service tests you get more time than you need to answer the questions. So don't be in a hurry. Read each word of instructions until you clearly understand the meaning. Study the examples, listen to all announcements and follow directions. Ask questions if you do not understand what to do.

3) Identify your papers

Civil service exams are usually identified by number only. You will be assigned a number; you must not put your name on your test papers. Be sure to copy your number correctly. Since more than one exam may be given, copy your exact examination title.

4) Plan your time

Unless you are told that a test is a "speed" or "rate of work" test, speed itself is usually not important. Time enough to answer all the questions will be provided, but this does not mean that you have all day. An overall time limit has been set. Divide the total time (in minutes) by the number of questions to determine the approximate time you have for each question.

5) Do not linger over difficult questions

If you come across a difficult question, mark it with a paper clip (useful to have along) and come back to it when you have been through the booklet. One caution if you do this – be sure to skip a number on your answer sheet as well. Check often to be sure that you have not lost your place and that you are marking in the row numbered the same as the question you are answering.

6) Read the questions

Be sure you know what the question asks! Many capable people are unsuccessful because they failed to read the questions correctly.

7) Answer all questions

Unless you have been instructed that a penalty will be deducted for incorrect answers, it is better to guess than to omit a question.

8) Speed tests

It is often better NOT to guess on speed tests. It has been found that on timed tests people are tempted to spend the last few seconds before time is called in marking answers at random – without even reading them – in the hope of picking up a few extra points. To discourage this practice, the instructions may warn you that your score will be "corrected" for guessing. That is, a penalty will be applied. The incorrect answers will be deducted from the correct ones, or some other penalty formula will be used.

9) Review your answers

If you finish before time is called, go back to the questions you guessed or omitted to give them further thought. Review other answers if you have time.

10) Return your test materials

If you are ready to leave before others have finished or time is called, take ALL your materials to the monitor and leave quietly. Never take any test material with you. The monitor can discover whose papers are not complete, and taking a test booklet may be grounds for disqualification.

VIII. EXAMINATION TECHNIQUES

1) Read the general instructions carefully. These are usually printed on the first page of the exam booklet. As a rule, these instructions refer to the timing of the examination; the fact that you should not start work until the signal and must stop work at a signal, etc. If there are any special instructions, such as a choice of questions to be answered, make sure that you note this instruction carefully.

2) When you are ready to start work on the examination, that is as soon as the signal has been given, read the instructions to each question booklet, underline any key words or phrases, such as least, best, outline, describe and the like. In this way you will tend to answer as requested rather than discover on reviewing your paper that you listed without describing, that you selected the worst choice rather than the best choice, etc.

3) If the examination is of the objective or multiple-choice type – that is, each question will also give a series of possible answers: A, B, C or D, and you are called upon to select the best answer and write the letter next to that answer on your answer paper – it is advisable to start answering each question in turn. There may be anywhere from 50 to 100 such questions in the three or four hours allotted and you can see how much time would be taken if you read through all the questions before beginning to answer any. Furthermore, if you

come across a question or group of questions which you know would be difficult to answer, it would undoubtedly affect your handling of all the other questions.

4) If the examination is of the essay type and contains but a few questions, it is a moot point as to whether you should read all the questions before starting to answer any one. Of course, if you are given a choice – say five out of seven and the like – then it is essential to read all the questions so you can eliminate the two that are most difficult. If, however, you are asked to answer all the questions, there may be danger in trying to answer the easiest one first because you may find that you will spend too much time on it. The best technique is to answer the first question, then proceed to the second, etc.

5) Time your answers. Before the exam begins, write down the time it started, then add the time allowed for the examination and write down the time it must be completed, then divide the time available somewhat as follows:
    - If 3-1/2 hours are allowed, that would be 210 minutes. If you have 80 objective-type questions, that would be an average of 2-1/2 minutes per question. Allow yourself no more than 2 minutes per question, or a total of 160 minutes, which will permit about 50 minutes to review.
    - If for the time allotment of 210 minutes there are 7 essay questions to answer, that would average about 30 minutes a question. Give yourself only 25 minutes per question so that you have about 35 minutes to review.

6) The most important instruction is to read each question and make sure you know what is wanted. The second most important instruction is to time yourself properly so that you answer every question. The third most important instruction is to answer every question. Guess if you have to but include something for each question. Remember that you will receive no credit for a blank and will probably receive some credit if you write something in answer to an essay question. If you guess a letter – say "B" for a multiple-choice question – you may have guessed right. If you leave a blank as an answer to a multiple-choice question, the examiners may respect your feelings but it will not add a point to your score. Some exams may penalize you for wrong answers, so in such cases only, you may not want to guess unless you have some basis for your answer.

7) Suggestions
    a. Objective-type questions
        1. Examine the question booklet for proper sequence of pages and questions
        2. Read all instructions carefully
        3. Skip any question which seems too difficult; return to it after all other questions have been answered
        4. Apportion your time properly; do not spend too much time on any single question or group of questions
        5. Note and underline key words – all, most, fewest, least, best, worst, same, opposite, etc.
        6. Pay particular attention to negatives
        7. Note unusual option, e.g., unduly long, short, complex, different or similar in content to the body of the question
        8. Observe the use of "hedging" words – probably, may, most likely, etc.

9. Make sure that your answer is put next to the same number as the question
10. Do not second-guess unless you have good reason to believe the second answer is definitely more correct
11. Cross out original answer if you decide another answer is more accurate; do not erase until you are ready to hand your paper in
12. Answer all questions; guess unless instructed otherwise
13. Leave time for review

b. Essay questions
1. Read each question carefully
2. Determine exactly what is wanted. Underline key words or phrases.
3. Decide on outline or paragraph answer
4. Include many different points and elements unless asked to develop any one or two points or elements
5. Show impartiality by giving pros and cons unless directed to select one side only
6. Make and write down any assumptions you find necessary to answer the questions
7. Watch your English, grammar, punctuation and choice of words
8. Time your answers; don't crowd material

8) Answering the essay question

Most essay questions can be answered by framing the specific response around several key words or ideas. Here are a few such key words or ideas:

M's: manpower, materials, methods, money, management
P's: purpose, program, policy, plan, procedure, practice, problems, pitfalls, personnel, public relations

a. Six basic steps in handling problems:
1. Preliminary plan and background development
2. Collect information, data and facts
3. Analyze and interpret information, data and facts
4. Analyze and develop solutions as well as make recommendations
5. Prepare report and sell recommendations
6. Install recommendations and follow up effectiveness

b. Pitfalls to avoid
1. Taking things for granted – A statement of the situation does not necessarily imply that each of the elements is necessarily true; for example, a complaint may be invalid and biased so that all that can be taken for granted is that a complaint has been registered
2. Considering only one side of a situation – Wherever possible, indicate several alternatives and then point out the reasons you selected the best one
3. Failing to indicate follow up – Whenever your answer indicates action on your part, make certain that you will take proper follow-up action to see how successful your recommendations, procedures or actions turn out to be
4. Taking too long in answering any single question – Remember to time your answers properly

EXAMINATION SECTION

EXAMINATION SECTION
TEST 1

DIRECTIONS: Each question or incomplete statement is followed by several suggested answers or completions. Select the one that BEST answers the question or completes the statement. *PRINT THE LETTER OF THE CORRECT ANSWER IN THE SPACE AT THE RIGHT.*

1. *Success is a relative term. You might think that owning a big house, and driving a Mercedes is the epitome of success. But then you'll meet someone who owns a bigger house, and a newer Mercedes, and you won't feel so successful anymore. Or you'll meet someone who lives in a small house, and drives an old car, but whose children are happy and well-adjusted, and you'll rethink your standards of success.*
   The writer above is primarily using which technique to make his point?

   A. Definition B. Persuasion
   C. Narration   D. Classification

   1.____

2. Hillary bought a book at United Books. Two days later, she saw the same book at Sparrow Books for $2 less than she had paid at United. As a result, she told all her friends that Sparrow's books were cheaper than United's. Hillary's flaw in logic is an example of

   A. ad hominem attack B. faulty deduction
   C. faulty induction   D. a logical fallacy

   2.____

Questions 3-5.

DIRECTIONS: Use the following citation to answer Questions 3 through 5.

Casey, Anna. "Writing My Days." New York Times Book Review. 9 Jan. 1980: 23. Rpt. in Writers Talk About Writing. Ed. Laramie Jones. New York: Songbird Press, 1982. 30-33.

3. Which of the following is true?

   A. The New York Times Book Review printed a review of Writers Talk About Writing on 9 Jan. 1980.
   B. The essay was initially published in the New York Times Book Review.
   C. Writers Talk About Writing is a compilation of essays from the New York Times Book Review.
   D. The essay was initially published by Songbird Press.

   3.____

4. Who wrote "Writing My Days"?

   A. Laramie Jones and Anna Casey
   B. The New York Times Book Review editors
   C. Laramie Jones
   D. Anna Casey

   4.____

5. Where does "Writing My Days" appear in Writers Talk About Writing?

   A. Not listed   B. 1982
   C. Pgs. 30-33   D. Pg. 23

   5.____

Questions 6-15.

DIRECTIONS: The following sentences in Questions 6 through 15 contain problems in grammar, usage, diction (choice of words), idiom, and punctuation. Some sentences are correct. No sentence contains more than one error. You will find that the error, if there is one, is underlined and lettered. Assume that all other elements of the sentence are correct and cannot be changed. If there is an error, select the one underlined part that must be changed in order to make the sentence correct. If there is no error, select answer D.

6. Americans waste vast amounts of paper . Because they don't think of paper as for-
    ‾A‾   ‾B‾   ‾C‾
   ests. No error
         ‾D‾

7. This all-purpose cleanser brightens pots and pans , including the copper-bottomed
                               ‾A‾   ‾B‾
   skillets mother uses so frequently . No error
                           ‾C‾   ‾D‾

8. I don't believe in space exploration . I believe that A the money should be spent on
                                        ‾A‾
   poor and destitute before it's used on rockets. No error.
                             ‾C‾   ‾D‾

9. The of Washington D.C., enjoy many museums , such as the Smithsonian, the Holo-
                                      ‾B‾
   caust Museum, and the National Gallery of Art. No error
                        ‾C‾   ‾D‾

10. Some believe that the signs , of the Zodiac can predict a person's romantic behav-
                                ‾B‾   ‾C‾
    ior. No error
         ‾D‾

11. Some people believes that even the most insignificant behaviors can be attributed to
                ‾A‾   ‾B‾
    the positioning of the stars on a person's birth date. No error
                                      ‾C‾   ‾D‾

12. Maya Angelou is a highly respected and popular poet . Who wrote a poem for Presi-
                       ‾A‾   ‾B‾
    dent Clinton's Inauguration Ceremony. No error
         ‾C‾   ‾D‾

3 (#1)

13. Before visiting my grandmother in the nursing home , I that nursing home just sat   13.____
                                                    A
    around all day and watched TV or took naps. No error D
                                                 ───────
                                                    D

14. Genelle likes to juggle in her spare can keep seven limes airborne while watching   14.____
           ─────   ───────────
             A   C
    old reruns of Lassie on television. No error
                                         ────────
                                             D

15. To make maple syrup is an important industry in Vermont. farmer drills a half-inch   15.____
    ───────
       A
    hole into the tree trunk a depth of about two inches. No error
                                                           ────────
                                                               D

16. Which of the following accurately interprets the information given in the dictionary entry   16.____
    below?
    rhetoric (reterik), n. [ME. rethorik <OFr. rhetorique <Lat. rhetorical

    A. Reterik is an acceptable variant spelling of *rhetoric*.
    B. Rhetoric is a transitive verb.
    C. Rhethorik is the English version of reterik.
    D. Old French rhetorique is derived from the latin rhetorica.

17. Which of the following accurately interprets the information given in the dictionary entry   17.____
    below?
    dun (dun), v. [Orig. unknown]; dun (dun) n., [ME dunn]

    A. In English, dun functions only as a noun.
    B. The origin of dun, used as a noun, is unknown.
    C. The origin of dun, used as a verb, is unknown.
    D. In English, dun functions only as a verb.

18. Which of the following accurately interprets the information given in the dictionary entry   18.____
    below?
    video (video), n. [Lat., imper. of videre, to see]

    A. Video is derived from the Latin imperative, *videre*.
    B. The definition of video is *to see*.
    C. Video is a Latin word.
    D. The abbreviation n. indicates that the word has multiple meanings.

Questions 19-25.

DIRECTIONS: In each of the following sentences, you are given two or more sentences to combine into one. After each set of sentences, there is a question that will help you decide how the sentences are to be combined. In combining some of the sentences, you will change the order of the original a great deal; in combining others, you will change the order only a little. Be sure that the new sentence you create is a complete sentence, that is contains all of the essential facts given in the original set of sentences, that is maintains the proper relationship of ideas, and that is clearly and effectively written.

19. No one wants to be forgotten. You can always write things worth reading. You can also do things worth writing. Your new sentence will begin with which of the following?   19.____

    A. Do things worth writing
    B. Being forgotten
    C. If you would not be forgotten
    D. Write things worth reading

20. I would sit alone on a pumpkin. It's better than sitting together and being crowded on a velvet cushion.   20.____
Which of the following will appear in your new sentence?

    A. sitting alone and being crowded
    B. cushion better than
    C. pumpkin, it's
    D. I would rather...than

21. People who deny freedom to others deserve it not for themselves. Under a just God, they will not long retain it. Which of the following is the BEST word to join the two sentences?   21.____

    A. But   B. And
    C. Even though   D. Furthermore

22. I like cheap hotels. They don't have phones. They do have television sets. They have loud air conditioners. They have interesting guests. Your new sentence will contain which of the following?   22.____

    A. because, even though
    B. and therefore
    C. cheap hotels don't have phones
    D. cheap hotels have guests

23. I hate my neighbors. I like to leave the doors and windows of my house open. I like to play loud music.   23.____
Your new sentence will begin with which of the following?

    A. So   B. Although
    C. Because   D. I hate

24. I have difficulty in math class. I consulted a friend in my class. She is good at math. 24.____
Your new sentence will contain which of the following?

    A. who is good at math in my class
    B. who is in my math class and good at math
    C. who is not difficult with math
    D. whose math is not difficult

25. I want not only to go away to school. I want to live in Italy. Your new sentence will contain 25.____
which of the following?

    A. to go away to school but to live
    B. to live in Italy and go away
    C. to live in school in Italy
    D. for Italy to go to school

KEY (CORRECT ANSWERS)

1. A		11. A
2. C		12. B
3. B		13. D
4. D		14. B
5. C		15. A
6. C		16. D
7. D		17. C
8. C		18. A
9. A		19. C
10. B		20. D

21. B
22. A
23. C
24. B
25. A

TEST 2

DIRECTIONS: Each question or incomplete statement is followed by several suggested answers or completions. Select the one that BEST answers the question or completes the statement. *PRINT THE LETTER OF THE CORRECT ANSWER IN THE SPACE AT THE RIGHT.*

Questions 1-2.

DIRECTIONS: Questions 1 and 2 are to be answered on the basis of the following sentence.

We are leaving tomorrow. We must close the windows. The lawn needs cutting. We must ask someone to bring in the paper.

1. Your new sentence will begin with which of the following?

    A. During   B. We are   C. After   D. Before

2. Your new sentence will contain which of the following?

    A. closing...cutting...and asking
    B. close...cut... and ask
    C. closed...to cut...and to ask
    D. closed...been cut...asked

3. Rover waited for his master. He waited at the intersection. He looked to the left. He looked to the right. He couldn't decide which way to go.
   Your new sentence will begin with which of the following?

    A. Unable to decide   B. Not deciding
    C. Waiting alone   D. Looking to the right

Questions 4-7.

DIRECTIONS: Questions 4 through 7 are to be answered on the basis of the following passage.

The Mirror (by Sylvia Plath)

I am silver and exact. (1) I have no preconceptions.(2) Whatever I see I swallow immediately.(3) Just as it is, unmisted by love or dislike.(4) I am not cruel, only truthful -- the eye of a little god, four cornered.(5) Most of the time I *meditate* on the opposite wall.(6) It is pink, with speckles.(7) I have looked at it so long I think it is a part of my heart.(8) But it flickers.(9) Faces and darkness separate us, over and over.

4. This passage depends most heavily on the use of which of the following?

    A. Description   B. Example
    C. Personification   D. Persuasion

5. The word that could best replace *meditate* in sentence 6 is

    A. mediate   B. ruminate   C. watch   D. stare at

6. The last lines refer to which of the following?

   A. People passing before the wall.
   B. Faces appearing in the mirror.
   C. The woman's heart.
   D. The woman's image in the mirror.

7. Who is the speaker?

   A. A man
   B. A woman
   C. The face in the mirror
   D. The mirror

Questions 8-17.

DIRECTIONS: The following sentences in Questions 8 through 17 contain problems in grammar, usage, diction (choice of words), idiom, and punctuation. Some sentences are correct. No sentence contains more than one error. You will find that the error, if there is one, is underlined and lettered. Assume that all other elements of the sentence are correct and cannot be changed. If there is an error, select the one underlined part that must be changed in order to make the sentence correct. If there is no error, select answer D.

8. <u>Curiously</u> peering at <u>their</u> images reflected in the placid water, the deer
        A   B

   <u>had stood</u> completely still. <u>No error</u>
        C   D

9. We live in a beautiful <u>place. Bald</u> eagles are common, ospreys even have park
                                 A

   <u>land,</u> nature trails and campgrounds. <u>No error</u>
        C   D

10. Val <u>knew</u> the presentation he planned to give <u>the boss</u> that afternoon probably
            A   B

    wouldn't be very <u>organized,</u> because he had been remiss in preparing for it. <u>No error.</u>
                          C   D

11. <u>Furthermore</u> Althea Gibson achieved international fame as the first African-American to
         A

    win the Wimbledon Tennis <u>Championship</u> the path she followed to that champion-
                                   B

    ship <u>was as unorthodox as</u> the champion herself. <u>No error.</u>
                 C   D

12. After the county had been ravaged by the worst tornado in decades, the President   12.____
    —A—   ——B——
    declared the entire region a Federal disaster area. No error
    ————C————   ——D——

13. After Toni scored the winning goal in the state championship soccer match, she   13.____
    —A—   ———B———
    had been lauded as a hero in the local papers. No error.
    ———C———   ———D———

14. Because Juanita neglected to lock her car door last night, the thief that stole her car   14.____
    ———A———   ——B——   ——C——
    stereo had an easy time of it. No error.
                                   ———D———

15. Although all pearls are coveted jewels, the complex process A of growing and harvest-   15.____
                                   ——A——
    ing rare black pearls place them among the most precious gems in the
                          ——B——   ——————C——————
    world. No error
           ———D———

16. Olga didn't know how to care for her cactus when she A bought it at the nursery; she   16.____
         ————A————   ————B————
    watered it so profusely that it drowned within a week. No error.
               —————C—————   ———D———

17. So to show his affection on their twentieth wedding anniversary, Walter gave Jean   17.____
    ————A————   —————B—————
    flowers and wrote her a card that said he would love her eternally. No error
                                              —————C—————   ———D———

18. Which of the following accurately interprets the information given in the dictionary entry   18.____
    below?
    cinder (sinder), n. 1. A burned or partly burned substance, such as coal, that is not
    reduced to ashes but is incapable of further combustion. 2. tr. v. -dered, -dering. To
    burn or reduce to cinders.

    A. *Sinder* is an acceptable alternate spelling of *cinder*.
    B. *Cindered* is the transitive verb form of cinder.
    C. The transitive verb form of cinder is *a burned, or partly burned substance*.
    D. The noun form of cinder is *to burn or reduce to cinders*.

19. Which of the following accurately interprets the information given in the dictionary entry below?
    obfuscate tr. v. -cated, -eating, -cates.
    1. to render obscure.   2. To darken, -obfuscation - n.; -obfuscatory - adj.

    A. *Obfuscates* is the plural noun form of obfuscate.
    B. *Obfuscate* is a noun.
    C. *Obfuscatory* is the transitive verb form of obfuscate.
    D. *Obfuscating* is the transitive verb form of obfuscate.

20. Which of the following accurately interprets the information given in the dictionary entry below?
    coerce (kours) tr. v. -erced, -ercing, -erces.
    1. To force to act or think in a given manner by pressure, threats, or intimidation; compel, -coercer, n.; -coercible, adj.

    A. *Kours* is the Middle English root of coerce.
    B. *Coerces* is the plural noun of coerce.
    C. *Coercer* is the noun form of coerce.
    D. *Coercible* is the transitive verb form of coerce.

21. Which of the following accurately interprets the information given in the dictionary entry below?
    curry (kure) tr.v. -ried, -rying, -ries. 1. To groom a horse with a curry comb. To seek or gain favor by fawning or flattery. [ME currein].

    A. *Kure* is a Middle English root of curry.
    B. *Currein* is a Middle English root of curry.
    C. *Curries* is the plural noun form of curry.
    D. *Kure* is the transitive verb form of curry.

22. Which of the following accurately interprets the information given in the dictionary entry below?
    heinous, adj. Grossly wicked or abominable. [ME <OFr. hainos] -heinously, adv.

    A. *Heinous* is an adjective.
    B. *Heinous* is an adverb.
    C. *Heinous* is both an adjective and an adverb.
    D. *Heinous* is derived from the old French word *heinously*.

23. Which of the following accurately interprets the information given in the dictionary entry below?
    macerate, v. -ated, -ating, -ates. -tr. 1. To make soft by soaking or steeping in a liquid. [Lat. macerare] -maceration, n.

    A. *Macerare* is an alternative spelling for macerate.
    B. *Macerate* is a noun.
    C. *Macerate* is a verb.
    D. *Macerates* is the plural noun form of macerate.

24. Which of the following is a primary source? A(n)

    A. biography written by another author
    B. interview included in a magazine article written by another author
    C. interview which you conducted
    D. article in a magazine

25. Which of the following is considered a secondary source?

    A. An interview which you conducted
    B. A laboratory experiment
    C. Artwork you examine for a project
    D. A biography written by another author

KEY (CORRECT ANSWERS)

1.	D	11.	A
2.	B	12.	D
3.	A	13.	C
4.	C	14.	C
5.	B	15.	B
6.	A	16.	D
7.	D	17.	A
8.	C	18.	B
9.	B	19.	D
10.	B	20.	C

21. B
22. A
23. C
24. C
25. D

TEST 3

DIRECTIONS: Each question or incomplete statement is followed by several suggested answers or completions. Select the one that BEST answers the question or completes the statement. *PRINT THE LETTER OF THE CORRECT ANSWER IN THE SPACE AT THE RIGHT.*

Questions 1-4.

DIRECTIONS: Questions 1 through 4 are to be answered on the basis of the following passage.

Since 1805, when members of the Lewis and Clark expedition first began shooting at the North American grizzly bear, the grizzly population in the lower forty-eight United States has declined steadily, from around 50,000 to fewer than 1,000 today.(1) The bears living in or near Yellowstone National Park almost disappeared in the early 1970's, but action by concerned groups and the Federal government has recently resulted in a growth spurt in the bear's population.(2)

In the twentieth century, because of constantly shrinking habitats and sources of food, the Yellowstone grizzly became largely dependent on people for survival.(3) Instead of developing its instincts for hunting and foraging, the grizzly fed mainly on the discarded sandwiches, chips, marshmallows and other foods found in the park garage dumps.(4) The grizzly's near-disappearance in the early 1970's was due to the closing of these dumps which contained as much as 4,800 tons of food in a given year by park officials.(5) Most grizzlies didn't know of any other way to feed themselves, and their numbers dropped sharply.(6).

1. This passage is best as which of the following?

    A. Persuasive   B. Descriptive   C. Expository   D. Narrative

2. What caused the near disappearance of the grizzlies in the early 1970's?

    A. The closing of the Yellowstone dumps
    B. The excessive hunting of grizzlies which began in 1805
    C. The shrinking habitat of the grizzly bear due to overdevelopment
    D. Intervention by the federal government.

3. *Instead of developing its instincts for hunting and foraging*
   The above is an example of which of the following?

    A. Independent clause   B. Phrase
    C. Coordinate clause   D. Subordinate clause

4. The main verb of the first sentence is

    A. when   B. began   C. has declined   D. shooting

5. *My Year in India* is a travel book written by author C.C. Collins. Where would you find this book in the library?

    A. Periodical index   B. Book index
    C. General index   D. Reference section

6. The *Congressional Quarterly Guide to U.S. Government Agencies* can be found in which of the following places?

   A. Book index
   B. Periodical index
   C. Reference section
   D. General index

7. Recent issues of *Time* magazine can be found in which of the following places?

   A. Book index
   B. Periodical index
   C. Reference section
   D. General index

8. The *Time-Life Guide to Building a House* can be found in which of the following places?

   A. Book index
   B. Periodical index
   C. Reference section
   D. General index

9. In order to find information about the important events which took place in a particular year, which of the following places should you look?

   A. Atlas
   B. Books
   C. Magazines
   D. Almanac

10. To research a report comparing the mineral concentrations of a wine valley in southern France to those of a wine valley in Northern California, you would consult a(n)

    A. atlas
    B. magazine
    C. reference book
    D. almanac

11. In order to gather information on the increasing occurrence of eating disorders in teen-age girls, you would consult

    A. a person suffering from an eating disorder at your school
    B. magazine articles profiling new treatments for eating disorders
    C. a periodical index
    D. a book index

12. In order to gather information on what it is like to struggle with an eating disorder, you would

    A. consult a doctor
    B. consult the school records database
    C. consult a reference book
    D. conduct a personal interview

Questions 13-14.

DIRECTIONS: Use the following citation to answer Questions 13 and 14.

American Cancer Society. <u>Handbook for Choosing Doctors.</u> New York: American Cancer Society., 1998.

13. Who is the author of the book?

    A. New York Chapter of the American Cancer Society
    B. The author is unlisted
    C. American Cancer Society
    D. The author is anonymous

14. Who is the publisher of the book?

    A. The publisher is unlisted
    B. The publisher is anonymous
    C. American Cancer Society
    D. New York Chapter of the American Cancer Society

Questions 15-25.

DIRECTIONS: In each of the following sentences, you are given two or more sentences to combine into one. After each set of sentences, there is a question that will help you decide how the sentences are to be combined. In combining some of the sentences, you will change the order of the original a great deal; in combining others, you will change the order only a little. Be sure that the new sentence you create is a complete sentence, that is contains all of the essential facts given in the original set of sentences, that is maintains the proper relationship of ideas, and that is clearly and effectively written.

15. The old man shouted. He was fed up with the salesman. The salesman had knocked on his door three times that day. Your new sentence will begin with which of the following?

    A. Shouting, the old man
    B. Out of control, the old man
    C. After knocking on his door
    D. Finally fed up with

16. My favorite chair is comfortable. It is shapeless. It is covered with horrible material. It is an eyesore. Your new sentence will contain which of the following?

    A. because
    B. since
    C. although
    D. which

17. I have hobbies. I like to sail. Sewing is fun. Painting is too.
    Your new sentence will contain which of the following?

    A. sailing, sewing and painting
    B. hobbies sailing, sewing and painting
    C. to sail, sewing and painting
    D. to sail, fun sewing and to paint

18. I was looking at my books. I noticed that *Little Women* was missing. Your new sentence will contain which of the following?

    A. even though
    B. while
    C. looking as I was
    D. noticing my looking

19. The little boy opened the cage. The parakeet flew out the window. I had forgotten to close the window. Your new sentence will begin with which of the following?

    A. The parakeet
    B. The little boy
    C. When
    D. I had

20. The parks report was very persuasive. It contained five pages of data. Your new sentence will contain which of the following?

    A. which contained
    B. persuasive it
    C. containing five
    D. persuasive and it

21. I walked into the homeless shelter. Men, women and children mingled about. Bags containing clothes and coats lay on the floor. Your new sentence will begin with which of the following?

    A. Mingling about the shelter
    B. Walking into the shelter
    C. Laying on the floor
    D. Containing clothes and coats

22. The scenery is beautiful at my grandfather's house. The woods are deep and lush. The lakes are blue. I love to spend spring break there. Your new sentence will contain which of the following?

    A. scenery of blue lakes and the woods are
    B. scenery is deep and lush
    C. deep and lush, and blue
    D. deep, lush woods, blue lakes and beautiful scenery

23. I had plowed a fifty acre patch. My brother would pour seed onto the path. I would water the acres. Your new sentence will begin with which of the following?

    A. I would   B. I had   C. After   D. Then

24. A committee was formed. Four teachers were appointed to the committee. They resolved the dispute. Your new sentence will begin with which of the following?

    A. Forming a committee
    B. Resolving the dispute
    C. Appointing four teachers
    D. Four teachers appointed

25. I love dogs. They are messy. They are hard to train. They chew up my shoes. Your new sentence will contain which of the following?

    A. chew messily and hard to train
    B. chewing, messy and hard to train
    C. messily hard to train and chewing
    D. messy, hard to train and chew

KEY (CORRECT ANSWERS)

1. C
2. A
3. D
4. C
5. B

6. C
7. B
8. A
9. D
10. A

11. C
12. D
13. C
14. D
15. D

16. C
17. A
18. B
19. C
20. A

21. B
22. D
23. C
24. D
25. D

TEST 4

DIRECTIONS: Each question or incomplete statement is followed by several suggested answers or completions. Select the one that BEST answers the question or completes the statement. *PRINT THE LETTER OF THE CORRECT ANSWER IN THE SPACE AT THE RIGHT.*

Questions 1-2.

DIRECTIONS: Use the following citation to answer Questions 1 and 2.

Samuels, Angela. "The Parable of Wheat and Weeds." The Writer at Work. Ed. Susan Edmonds. New York: Small Tree Press, 1980. 27-32.

1. Who wrote "The Parable of Wheat and Weeds"? 1.____

    A. Angela Samuels
    B. Susan Edmonds
    C. Angela Samuels and Susan Edmonds
    D. Small Tree Press

2. Susan Edmonds' role is editor of the 2.____

    A. story, "The Parable of Wheat and Weeds"
    B. novel, The Writer at Work
    C. anthology, The Writer at Work
    D. anthology, "The Parable of Wheat and Weeds

3. Sevarra, Thomas. Introduction. A Few Good Voices off the Prairie. By Kennedy Coombs. New York: Littleton Press, 1990. 8-10. 3.____
What is Thomas Severra's relationship to A Few Good Voices off the Prairie?
He

    A. wrote the introduction
    B. wrote the book
    C. wrote the introduction and edited the book
    D. edited the book

4. Milosz, Czeslaw. Gray Days. Trans. Shannon Raffel. The Critical Tradition; Contemporary Trends in Polish Poetry. Ed. David Riven. New York: Knopf, 1992. 64-73. Which of the following is true of Czeslaw Milosz? 4.____
He

    A. edited The Critical Tradition; Contemporary Trends in Polish Poetry
    B. translated The Critical Tradition; Contemporary Trends in Polish Poetry
    C. wrote The Critical Tradition: Contemporary Trends in Polish Poetry
    D. wrote Gray Days

5. Referring to the citation in Question 4 above, which of the following is true of Shannon Raffel? 5.____
She

A. edited The Critical Tradition: Contemporary Trends in Polish Poetry
B. translated The Critical Tradition: Contemporary Trends in Polish Poetry
C. wrote The Critical Tradition: Contemporary Trends in Polish Poetry
D. wrote The Gray Days

6. Referring to the citation in Question 4 above, which of the following is true of David Riven?
He

A. edited The Critical Tradition: Contemporary Trends in Polish Poetry
B. translated The Critical Tradition: Contemporary Trends in Polish Poetry
C. wrote The Critical Tradition: Contemporary Trends in Polish Poetry
D. wrote The Gray Days

6.____

7. Which of the following most determines the tone of an essay?

A. Purpose   B. Organization   C. Audience   D. Subject

7.____

8. Outlining is part of which stage of the writing process?

A. Purpose   B. Organization   C. Audience   D. Subject

8.____

9. Peer-editing is part of which stage of the writing process?

A. Researching   B. Revising   C. Brainstorming   D. Drafting

9.____

Questions 10-15.

DIRECTIONS: Use the following pronunciation key (American Heritage Dictionary) to answer Questions 10 through 15.

ă pat pit caught, paw
ā pay pie, by took

ĕ pet pot boot

ē bee toe

ə about, item, edible, gallop, circus

10. schedule (skĕj'ool, -əl; Brit. shĕd'yool)n. Which of the following accurately interprets the information given in the dictionary entry above? The

A. British and American pronunciations of schedule is uniform
B. British pronunciation of schedule is different from the standard American pronunciation
C. British use schedule as a noun, whereas the Americans use it as another part of speech
D. American use schedule as a noun, whereas the British use it as another part of speech

10.____

11. Schistosome (schis-to-some) (shĭs´tə-sōm´) n. 11.____
    The middle syllable of schistosome (to) is pronounced like the

    A. e in bee   B. o in pot
    C. o in toe   D. e in item

12. Integument (in-teg-u-ment) (ĭn-tĕg´yŏŏ-mənt) n. 12.____
    The third syllable of integument (u) is pronounced like the

    A. oo in took   B. o in toe
    C. u in cut   D. oo in boot

13. obi (ō´bē) n. 13.____
    The pronunciation of obi rhymes with

    A. toe   B. pie
    C. the e in pet   D. bee

14. Intine (in-tine) (ĭn´tēn´) n. 14.____
    The pronunciation of intine rhymes with

    A. tone   B. gone   C. seen   D. line

15. Anorthosite (an-or-tho-site) (ăn-ôr´thə-sīt´) n. The last syllable of anorthesite 15.____
    rhymes with

    A. meet   B. bite   C. pit   D. pet

16. On his first day of college classes, Rumeal attended English class and noticed that his 16.____
    instructor did not have a syllabus prepared. As a result, Rumeal called home and told his
    parents that his college professors were lazy.
    Rumeal's flaw in logic is an example of

    A. ad hominem attack   B. faulty deduction
    C. faulty induction   D. a logical fallacy

17. Carmen knew that her college professors were opposed to the new policy on attendance. 17.____
    When she met a young man in the student union who also said he was opposed to the
    policy, Carmen knew that he was a professor.
    Carmen's flaw in logic is an example of

    A. ad hominem attack   B. faulty deduction
    C. faulty induction   D. a logical fallacy

18. After she walked under a ladder and crossed the path of a black cat on Friday the thir- 18.____
    teenth, Amy went home and locked her door.
    Amy's flaw in logic is an example of

    A. a hasty generalization   B. faulty deduction
    C. ad hominem attack   D. a logical fallacy

19. After seeing her favorite television character, a doctor, support a brand of pain medication that she didn't use, Jordan decided to switch brands.
    Jordan's decision is an example of

    A. ad hominem attack
    B. a faulty use of authority
    C. hasty generalization
    D. a logical fallacy

    19.____

20. Every evening, little Ernie Simms rushes with his mother to the beach in order to see the sunset. Ernie believes that if he isn't there, the sun won't be able to set. Ernie's reasoning is an example of

    A. ad hominem attack
    B. hasty generalization
    C. a faulty use of authority
    D. a doubtful cause

    20.____

21. Claire refuses to quit smoking. She argues that people who drive cars have much higher mortality rates than people who don't drive cars, but no one is forcing them to quit driving.
    Claire's argument is an example of

    A. a false analogy
    B. hasty generalization
    C. a faulty use of authority
    D. a doubtful cause

    21.____

Questions 22-25.

DIRECTIONS: Questions 22 through 25 are to be answered on the basis of the following passage.

Civil Disobedience, Henry David Thoreau

I heartily accept the motto - "That government is best which governs least," and I should like to see it acted up to more rapidly and systematically.(1) Carried out, it finally amounts to this which also I believe - "That government is best which governs not at all," and when men are prepared for it, that will be the kind of government which they will have.(2) Government is at best but an expedient; but most governments are usually, and all governments are sometimes, inexpedient.(3) The objections which have been brought against a standing army, and they are many and weighty, and deserve to prevail, may also at last be brought against a standing government.(4)

22. In sentence 3, which of the following would best replace the word *expedient*?

    A. Expedition
    B. Stopgap
    C. Choice
    D. Measure

    22.____

23. The main verb(s) of the first sentence is/are

    A. accept and like
    B. is
    C. governs
    D. to see

    23.____

24. Which of the following is used most often by the writer?

    A. Shifts of topic   B. Shifts of diction
    C. Coordination   D. Imagery

25. The tone of this piece is best characterized as

    A. ironic   B. colloquial
    C. expository   D. argumentative

KEY (CORRECT ANSWERS)

1.	A	11.	D
2.	C	12.	A
3.	A	13.	D
4.	D	14.	C
5.	B	15.	B
6.	A	16.	C
7.	C	17.	B
8.	D	18.	A
9.	B	19.	B
10.	B	20.	D

21. A
22. B
23. A
24. C
25. D

EXAMINATION SECTION
TEST 1

DIRECTIONS: Each question or incomplete statement is followed by several suggested answers or completions. Select the one that BEST answers the question or completes the statement. *PRINT THE LETTER OF THE CORRECT ANSWER IN THE SPACE AT THE RIGHT.*

Questions 1-11.

DIRECTIONS: The following sentences in Questions 1 through 11 contain problems in grammar, usage, diction (choice of words), idiom, and punctuation. Some sentences are correct. No sentence contains more than one error. You will find that the error, if there is one, is underlined and lettered. Assume that all other elements of the sentence are correct and cannot be changed. If there is an error, select the one underlined part that must be changed in order to make the sentence correct. If there is no error, select answer D.

1. Halfway through his <u>speech,</u> Val forgot what he'd planned to say and began to
                                   A
   ramble, saying whatever came to <u>mind,</u> it was obvious to everyone listening that
                                             B
   he <u>hadn't prepared</u> his speech carefully. <u>No error</u>
        C   D

1.____

2. Although Gwendolyn Brooks <u>had received</u> much praise from fellow poets
                                         A
   throughout her illustrious career, the people who <u>have had</u> the most direct
                                                     B
   influence upon her work are <u>parents</u>. <u>No error</u>
                           C   D

2.____

3. Tom did not feel well the morning after the big <u>party,</u> and <u>decides</u> that in the
                                        A   B
   future he <u>would drink</u> alcohol only in moderation. <u>No error</u>
            C   D

3.____

4. After several months of <u>steadily</u> dropping sales, the <u>executives</u> <u>were forced</u> to
                    A   B   C
   acknowledge the failure of their advertising campaign. <u>No error</u>
                                                   D

4.____

5. The factory strike lasted <u>so long a time</u> that the management and <u>workers</u>
                             A   B
   agreed to hire an impartial judge to decide <u>upon</u> a fair solution to their
                                             C
   dispute. <u>No error</u>
            D

5.____

6. People who watch the display of fireflies on a clear summer evening are actually
   witnessing a complex chemical reaction called bioluminescence, turn certain
     A   B
   organisms into living light bulbs. No error
     C   D

7. Since the beginning of this century many members of the Caughnawaga
                                              A
   Mohawk tribe make their living high above New York City. No error
           B   C   D

8. Maria Tallchief, the daughter of a full-blood Osage Indian, will perhaps
   mostly be remembered as America's first internationally celebrated
     A   B
   prima ballerina. No error
     C   D

9. Angela's parents were stern and old-fashioned they considered it improper for
     A   B   C
   her to call boys on the telephone. No error
                                        D

10. Although former congresswoman Barbara Jordan led a life marked by
                     A
    groundbreaking accomplishments, her insistence that she was no different
                   B
    from anyone else may be her greatest lesson. No error
                      C   D

11. The old man was a hermit who lived by himself at a cabin in the woods;
                              A   B
    nobody in town had ever spoken with him. No error
                    C   D

12. Quotation marks should be used for which of the following?
    A. Paraphrasing quotations
    B. Summarizing another person's ideas
    C. Direct quotations
    D. To emphasize an idea

13. Which of the following is CORRECTLY punctuated?
    A. Her story was titled, "Apples in Autumn".
    B. Her story was titled, "Apples in Autumn."
    C. Her story was titled "Apples in Autumn".
    D. Her story was titled; "Apples in Autumn."

14. (qtd. in Smith 27) 14._____
    What does the above parenthetical reference indicate about the source?
    A. Information regarding the quotation can be found in footnote 27.
    B. Smith is the author of the quotation.
    C. The source is direct.
    D. The source is indirect.

15. The Modern Language Association (MLA) format for documenting sources 15._____
    uses which of the following?
    A. References page
    B. Works Cited page
    C. Bibliography page
    D. All are acceptable

16. A direct quote is MOST beneficial in an essay when you 16._____
    A. want to emphasize a person's opinions
    B. need to include a long passage in order to selectively record a person's main ideas
    C. want to outline a person's general argument
    D. want to provide lengthy background information on a person's expertise

17. If you are writing a research essay on a new development in medical technology 17._____
    and you need the most current information available, where should you look?
    A. Library Reference Section
    B. Library Periodical Index
    C. Library Book Index
    D. Internet

18. www.ncu.edu 18._____
    What does the above internet address indicate?
    The site is
    A. in northern California
    B. affiliated with an educational institution
    C. affiliated with a government institution
    D. affiliated with a publishing institution

Questions 19-22.

DIRECTIONS: Questions 19 through 22 are to be answered on the basis of the following passage.

So This Was Adolescence by Annie Dillard

For as long as I could remember, I had been transparent to myself, unselfconscious, learning, doing, most of every day.(1) Now I was in my own way; I myself was a dark object I could not ignore.(2) I couldn't remember how to forget myself.(3) I didn't want to think about myself, to reckon myself in, to deal with myself every livelong minute on top of everything else – but swerve as I might, I couldn't avoid it.(4) I was a boulder blocking my own path.(5) I was a dog barking between my own ears, a barking dog who wouldn't hush.(6)

19. This excerpt can BEST be classified as which of the following? 19.____
    A. Narrative   B. Descriptive
    C. Argumentative   D. Explanatory

20. The imagery in this excerpt depends MOST heavily on which of the following? 20.____
    A. Exaggeration   B. Comparison   C. Metaphor   D. Simile

21. What has changed for the author in this paragraph? 21.____
    She
    A. doesn't know
    B. has recalled a painful memory
    C. has experienced a nervous breakdown
    D. has grown self-conscious

22. The phrase *reckon myself in* in sentence 5 is BEST characterized as which of the following? 22.____
    A. Formal   B. Colloquial   C. Poetic   D. Abstract

Questions 23-25.

DIRECTIONS: Questions 23 through 25 are to be answered on the basis of the following passage.

People Have Multiple Intelligences by Howard Gardner

Intelligence is not an absolute such as height that can be measured simply, largely because people have multiple intelligences rather than one single intelligence.(1) In all, I have identified seven forms of intelligence.(2) The two that are valued most highly in this society are linguistic and logical-mathematical intelligences.(3) When people think of someone as smart, they are usually referring to those two, because individuals who possess linguistic and logical-mathematical abilities do well on tests that supposedly measure intelligence.(4)

23. The effect of this excerpt depends MOST heavily on the use of which of the following? 23.____
    A. Multiple examples   B. Definition
    C. Narration   D. Imagery

24. The main verb of the first sentence is 24.____
    A. is   B. can be   C. is and have   D. have

25. The phrase *linguistic intelligence* in sentence 3 refers to which of the following? 25.____
    A. Spatial and language abilities   B. Knowledge of multiple languages
    C. Language abilities   D. Public speaking abilities

5 (#1)

KEY (CORRECT ANSWERS)

1.	B	11.	B
2.	A	12.	C
3.	B	13.	B
4.	D	14.	D
5.	A	15.	B
6.	B	16.	A
7.	C	17.	D
8.	A	18.	B
9.	C	19.	A
10.	D	20.	C

21.	D
22.	B
23.	B
24.	A
25.	C

TEST 2

DIRECTIONS: Each question or incomplete statement is followed by several suggested answers or completions. Select the one that BEST answers the question or completes the statement. *PRINT THE LETTER OF THE CORRECT ANSWER IN THE SPACE AT THE RIGHT.*

Questions 1-6.

DIRECTIONS: Questions 1 through 6 are to be answered on the basis of the following passage.

Declaration of Sentiments and Resolutions by Elizabeth Cady Stanton

    When, in the course of human events, it becomes necessary for one portion of the family of man to assume among the people of the earth a position different from that which they have hitherto occupied, but one to which the laws of nature and nature's God entitle them, a decent respect to the opinions of mankind requires that they should declare the causes that impel them to such a course.(1)
    We hold these truths to be self-evident: that all men and women are created equal; that they are endowed by their creator with certain inalienable rights; that among these are life, liberty and the pursuit of happiness; that to secure these rights governments are instituted, deriving their just powers from the consent of the governed.(2)

1. This passage is BEST characterized as
   A. interpretive   B. narrative   C. an allegory   D. persuasive

2. *...from that which they have hitherto occupied, but one to which the laws of nature and of nature's God entitle them, a decent respect to the opinions of mankind requires that they should declare the causes that impel them to such a course...*
   The above excerpt from the first sentence relies MOST heavily on which of the following?
   A. Parallel construction   B. Example
   C. Imagery   D. Coordination

3. In sentence 1, the word *hitherto* is BEST replaced by
   A. will one day   B. again   C. previously   D. never

4. What point of view is this excerpt written in?
   A. First person singular   B. First person plural
   C. Third person singular   D. Third person plural

5. Which of the following BEST expresses the main purpose of this excerpt?
   A. To explain the illegal actions this political group is planning to take
   B. To explain the need for women's legal rights
   C. To argue for the legal rights of women
   D. To argue for the legal rights of men and women

6. This excerpt, from sentence 2, is an example of a(n)
   A. noun phrase
   B. dangling modifier
   C. dependent clause
   D. independent clause

Question 7.

DIRECTIONS: Question 7 contains problems in grammar, usage, diction (choice of words), idiom, and punctuation, or it can be correct. The sentence does not contain more than one error. You will find that the error, if there is one, is underlined and lettered. Assume that all other elements of the sentence are correct and cannot be changed. If there is an error, select the one underlined part that must be changed in order to make the sentence correct. If there is no error, select answer D.

7. <u>Although</u> scientists have succeeded in creating robots able to process huge
     A

   amounts of information, the <u>are</u> still struggling to create one <u>who's</u> reasoning
                     B   C

   ability matches that of a human baby. <u>No error</u>
                                                        D

8. One Sunday, Katy Smith noticed that her new neighbor did not leave home to go to church. As a result, Katy concluded that her neighbors were atheists. Katy's flaw in logic is an example of
   A. ad hominem attack
   B. faulty deduction
   C. faulty induction
   D. a logical fallacy

Questions 9-14.

DIRECTIONS: In each of the following sentences, you are given two or more sentences to combine into one. After each set of sentences, there is a question that will help you decide how the sentences are to be combined. In combining some of the sentences, you will change the order of the original a great deal; in combining others, you will change the order only a little. Be sure that the new sentence you create is a complete sentence, that it contains all of the essential facts given in the original set of sentences, that it maintains the proper relationship of ideas, and that is clearly and effectively written.

9. My grandfather has dramatic mood swings. He was diagnosed as manic-depressive.
   Your new sentence will contain which of the following?
   A. swings, he
   B. manic-depressive grandfather
   C. grandfather, who
   D. with dramatic mood swings, my grandfather

10. A politician thinks of the next election. A statesman thinks of the next generation.
    Which of the following is the BEST word to join the two sentences?
    A. whereas   B. furthermore   C. hitherto   D. although

11. Ulysses was written by James Joyce. It is an important book. It examines the human psyche.
    Your new sentence will begin with which of the following?
    A. The human psyche, an important
    B. James Joyce, an important
    C. Ulysses, an important
    D. Ulysses and James Joyce

12. I visited my friend Anna. She owns a wolf. It ate my steak one night.
    Your new sentence will begin with which of the following?
    A. After
    B. When
    C. I visited
    D. My friend Anna, who

13. I had a job in high school. I worked for a family. I babysat their children. I was responsible for house-cleaning.
    Your new sentence will contain which of the following?
    A. babysitting and housecleaning
    B. babysat their children and was responsible for
    C. responsible for housecleaning and to babysit
    D. to babysit and for housecleaning

Questions 14-17.

DIRECTIONS: Question 14 through 17 are to be answered on the basis of the following passage.

Asking How Much is Enough by Alan Durning

Consumption has become a central pillar of life in industrial lands and is even embedded in social values.(1) Opinion surveys in the world's two largest economies—Japan and the United States show consumerist definitions of success becoming ever more prevalent.(2)
In Taiwan, a billboard demands "Why Aren't You a Millionaire Yet?"(3) The Japanese speak of the "new three sacred treasures": color television, air conditioning and the automobile.(4)
The affluent life-style born in the United States is emulated by those who can afford it around the world.(5) And many can: the average person today is 4.5 times richer than were his or her great-grandparents at the turn of the century.(6)

14. The effect of this passage depends MOST heavily on the use of which of the following?
    A. Definition of terms   B. Narrative scene
    C. Extended example   D. Multiple examples

15. In sentence 2, the phrase *consumerist definitions of success* MOST NEARLY means which of the following?
Success
   A. determined by consumer surveys
   B. that is measured by material wealth
   C. that includes spiritual and psychological considerations
   D. measured by greed

15.____

16. In sentence 5, the word *affluent* is BEST replaced by which of the following?
    A. Frugal   B. Wasteful   C. Wealthy   D. Luxurious

16.____

17. This passage can BEST be characterized as which of the following?
    A. Narrative   B. Expository   C. Persuasive   D. Symbolic

17.____

Questions 18-23.

DIRECTIONS: Questions 18 through 23 are to be answered on the basis of the following passage.

Nonmoral Nature by Stephen Jay Gould

When the Right Honorable and Reverend Francis Henry, earl of Bridgewater, died in February, 1829, he left $8,000 to support a series of books "on the power, wisdom and goodness of God, as manifested in the creation."(1) William Buckland, England's first official academic geologist and later dean of Westminster, was invited to compose one of the nine Bridgewater Treatises.(2) In it he discussed the most pressing problem of natural theology: If God is benevolent and the Creation displays his "power, wisdom and goodness," then why are we surrounded with pain, suffering, and apparently senseless cruelty in the animal world?(3)

18. What is the main verb in the first sentence?
    A. to support   B. left and died   C. died   D. left

18.____

19. In sentence 3, the word *benevolent* is BEST replaced by
    A. good   b. mild   C. just   D. stern

19.____

20. This passage is BEST described as
    A. persuasive   B. narrative   C. expository   D. comparative

20.____

21. The phrase *pain, suffering, and apparently senseless cruelty* from sentence 3 is an example of
    A. a subordinate clause   B. parallel construction
    C. an independent clause   D. a phrase

21.____

22. Which of the following BEST expresses the main idea of the excerpt?
    A. Historians who believed that nature reflected God's goodness were often disappointed.
    B. Historians believed that nature reflected God's goodness, but they were wrong
    C. God is good, and nature reflects this goodness.
    D. If God is good, then why doesn't nature reflect this goodness?

    22.____

23. ...England's first official academic geologist and later dean of Westminster...
    The above excerpt, from sentence 2, is an example of which of the following?
    A. A dependent clause   B. An independent clause
    C. A phrase   D. Parallel construction

    23.____

Question 24.

DIRECTIONS: See directions for Question 7.

24. <u>After</u> the basketball team lost by forty points, the angry A coach gathered <u>it</u>
     A   B
    into the locker room and told <u>them their</u> performance had been a disgrace.
                                            C
    <u>No error</u>
    D

    24.____

Question 25.

DIRECTIONS: See directions for Questions 9-14.

25. I saw him far down the road. He rode an old dusty horse. An old song played on the radio. I sat on the upper rail of our small corral.
    Your new sentence will begin with which of the following?
    A. Riding an old dusty horse   B. I was on the upper rail
    C. The song playing on the radio   D. Seeing him far down the road

    25.____

KEY (CORRECT ANSWERS)

1.	D	11.	C
2.	A	12.	B
3.	C	13.	A
4.	B	14.	D
5.	C	15.	B
6.	D	16.	C
7.	C	17.	B
8.	C	18.	D
9.	C	19.	A
10.	A	20.	C

21.	B
22.	D
23.	C
24.	B
25.	B

TEST 3

DIRECTIONS: Each question or incomplete statement is followed by several suggested answers or completions. Select the one that BEST answers the question or completes the statement. *PRINT THE LETTER OF THE CORRECT ANSWER IN THE SPACE AT THE RIGHT.*

Questions 1-9.

DIRECTIONS: In each of the following sentences, you are given two or more sentences to combine into one. After each set of sentences, there is a question that will help you decide how the sentences are to be combined. In combining some of the sentences, you will change the order of the original a great deal; in combining others, you will change the order only a little. Be sure that the new sentence you create is a complete sentence, that is contains all of the essential facts given in the original set of sentences, that is maintains the proper relationship of ideas, and that is clearly and effectively written.

1. Bhavesh runs in front of the trains. Bhavesh is crazy.
   Your new sentence will contain which of the following?
   A. whose   B. that   C. who   D. whom

2. Frank is frustrated by how slow his bicycle is. Frank bought a new Toyota.
   Your new sentence will begin with which of the following?
   A. Buying a new Toyota   B. His bicycle being frustrating
   C. The new Toyota   D. Frank, frustrated

3. The police officer met his informer. They met at a diner in another city. No one from the neighborhood went there.
   Your new sentence will contain which of the following?
   A. away from the neighborhood   B. meeting at a neighborhood diner
   C. informer at an out-of-the-way   D. informing in the neighborhood

4. That window was fine yesterday. Today it is broken.
   Your new sentence will contain which of the following?
   A. which   B. that   C. it   D. its

5. There was a fight. Three students were suspended. No one was hurt.
   Your new sentence will begin with which of the following?
   A. Fighting with each other   B. Three students were
   C. Suspended for fighting   D. Unhurt from fighting

6. The town of Happy is four square miles. It is bounded on the North by Holler Creek, and on the South by an Interstate. Seven hundred people live there.
   Your new sentence will begin with which of the following?
   A. Four square miles and called Happy
   B. Bounded by Holler Creek
   C. Seven hundred people
   D. Bounded on the South by an Interstate

7. The horse was a nice, friendly horse. It never caused any trouble. It let me slip the bridle off. It stood quietly as I combed the burrs from its hide.
Your new sentence will contain which of the following?
   A. standing quietly as I combed
   B. horse, it never caused
   C. letting me slip the bridle off
   D. which was nice and friendly and had never caused any trouble

8. There was an emergency with the patient. Two doctors were called in to operate. The patient lived.
Your new sentence will begin with which of the following?
   A. Called in to operate
   B. Two doctors were
   C. The patient's emergency
   D. Living through the surgery

9. The losing team was made up of superstars. These superstars acted as isolated individuals on the court.
Your new sentence will contain which of the following?
   A. superstars, these
   B. losing team superstars these
   C. superstars who
   D. acting isolated on the superstar court

10. Ernest was surprised to discover that Angela was a smoker. She didn't have yellow teeth or a terrible cough.
Ernest's flaw in logic is an example of
   A. ad hominem attack
   B. faulty deduction
   C. faulty induction
   D. a logical fallacy

Questions 11-15.

DIRECTIONS: Questions 11 through 15 are to be answered on the basis of the following passage.

On the Ball, by Roger Angell

It weighs just over five ounces and measures between 2.86 and 2.94 inches in diameter.(1) It is made of a composition-cork nucleus encased in two thin layers of rubber, one black and one red, surrounded by 121 yards of tightly wrapped blue-gray wool yarn, 45 yards of white wool yarn 53 more yards of blue-gray wool yarn, 150 yards of fine cotton yarn, a coat of rubber cement, and a cowhide (formerly horsehide) exterior which is held together with 216 slightly raised red cotton stitches.(2)

11. The effect of this passage relies MOST heavily on which of the following?
    A. Argument
    B. Extended example
    C. Description
    D. Narration

12. ...*by 121 yards of tightly wrapped blue-gray wool, 45 yards of white wool yarn,* 12._____
    53 more yards of blue-gray wool yarn...
    The above excerpt, taken from sentence 2, is an example of
    A. parallel construction   B. non-parallel construction
    C. an independent clause   D. a dependent clause

13. The main verb of sentence 2 is   13._____
    A. surrounded   B. is made   C. wrapped   D. is held

14. This passage is BEST characterized as   14._____
    A. narrative   B. ironic
    C. argumentative   D. informative

15. Which of the following techniques is MOST frequently used by the writer?   15._____
    A. Vivid detail   B. Extended examples
    C. Imagery   D. Simile

16. In competition against a rival bookstore, the owner of the smaller store   16._____
    began running ads about his competitor's gambling history.
    This is an example of a(n)
    A. false analogy   B. hasty generalization
    C. faulty use of authority   D. ad hominem attack

17. An unpopular monarch was criticized for being too authoritarian with his   17._____
    subjects. He replied by saying, "Would you prefer anarchy instead?"
    His reasoning is an example of a
    A. false analogy   B. slippery slope argument
    C. faulty dilemma   D. doubtful cause

Questions 18-22.

DIRECTIONS: The following sentences in Questions 18 through 22 contain problems in
              grammar, usage, diction (choice of words), idiom, and punctuation. Some
              sentences are correct. No sentence contains more than one error. You will
              find that the error, if there is one, is underlined and lettered. Assume that all
              other elements of the sentence are correct and cannot be changed. If there is
              an error, select the one underlined part that must be changed in order to make
              the sentence correct. If there is no error, select answer D.

18. In the past few <u>decades,</u> while much of the <u>worlds</u> imagination has focused on   18._____
                        A   B
    the possibilities of outer space some scientists <u>have been</u> exploring a different
                                                         C
    frontier —the ocean floor. <u>No error</u>
                                  D

19. Many treasure hunters and archaeologists believe the sea floor around the   19.____

    Azores, a group of islands west of Portugal, still harbor some of the richest
      A   B   C

    sunken treasure in the world. No error
                                    D

20. Throughout the Age of Exploration, explorers like Columbus and Vespucci   20.____
                        A   B

    relied on the Trade Winds of the North Atlantic to fuel and sustain their long
                    C

    journeys. No error
                D

21. The undersea canyon that began just west of the Monterey peninsula in   21.____
                              A   B

    California has provided marine biologists a rare opportunity to study the
                                                                   C

    life of the deep ocean up close. No error
                                       D

22. Though they may not realize it, many modern restaurants have adopted menus   22.____
                                                              A   B

    reminiscent of an old Swedish tradition called the smorgasbord. No error
                                                        C   D

23. Sylvia was sad when she heard that Mr. Roe had had a heart attack. She   23.____
    wasn't surprised, however, since Mr. Roe did not like to see his doctor anymore
    than necessary.
    Sylvia's flaw in logic is an example of
       A. a logical fallacy   B. faulty deduction
       C. faulty induction   D. ad hominem attack

24. Cynthia couldn't believe that, at 6'9" tall, Thomas didn't play basketball.   24.____
    Cynthia's flaw in logic is an example of
       A. ad hominem attack   B. faulty deduction
       C. faulty induction   D. a logical fallacy

Question 25.

DIRECTIONS: See directions for Questions 1-9.

25. Every student should have access to a computer. Access to the internet should   25.____
    be free.
    Which of the following is the BEST word to join the two sentences?
       A. and   B. however   C. therefore   D. furthermore

KEY (CORRECT ANSWERS)

1.	C	11.	C
2.	D	12.	A
3.	C	13.	B
4.	A	14.	D
5.	B	15.	A
6.	C	16.	D
7.	D	17.	C
8.	B	18.	B
9.	C	19.	C
10.	B	20.	D

21. A
22. D
23. B
24. B
25. D

TEST 4

DIRECTIONS: Each question or incomplete statement is followed by several suggested answers or completions. Select the one that BEST answers the question or completes the statement. *PRINT THE LETTER OF THE CORRECT ANSWER IN THE SPACE AT THE RIGHT.*

Questions 1-6.

DIRECTIONS: Questions 1 through 6 are to be answered on the basis of the following passage.

Finding a Voice, by Eudora Welty

    Through learning at my later date things I hadn't known, or had escaped or possibly feared realizing, about my parents—and myself—I glimpse our whole family life as if it were freed of that clock time which spaces us apart so inhibitingly, divides young and old, keeps our living through the same experiences at separate distances.(1)
    It is our inward journey that leads us through time—forward or back,, seldom in a straight line, most often spiraling.(2) Each of us is moving, changing, with respect to others.(3) As we discover, we remember; remembering, we discover; and most intensely do we experience this when our separate journeys converge.(4)

1. The main verb in the first sentence is
   A. spaces   B. hadn't known and had escaped
   C. learning   D. glimpse

                                                                                                 1.____

2. *Through learning at my later date things I hadn't known.*
The above excerpt, taken from sentence 1, is an example of which of the following?
   A. Parallel construction   B. An independent clause
   C. A dependent clause   D. A phrase

                                                                                                 2.____

3. *As we discover, we remember; remembering, we discover.*
The above excerpt, taken from sentence 4, is an example of which of the following?
   A. Parallel construction   B. An independent clause
   C. A dependent clause   D. A phrase

                                                                                                 3.____

4. *...forward or back, seldom in a straight line, most often spiraling...*
The above excerpt, taken from sentence 2, is an example of which of the following?
   A. Parallel construction   B. An independent clause
   C. A dependent clause   D. A phrase

                                                                                                 4.____

5. In sentence 4, the word *converge* is BEST replaced with
   A. separate   B. come together
   C. subordinate   D. end

                                                                                                 5.____

6. The author's main point is BEST summarized by which of the following statements? 6.____
   A. Time is the dominant force in our lives.
   B. Time is irrelevant in our lives.
   C. Our lives are better measured by emotional time than chronological time.
   D. Our lives are better measured by chronological time than emotional time.

Questions 7-13.

DIRECTIONS: In each of the following sentences, you are given two or more sentences to combine into one. After each set of sentences, there is a question that will help you decide how the sentences are to be combined. In combining some of the sentences, you will change the order of the original a great deal; in combining others, you will change the order only a little. Be sure that the new sentence you create is a complete sentence, that is contains all of the essential facts given in the original set of sentences, that is maintains the proper relationship of ideas, and that is clearly and effectively written.

7. The rodeo arena was crowded. The crowd made no impression on me. 7.____
   Your sentence will begin with which of the following?
   A. And   B. However   C. Although   D. Furthermore

8. People turn on the television. Three hours later, people find themselves still in front of the television. They've eaten many bags of snacks. 8.____
   Your new sentence will contain which of the following?
   A. are eating   B. people find themselves
   C. they've eaten   D. hours, and many bags

9. Watching television is a popular way to spend leisure time. It makes people apathetic. 9.____
   Which of the following is the BEST word to join the two sentences?
   A. and   B. but   C. because   D. furthermore

10. I don't like seafood. My mother doesn't like seafood either. 10.____
    Your new sentence will contain which of the following?
    A. Either…or   B. Either…nor   C. Neither…nor   D. Neither…or

11. Thurmount means "gateway to the mountains." It is minutes from the Blue Ridge mountains. It is also minutes from the historic town of Surley. 11.____
    Your new sentence will begin with which of the following?
    A. Thurmount, which means
    B. Minutes from Surely, the historic town
    C. Gateway to the mountains, Thurmount
    D. Surley and the Blue Ridge mountains close by

12. Her job was to sell to vendors. She also helped with marketing. There were 12.____
    some advertising opportunities, too.
    Your new sentence will contain which of the following?
    A. to sell to vendors, market and sometimes advertising
    B. selling to vendors, to market and some advertising
    C. selling to vendors, marketing and some advertising
    D. to sell, marketing and advertising

13. I want not only to survive. I want to live. 13.____
    Your new sentence will contain which of the following?
    A. want to live   B. survive and live
    C. and   D. but also

Questions 14-20.

DIRECTIONS: The following sentences in Questions 14 through 20 contain problems in grammar, usage, diction (choice of words), idiom, and punctuation. Some sentences are correct. No sentence contains more than one error. You will find that the error, if there is one, is underlined and lettered. Assume that all other elements of the sentence are correct and cannot be changed. If there is an error, select the one underlined part that must be changed in order to make the sentence correct. If there is no error, select answer D.

14. Among the Tlingit people of Western Canada, the tradition of the potlatch 14.____

    <u>was used</u> to redistribute wealth within the <u>tribe,</u> and <u>marked</u> all ceremonial
       A   B   C

    occasions. <u>No error</u>
                  D

15. One of the <u>great,</u> and least publicized, <u>legacies</u> of Native American culture 15.____
              A   B

    <u>has been</u> the worldwide cultivation of food staples such as tomatoes, potatoes,
       C

    and corn through careful farming methods. <u>No error</u>
                                                                       D

16. Although the <u>Japanese art of Bonsai</u> began <u>more then</u> 1,000 years ago, it has 16.____
                                 A   B

    become a modern antidote to the cramped <u>gardens</u> of densely populated urban
                                                           C

    areas. <u>No error</u>
            D

17. Feng Shui, the ancient Chinese science of studying the natural <u>environment's</u>　　　　17.____
　　　　　　　　　　　　　　　　　　　　　　　　　　　　　　　　　　　　A
<u>affect</u> on a person's well-being, <u>has gained</u> new popularity in the design and
　B　　　　　　　　　　　　　　　　　C
decoration of buildings. <u>No error</u>
　　　　　　　　　　　　　　　D

18. Karala had to write her article more <u>quick</u> <u>than</u> the other <u>reporters,</u> because　　　18.____
　　　　　　　　　　　　　　　　　　　　　A　　B　　　　　　　　C
her flight was scheduled to leave an hour after the deadline. <u>No error</u>
　　　　　　　　　　　　　　　　　　　　　　　　　　　　　　　　　D

19. After careful <u>consideration,</u> the committee <u>have</u> decided to extend <u>our</u>　　　　19.____
　　　　　　　　　　A　　　　　　　　　　　　　　　B　　　　　　　　　　　C
contract for another four years. <u>No error</u>
　　　　　　　　　　　　　　　　　　　　D

20. Of the eight <u>attorneys</u> at the law <u>firm,</u> Martha is the <u>most qualified</u> to handle　　20.____
　　　　　　　　　　A　　　　　　　　　　B　　　　　　　　　　C
this case. <u>No error</u>
　　　　　　　　　D

Questions 21-25.

DIRECTIONS:　Questions 21 through 25 are to be answered on the basis of the following passage.

Letter From Birmingham Jail, Martin Luther King, Jr.

　　I have earnestly worked and preached against violent tension, but there is a type of constructive nonviolent tension that is necessary for growth.(1) Just as Socrates felt that it was necessary to create a tension in the mind so that individuals could rise from the bondage of myths and half-truths to the unfettered realm of creative analysis and objective appraisal, we must see the need for having nonviolent gadflies to create the kind of tension in society that will help men rise from the dark depths of prejudice and racism to the majestic heights of understanding and brotherhood.(2)

21.　*...mind so that individuals could rise from the bondage of myths and half-truths*　　21.____
　　　to the unfettered realm of creative analysis and objective appraisal...
　　　The above excerpt from sentence 2 contains examples of which of the
　　　following?
　　　　A. Coordination　　　　　　　　　B. Prepositional phrasing
　　　　C. Dangling modifiers　　　　　　D. Parallel construction

22.　In sentence 2, the word *gadflies* is BEST replaced by　　　　　　　　　　　　　22.____
　　　　A. soldier　　　　　　　　　　　　B. protester
　　　　C. underachievers　　　　　　　　D. indigent men

23. This passage is BEST characterized as which of the following? 23.____
    A. Moral argument B. Narrative episode
    C. Poetic statement D. A tribute

24. The writer depends MOST heavily on which of the following devices? 24.____
    A. Hyperbole B. Understatement
    C. Metaphor and simile D. Personification

25. Based on the tone and style of the excerpt, what can you infer about the 25.____
    writer's feelings for his intended audience?
    He
    A. believes they are ignorant B. hates them
    C. agrees with their views D. disagrees with their view

KEY (CORRECT ANSWERS)

1.	D		11.	A
2.	C		12.	C
3.	A		13.	D
4.	D		14.	C
5.	B		15.	A
6.	C		16.	B
7.	C		17.	B
8.	D		18.	A
9.	B		19.	B
10.	C		20.	D

21. D
22. B
23. A
24. C
25. D

EXAMINATION SECTION
TEST 1

DIRECTIONS: Each question or incomplete statement is followed by several suggested answers or completions. Select the one that BEST answers the question or completes the statement. *PRINT THE LETTER OF THE CORRECT ANSWER IN THE SPACE AT THE RIGHT.*

Questions 1-3.

DIRECTIONS: In each of the following sentences, you are given two or more sentences to combine into one. After each set of sentences, there is a question that will help you decide how the sentences are to be combined. In combining some of the sentences, you will change the order of the original a great deal; in combining others, you will change the order only a little. Be sure that the new sentence you create is a complete sentence, that is contains all of the essential facts given in the original set of sentences, that is maintains the proper relationship of ideas, and that is clearly and effectively written.

1. Finding a job is hard. The job market is competitive. You must be sharp in the job market. It can eat up your confidence.
   Your new sentence will contain which of the following?
   A. sharp and confident
   B. sharp market with confidence
   C. competitive, sharp, confident market
   D. hard market

2. I like to ski. I like to snowboard. I like making Adirondack chairs.
   Your new sentence will contain which of the following?
   A. skiing, snowboarding and to make
   B. skiing, snowboarding, and making
   C. to snowboard, ski and making
   D. make, ski and snowboarding

3. Our waitress was costumed in a kimono. She had painted her face white. She had arranged her hair in an upswept lacquered beehive.
   Your new sentence will begin with which of the following?
   A. Wearing her hair
   B. In a kimono, with painted face and lacquered beehive
   C. Our waitress, who
   D. Painting her face

Questions 4-20.

DIRECTIONS: The following sentences in Questions 4 through 20 contain problems in grammar, usage, diction (choice of words), idiom, and punctuation. Some sentences are correct. No sentence contains more than one error. You will find that the error, if there is one, is underlined and lettered. Assume that all other elements of the sentence are correct and cannot be changed. If there is an error, select the one underlined part that must be changed in order to make the sentence correct. If there is no error, select answer D.

4. The <u>Sioux Indians</u> wasted no part of a bison kill, and even used <u>it's</u> bones to
      A   B
make knives, cooking <u>tools,</u> and sewing needles. <u>No error</u>
                           C   D

4.____

5. Due to <u>Lily's</u> years of care and grooming, her <u>sleek</u> healthy Holstein won the
        A   B
dairy cattle competition at the <u>state fair</u>. <u>No error</u>
                              C   D

5.____

6. Due to the changing nature of the cattle <u>industry,</u> <u>there</u> <u>are not</u> real cowboys
                                                        A   B   C
left in America. <u>No error</u>
                      D

6.____

7. This <u>weekend,</u> the gas <u>company's</u> bowling team, made up of both managers
       A   B
and workers, won <u>their</u> fifth straight championship. <u>No error</u>
                  C   D

7.____

8. The <u>grizzly bears</u> of Yellowstone National Park have begun to relearn their
      A
old hunting and foraging techniques, <u>however</u> there <u>has been</u> an increase
                                        B   C
in the bear population. <u>No error</u>
                            D

8.____

9. You must exercise, <u>eating sensibly</u> and <u>think positively</u> if you want to <u>lose</u>
                          A   B   C
weight. <u>No error</u>
          D

9.____

10. If Carlton <u>Was</u> to put any more weight on that <u>hayrack</u>, it <u>would</u> surely be
           A   B   C
too heavy for the tractor to pull. <u>No error</u>

10.____

11. Diving from her chair into the pool's deep end, the lifeguard had saved the
                                        A   B   C
    children. No error
             D

    11.____

12. Hank made Sheila and I promise to meet him at the fairgrounds when the
                      A   B
    state fair came to town. No error
              C   D

    12.____

13. Luther put his children to bed, read them a story, and kissed them good
                                 A   B   C
    night. No error
          D

    13.____

14. Our kitchen table, along with the Adirondack chairs in the yard, were made
                 A   B
    by my grandfather, who is a skilled carpenter. No error
           C   D

    14.____

15. The tenants of the apartment complex wanted to show their appreciation for
         A
    the work of Arthur, the building superintendent at his retirement party they
                                       B
    gave him a gold watch, a plaque and a certificate. No error
      C   D

    15.____

16. My Aunt Audrey used to have a gold tooth that shined brightly whenever she
                                A   B   C
    laughed. No error
              D

    16.____

17. The only person in the county who's relatives are all natives, Abel makes
                                     A   B
    sure everyone knows it. No error
                    C   D

    17.____

18. After Luc scored the goal that won the hockey game, his teammates treated
                              A   B
    him as if he was a king. No error
            C   D

    18.____

19. Mr. Lopez was angry when he discovered the latch on the corral gate
                                   A
    had been broken by one of his ranch hands. No error
         B   C   D

    19.____

20. Stewart burned the gravy and ruined the <u>dinner,</u> but we told him not to worry 20.____
                                                                  A

    <u>because</u> none of us are <u>are perfect cooks</u>. <u>No error</u>
       B   C   D

21. Susanne refused to allow her son to buy a red car because she knew it would result in more speeding tickets for him. Susanne's flaw in logic is an example of 21.____
    - A. ad hominem attack
    - B. faulty deduction
    - C. faulty induction
    - D. hasty generalization

Questions 22-25.

DIRECTIONS: Use the following information to answer Questions 22 through 25.

    003.42   Schuster, Mary B
    CAM   Student's Guide to Home Sewing Projects/Mary Schuster—
                     Bedford, Mass.: Addison-Wesley Pub. Co.
                     c. 1998.
                     ix, 254 p.: ill., 36 cm.
                     ISBN 0-000-00836-2 (pbk)
                     1. Crafts – Sewing
                     2. Home – Craft Projects
                     3. Mary Schuster

22. What do the numbers 003.42 (along the lefthand margin) represent? 22.____
    - A. Library of Congress number
    - B. Size of the book (in height and depth)
    - C. The number of pages in the book
    - D. Library call numbers

23. ix, 254 p.: ill., 36 cm. 23.____
    What does the above line indicate?
    - A. Volume number, Library of Congress number, and height of book
    - B. Number of pages, use of illustrations, and height of book
    - C. Volume number, number of pages, and height of book
    - D. Number of pages, location of book, and height of book

24. Bedford, Mass.: Addison-Wesley Pub. Co.© 1998 24.____
    What does the above information indicate?
    - A. Publisher and year that book was accepted for publication
    - B. Location of publisher, publisher, and year that book was accepted for publication
    - C. Location of publisher, publisher, and year of publication
    - D. Publisher and year publishing house was established

25.
1. Crafts – Sewing
2. Home – Craft Projects
3. Mary Schuster

What does the above information indicate?
   A. Other Library of Congress listings for the same book
   B. Subjects related to the book's subject
   C. Other books by the same author
   D. Other library catalog listings for the same book

25._____

KEY (CORRECT ANSWERS)

1.	A		11.	C
2.	B		12.	A
3.	C		13.	D
4.	B		14.	B
5.	D		15.	B
6.	C		16.	B
7.	C		17.	A
8.	B		18.	C
9.	A		19.	D
10.	A		20.	C

21.	B
22.	D
23.	B
24.	C
25.	D

TEST 2

DIRECTIONS: Each question or incomplete statement is followed by several suggested answers or completions. Select the one that BEST answers the question or completes the statement. *PRINT THE LETTER OF THE CORRECT ANSWER IN THE SPACE AT THE RIGHT.*

Questions 1-5.

DIRECTIONS: Questions 1 through 5 are to be answered on the basis of the following passage.

No Name Woman, Maxine Hong Kingston

The round mooncakes and round doorways, the round tables of graduated size that fit one roundness inside another, round windows and rice bowls—these talismans had lost their power to warn this family of the law: a family must be whole, faithfully keeping the descent line by having sons to feed the old and the dead, who in turn look after the family.(1) The villagers came to show my aunt and her lover-in-hiding a broken house.(2) The villagers were speeding up the circling of events because she was too shortsighted to see that her infidelity had already harmed the village, that waves of consequences would return unpredictably, sometimes in disguise, as now, to hurt her.(3)

1. This passage is BEST characterized as which of the following?
   A. Persuasive   B. Narrative
   C. Classification   D. Definition   1.____

2. The author relies MOST heavily on which of the following?
   A. Definition   B. Hyperbole
   C. Personification   D. Imagery   2.____

3. In sentence 1, the word *talismans* is BEST replaced by which of the following?
   A. Objects   B. Images   C. Symbols   D. Superstitions   3.____

4. ...that her infidelity had already harmed the village, that waves of consequences would return unpredictably...
The above excerpt, from sentence 3, contains examples of which of the following?
   A Fragments   B. Dangling modifiers
   C. Parallel construction   D. Coordination   4.____

5. What is the MAIN verb of the first sentence?
   A. had lost   B. fit   C. to warn   D. graduated   5.____

Questions 6-9.

DIRECTIONS: Questions 6 through 9 are to be answered on the basis of the following passage.

Winged: The Creatures on My Mind, Ursula K. LeGuin

   Gulls on Klatsand Beach, on any North Pacific shore, are all alike in their two kinds: white adults with black wingtips and yellow bills; and yearlings, adult-sized but with delicately figured brown features.(1) They soar and cry, swoop, glide, dive, squabble, and grab; they stand in their multitudes at evening in the sunset shallows of the creek mouth before they rise in silence to fly out to sea, where they will sleep the night afloat on waves far out beyond the breakers, like a fleet of small white ships with sails furled and no riding lights.(2)

6. This passage is BEST characterized as
   A. narrative   B. ironic   C. persuasive   D. descriptive

7. Which of the following is used MOST frequently by the writer?
   A. Irony
   B. Imagery
   C. Subordination
   D. Simile

8. The final image of the gulls, in sentence 2, suggests which of the following?
   A. Isolation
   B. Foreboding
   C. Communal identity
   D. Individual identity

9. In sentence 1, the word *yearlings* is BEST replaced by
   A. adolescents   B. children   C. aged adults   D. young males

Questions 10-13.

DIRECTIONS: Questions 10 through 13 are to be answered on the basis of the following passage.

Leisure Will Kill You, Art Buchwald

   This country is producing so much leisure equipment for the home that nobody has any leisure time anymore to enjoy it.(1) A few months ago I bought a television tape recorder to make copies of programs when I was out of the house.(2)
   Last week I recorded the Nebraska-Oklahoma football game.(3) When I came home in the evening, I decided to play it back.(4) But my son wanted to play "Baseball" on the TV screen with his Atari Computer.(5) We finished four innings when my wife came in the room and asked me if I would like to listen to the Vienna Opera on our hi-fi stereo set.(6)

10. The tone of this passage is BEST described as
    A. sarcastic
    B. argumentative
    C. ironic
    D. sentimental

11. The effect of the passage relies MOST heavily on which of the following? 11._____
    A. Definition   B. Metaphor   C. Argument   D. Example

12. The MAIN verb in sentence 6 is 12._____
    A. finished   B. came   C. asked   D. would like

13. Which of the following BEST describes the author's writing style? 13._____
    A. Academic   B. Direct   C. Abstract   D. Poetic

Questions 14-17.

DIRECTIONS: Questions 14 through 17 are to be answered on the basis of the following passage.

The Women, Harriet Jacobs

I would ten thousand times rather that my children should be the half-starved paupers of Ireland than to be the most pampered among the slaves of America.(1) I would rather drudge out my life on a cotton plantation, till the grave opened to give me rest, than to live with an unprincipled master and a jealous mistress.(2) The felon's home in a penitentiary is preferable.(3) He may repent, and turn from the error of his ways, and so find peace, but it is not so with a favorite slave.(4) She is not allowed to have any pride or character.(5) It is deemed a crime in her to wish to be virtuous.(6)

14. The effect of this passage relies MOST heavily on which of the following? 14._____
    A. Argument   B. Imagery
    C. Extended example   D. Comparison

15. The word *pampered*, in sentence 1, is BEST replaced with 15._____
    A. coddled   B. rich   C. abused   D. large

16. The underlined excerpt from sentence 2 is an example of 16._____
    A. an independent clause   B. a dependent clause
    C. a phrase   D. parallel construction

17. This passage can BEST be characterized as 17._____
    A. persuasive   B. ironic   C. sarcastic   D. poetic

Questions 18-25.

DIRECTIONS: The following sentences in Questions 18 through 25 contain problems in grammar, usage, diction (choice of words), idiom, and punctuation. Some sentences are correct. No sentence contains more than one error. You will find that the error, if there is one, is underlined and lettered. Assume that all other elements of the sentence are correct and cannot be changed. If there is an error, select the one underlined part that must be changed in order to make the sentence correct. If there is no error, select answer D.

18. Saku, the anchor of the women's crew team, has the strongest forearms I
          A   B
ever saw. No error
  C   D

19. Carlos, who visited the museum to see the collection of Olmec figurines, was
    A   B
amazed by the mystical expressions on their faces. No error
       C   D

20. I want all employees to attend the company picnic this afternoon, so post the
             A   A
notice however it can be seen by everyone. No error
       C   D

21. Whenever Rakesh and me go to the community center, we like to sit near
                        A   B   C
the baby pool and watch the children play. No error

22. Everyone knew Irina was an experienced pilot and they wondered why she
             A   B
hadn't filed a flight plan before leaving for Bermuda. No error
                                               C   D

23. Its not a good idea to disturb my father when he is napping. No error
    A   B   C   D

24. The committee are opposed to the new dress code which requires men
                   A   B   C
to wear suits and women to wear skirts. No error
                                           D

25. After mowing Mr. Tanner's lawn, I went to the pool to meet my friends.
                      A   B   C
No error
  D

KEY (CORRECT ANSWERS)

1.	B	11.	D
2.	D	12.	A
3.	C	13.	B
4.	C	14.	D
5.	A	15.	A
6.	D	16.	C
7.	B	17.	A
8.	C	18.	C
9.	A	19.	D
10.	C	20.	C

21.	A
22.	D
23.	A
24.	A
25.	D

TEST 3

DIRECTIONS: Each question or incomplete statement is followed by several suggested answers or completions. Select the one that BEST answers the question or completes the statement. *PRINT THE LETTER OF THE CORRECT ANSWER IN THE SPACE AT THE RIGHT.*

1. *The Irish Elk, now extinct, was neither exclusively Irish, nor an elk.(1) Although the Guiness book of world records honors the American moose's antlers, the size of the Irish Elk's antlers has never even been approached in the history of life.(2)*
   Which of the following would be the MOST suitable sentence to insert immediately after sentence 1 in the above paragraph?
   A. Before attracting the attention of scientists, they had been used as gateposts.
   B. By some accounts, their antlers were over eight wide.
   C. It was the largest deer that ever lived, and its enormous antlers were even more impressive.
   D. We now know that the giant deer ranged as far east as Siberia and China and as far south as Northern Africa.

   1.____

2. *Cornbread is a food that originated during the settlement of the American Midwest, and is still popular in both urban and rural sections of the country's interior. Unlike most American foods, which were variations of dishes that pioneers brought from their home countries, cornbread originated on this continent, in the Kansas territory, as a direct descendant of the "ashcake" of the Kansas Indians.*
   Which of the following would be the MOST suitable sentence to conclude this paragraph?
   A. For many years this method of baking cornbread remained unchanged by people who settled the frontier.
   B. Ashcake was mixed from cornmeal and water, made into thick cakes, and baked directly on the cinders and ashes of prairie camp fires.
   C. Today corn-dodger days are remembered in Illinois by occasional corn-dodger dinners.
   D. Illinois pioneers created a variation of cornbread, a small loaf called the corn-dodger.

   2.____

Questions 3-15.

DIRECTIONS: In each of the following sentences, you are given two or more sentences to combine into one. After each set of sentences, there is a question that will help you decide how the sentences are to be combined. In combining some of the sentences, you will change the order of the original a great deal; in combining others, you will change the order only a little. Be sure that the new sentence you create is a complete sentence, that is contains all of the essential facts given in the original set of sentences, that is maintains the proper relationship of ideas, and that is clearly and effectively written.

3. The particles are known as *stealth liposomes*. They can hide in the body a long time without detection.
   Your new sentence will begin with which of the following?
   A. Stealthy liposomes
   B. Hiding in the body
   C. Known as
   D. Particles hiding in the body without detection

4. Cory felt like a soldier. He felt like a soldier who had been comfortably wounded. A soldier who knows the war, for him, is over. Cory felt a heavy, sighing peace.
   Your new sentence will begin with which of the following?
   A. Cory felt a heavy, sighing peace
   B. Feeling a heavy, sighing peace, the soldier
   C. Comfortably wounded and knowing
   D. Knowing that war was over for him

5. Six boys ran over the hill. The six boys breathed hard. They worked their arms as they ran.
   Your new sentence will begin with which of the following?
   A. Arms at work   B. The six boys breathed
   C. Running over the hill D. With their hearts pounding

6. Stress is hard on body and soul. Some people suffer from being unable to sleep. Some people have low self-esteem. Some people have nervous breakdowns.
   Your new sentence will contain which of the following?
   A. sleeplessness, low self-esteem and even nervous breakdowns
   B. unable to sleep, low self-esteem and nervous breakdowns
   C. no sleeping, low self-esteem and to have a nervous breakdown
   D. to have nervous breakdowns and sleeplessness and low self-esteem

7. Susan went from the new part of the library through to the old part. Susan walked around awhile. She went to the periodicals section.
   Your new sentence will contain which of the following?
   A. however   B. afterwards   C. therefore   D. during

8. I had made a decision. It was time to prove myself. I was scared.
   Your new sentence will begin with which of the following?
   A. However,   Therefore   C. And   D. Even though

9. Mrs. Stevenson was a heavyset woman. Mrs. Stevenson lived in a yellow house behind the elementary school
   Your new sentence will contain which of the following?
   A. she   B. that   C. whom   D. who

10. People come home from work feeling tired. People turn on the television. People watch the evening news.
    Your new sentence will contain which of the following?
    A. people turn and watch
    B. tired people turn
    C. tired and they
    D. working tired

11. I walked to the ticket window at the train station. I laid my money on the counter. I could not decide where to go.
    Your new sentence will begin with which of the following?
    A. Not deciding
    B. Unable to decide
    C. Laying my money on the counter
    D. My money on the counter

12. Some people attend college for the wrong reasons. Some only want to have fun. Some want to find a mate. Some would rather not get a job.
    Your new sentence will contain which of the following?
    A. not get jobs, have fun or find a mate
    B. having fun, find a mate or put off getting a job
    C. have fun, find a mate or put off getting a job
    D. having fun, finding mates and getting jobs

13. I will always remember my elementary school uniforms. The girls wearing blue skirts. The boys had to wear blue pants.
    Your new sentence will contain which of the following?
    A. wearing skirts and pants, boys and girls, of blue
    B. the wearing of blue skirts for girls, and boys wore
    C. wearing blue skirts and the boys wore
    D. wearing blue skirts, the boys wearing

14. Eva went to class. She picked up Yolanda at the marina.
    Which of the following is the BEST word to join the two sentences?
    A. then
    B. than
    C. so than
    D. because

15. Bay Street is located in the heart of downtown Nassau. It houses the straw market.
    Your new sentence will begin with which of the following?
    A. Downtown Nassau
    B. Housing the straw market on Bay Street
    C. Bay Street, located
    D. Locating at Bay Street

16. During his campaign for City Council, Adam decided to focus on the fact that his opponent had been married and divorced three times.
    Adam's decision is an example of
    A. ad hominem attack
    B. faulty deduction
    C. hasty generalization
    D. a logical fallacy

Questions 17-23.

DIRECTIONS: Questions 17 through 23 are to be answered on the basis of the following passage.

Of Cruelty and Clemency, Niccolo Machiavelli

From this arises the question whether it is better to be loved more than feared, or feared more than loved.(1) The reply is, that one ought to be both feared and loved, but as it is difficult for the two to go together, it is much safer to be feared than loved, if one of the two has to be wanting.(2) For it may be said of men in general that they are ungrateful, voluble dissemblers, anxious to avoid danger, and covetous of gain; as long as you benefit them, they are entirely yours; they offer you their blood, their goods, their life, and their children, as I have before said, when the necessity is remote; but when it approaches, they revolt.(3)

17. This paragraph is BEST characterized as
    A. interpretive   B. symbolic   C. explanatory   D. persuasive

18. The MAIN verb of the first sentence is
    A. arises   B. loved   C. feared   D. to be

19. In sentence 1, the phrase *loved more than feared, and feared more than loved* is an example of
    A. a noun phrase   B. parallel construction
    C. simile   D. metaphor

20. In sentence 2, the word *wanting* is BEST replaced with
    A. required   B. present   C. needed   D. absent

21. In sentence 3, the phrase *ungrateful, voluble dissemblers* contains which of the following?
    A. Coordinate nouns   B. Coordinate adjectives
    C. Subordinate adverbs   D. Subordination

22. Sentence 3 of this passage relies MOST heavily on which of the following?
    A. Subordination   B. Coordination
    C. Imagery   D. Metaphor

23. The main point of this passage is BEST expressed by which of the following statements?
    A. Men are best controlled through love, whereas women are best controlled through fear.
    B. Men are best controlled through fear, whereas women are best controlled through love.
    C. Because men are basically untrustworthy, it is easier to control them through fear than through love.
    D. Because men are basically trustworthy, it is better to control them through love than through fear.

24. Little Susan Richter hates to take her evening bath. One night, Susie's mother scolded Susie for standing too close to the oven. She explained that she didn't want Susie to get hurt. Susie countered by asking why her mother didn't let her escape her evening bath rituals, since she could fall in the tub and hurt herself. Susie's reasoning is an example of
    A. a false analogy
    B. hasty generalization
    C. a faulty use of authority
    D. a doubtful cause

24.____

25. *During World War II, important military communications often took place in code, so that messages could not be intercepted and translated by enemy forces.(1) This problem was solved by a man named Philip Johnston, who grew up on a Navajo Indian Reservation in the American Southwest.(2)*
    Which of the following would be MOST suitable to insert after sentence 1 in the above paragraph?
    A. Johnston's idea was used by the military, and the Navajo codetalkers devised a code so effective that it was not declassified by the military until more than twenty years later.
    B. The American military faced a significant problem: the similarities between the English and German languages would make English codes easy for a German to translate, and many Japanese soldiers who had graduated from American universities were used as codebreakers.
    C. Johnston's idea was to use Navajo soldiers as code-talkers; the Navajo language was tonal, meaning that its vowels rise and fall, changing meaning with different pitches that cannot be communicated in writing.
    D. Devising an effective code was a problem the American military had to solve.

25.____

KEY (CORRECT ANSWERS)

1.	C		11.	B
2.	B		12.	C
3.	C		13.	D
4.	A		14.	A
5.	D		15.	C
6.	A		16.	A
7.	B		17.	D
8.	D		18.	A
9.	D		19.	B
10.	C		20.	D

21.	B
22.	A
23.	C
24.	A
25.	B

TEST 4

DIRECTIONS: Each question or incomplete statement is followed by several suggested answers or completions. Select the one that BEST answers the question or completes the statement. *PRINT THE LETTER OF THE CORRECT ANSWER IN THE SPACE AT THE RIGHT.*

Questions 1-5.

DIRECTIONS: Questions 1 through 5 are to be answered on the basis of the following passage.

Think About It, Frank Conroy

    Indeed, in our intellectual lives, our creative lives, it is perhaps those problems that will never resolve that rightly claim the lion's share of our energies.(1) The physical body exists in a constant state of tension as it maintains homeostasis, and so too does the active mind embrace the tension of never being certain, never being absolutely sure, never being done, as it engages the world.(2) That is our special fate, our inexpressibly valuable condition.(3)

1. The MAIN verb in sentence 1 is
   A. is and claim   B. claim   C. is   D. resolve

2. The passage is BEST described as which of the following?
   A. Persuasive   B. Expository   C. Ironic   D. Poetic

3. *...never being certain, never being absolutely sure, never being done...*
   The above excerpt, taken from sentence 2, is an example of which of the following?
   A. Coordinate independent clauses   B. An independent clause
   C. A dependent clause   D. Parallel construction

4. In sentence 2, the word *homeostasis* is BEST replaced by
   A. balance   B. dominance
   C. subordination   D. confusion

5. Which of the following BEST summarizes the writer's main point?
   A. The state of being uncertain requires a great deal of energy.
   B. We should avoid uncertainty at all costs.
   C. Uncertainty is the basis of our most important creativity.
   D. Uncertainty is the basis of our most debilitating insecurities.

6. Although Althea had heard that the new park was beautiful, she refused to take her son there since it was in the city and Althea had heard that city parks were dangerous.
   Althea's flaw in logic is an example of
   A. ad hominem attack   B. faulty deduction
   C. faulty induction   D. a logical fallacy

2 (#4)

Questions 7-11.

DIRECTIONS: Questions 7 through 11 are to be answered on the basis of the following passage.

The Collective Unconscious, Karl Jung

   The collective unconscious is a part of the psyche which can be negatively distinguished from a personal unconscious by the fact that it does not, like the latter, owe its existence to personal experience and consequently is not a personal acquisition.(1) While the personal unconscious is made up essentially of contents which have at one time been conscious but which have disappeared from consciousness, and therefore have never been individually acquired, but owe their existence exclusively to heredity.(2) Whereas the personal unconscious consists for the most part of complexes, the content of the collective unconscious is made up essentially of archetypes.(3)

7. The effect of this passage relies MAINLY on the use of
   A. definition   B. narration   C. analogy   D. metaphor

8. This passage is BEST characterized as
   A. psychological   B. narrative   C. persuasive   D. analytical

9. In sentence 1, the word *acquisition* is BEST replaced by
   A. accomplishment   B. attainment
   C. possession   D. means

10. *While the personal unconscious is made up essentially of contents which have at one time been conscious.*
    The above excerpt from sentence 2 is an example of which of the following?
    A. Noun phrase   B. Parallel construction
    C. Subordinate clause   D. Independent clause

11. Which of the following BEST describes the primary difference between the personal and the collective unconscious?
    A. The personal unconscious is based on individual experience while the collective unconscious is not.
    B. The collective unconscious is based on individual experience while the personal unconscious is not.
    C. The collective unconscious is beyond human understanding, whereas the personal unconscious is within the bounds of human understanding.
    D. The personal unconscious is unreliable, whereas the collective unconscious is reliable.

12. *Following its discovery in 1492, the New World's exploration includes in its history many stories of ambitious, sometimes greedy explorers who exploited the new land and its people in order to achieve wealth and fame.(1) Pizarro's harshness is perhaps best illustrated by his treatment of Atahualpa, emperor of*

3 (#4)

the Incan empire.(2) The Incas were a native civilization that ranged over most of western South America, and were known for their sophisticated technology, roads, and architecture.(3)

Which of the following would be the MOST suitable sentence to insert immediately after sentence 2 in the above paragraph?
- A. Beginning in 1531 with fewer than two hundred men, Pizarro took less than two years to conquer the Incas and capture Atahualpa at his palace in the city of Cuzco.
- B. As it turned out, the Incan empire contained enough gold to fill many rooms.
- C. Pizarro made many enemies during the years of his brutal career.
- D. Of all these men, one of the most ruthless and coldblooded was Francisco Pizarro, the Spanish conquistador.

13. *The name "Piltdown Man" refers to a skull, unearthed from the English countryside, that was brought before the London Geological Society in 1912.(1) This unusual size and shape led many scientists to proclaim the skull was hard evidence of the common ancestry of apes and humans, and the skull was placed in the British Museum.(2)*

    Which of the following would be the MOST suitable sentence to insert immediately after <u>sentence 1</u> in the above paragraph?
    - A. In an effort to fool the world's scientists, somebody had buried a human skull with an ape's jawbone, and pulled off a practical joke that lasted more than forty years.
    - B. The skull had a large cranium, which suggested a brain like a human's, but its jawbone was unusually long and heavy, with pronounced canine teeth.
    - C. It wasn't until many years after the skull's discovery that a few skeptics were able to prove what they had long suspected Piltdown Man was a fake.
    - D. The presenter was Sir Edmund Georges, a prominent English geologist.

14. *It seems appropriate, then, that ketchup, a sauce made from tomatoes, has become a sort of All-American addition to foods such as hot dogs and hamburgers. In spite of the tomato's origin, however, ketchup isn't even close to being All-American.*

    Which of the following would be the MOST suitable to insert at the <u>beginning</u> of the above paragraph?
    - A. Tomatoes originated in North America, and were cultivated for centuries by natives before becoming popular in other parts of the world.
    - B. Ketchup is believed to have come from a Malaysian pickled fish sauce called "kechap" and a similar Chinese sauce called "ke-tsiap."
    - C. Tomatoes have a diverse history and origin.
    - D. Nobody knows for sure, but it is assumed that these sauces made the immigration from the Far East to America and were eventually changed into what we now call ketchup.

15. *Because the temperature during atmospheric re-entry is so incredibly hot, it took NASA's engineers some time to find a substance capable of protecting the shuttles. Eventually, the engineers were led to a material that is as old as our most ancient civilizations—glass.*
    Which of the following would be the MOST suitable to insert at the beginning of the above paragraph?
    A. One of the most easily manipulated substances on earth, glass can be made into ceramic tiles that are composed of over 90% air.
    B. These ceramic tiles are such effective insulators that when a tile emerges from the oven in which it was fired, it can be held safely in a person's hand.
    C. NASA's space shuttles are the first spacecraft ever designed to leave and re-enter the Earth's atmosphere while remaining intact.
    D. NASA astronauts require protection from the heat generated by re-entering the Earth's atmosphere.

15.____

Questions 16-20.

DIRECTIONS: Questions 16 through 20 are to be answered on the basis of the following passage.

A Bend in the Road, Colin Fletcher

When we contemplate such rents in the fabric as Los Angeles and the Love Canal, Beirut, and Chernobyl, Ethiopia and the East Bronx, most of us tend to bleat about politicians or multinationals or drug cartels or other handy breeds of "them."(1) Indictments of this kind are easy and exculpating and slightly titillating; but perhaps we should be looking closer to home.(3)

16. In sentence 1, the word *rents* is BEST replaced by
    A. upheavals   B. mistakes   C. rips   D. surprises

16.____

17. *...as Los Angeles and the Love Canal, Beirut and Chernobyl, Ethiopia and the East Bronx...*
    The above excerpt, from sentence 2, is an example of which of the following?
    A. Parallel construction   B. An independent clause
    C. A dependent clause   D. Coordinate clauses

17.____

18. In the context of this passage, the word *bleat*, in sentence 1, is BEST characterized as
    A. academic   B. technical   C. poetic   D. colloqial

18.____

19. This passage is BEST characterized as which of the following?
    A. Poetic   B. Expository   C. Narrative   D. Persuasive

19.____

20. In sentence 1, the MAIN verb is
    A. rents   B. contemplate   C. tend   D. bleat

20.____

21. *Archimedes, the ancient Greek scientist, once used the exclamation "Eureka (I have found it)!" in such dramatic fashion that it is still part of the English language today.(1) Archimedes' benefactor, Hiero, wanted to know if his crown was made of pure gold or had been diluted with an amount of silver, and he assigned Archimedes the problem.(2)*
    Which of the following would be MOST suitable to insert after sentence 2 in the above paragraph?
    A. He knew that gold and silver had different densities, and that pieces of gold and silver that weighed the same would displace different amounts of water.
    B. Archimedes was thinking about the problem when he stepped into his bathtub, and some of the water overflowed, giving him inspiration he needed to find a solution.
    C. When he realized he could use this principle to answer Hiero's question, he ran into the streets shouting, "Eureka!" without remembering to put on his clothes.
    D. Archimedes was a very successful scientist in his time.

22. *Many white Americans, who then dictated the tastes of society, were wary of music that was played almost exclusively in black clubs in the poorer sections of cities and towns. However, jazz didn't take long to develop from early ragtime melodies into more complex, sophisticated forms, such as Charlie Parker's "bebop" style of jazz.*
    Which of the following would be MOST suitable to insert at the beginning of the above paragraph?
    A. After charismatic band leaders such as Duke Ellington and Count Basie brought jazz to a larger audience, white audiences began to accept and even to enjoy the new American art form.
    B. Soon, by the 1940's, jazz was the most popular type of music among American intellectuals and college students.
    C. Jazz soon developed into very complicated and sophisticated forms.
    D. In the early days of jazz, it was considered "lowdown" music, or music that was played only in rough, disreputable bars and taverns.

23. *The computer technology known as virtual reality, now in its very first stages of development, is already revolutionizing some aspects of contemporary life.(1) No more than a computer program that is designed to build and display graphic images, the virtual reality program takes graphic programs a step further by sensing a person's head and body movements.(2)*
    Which of the above would be MOST suitable to insert after sentence 2 in the above paragraph?
    A. A virtual reality program responds to these movements by adjusting the images that a person sees on a screen or through goggles, creating an "interactive" world.
    B. Plastic surgeons have already begun to use virtual reality to map out the complex nerve and tissue structures of a particular patient's face, in order to prepare for delicate surgery.

C. This ability to sense real movement is truly revolutionary.
D. Virtual reality computers are also being used by the space program, most recently to simulate conditions for the astronauts who were launched on a repair mission to the Hubble telescope.

24. *The macaws of South America are not only among the largest and most beautifully colored of the world's flying birds, but they are also one of the smartest.(1) For example, all macaws flock to riverbanks at certain times of the year to eat the clay that is found in river mud.(2)*
Which of the following would be MOST suitable to insert <u>after sentence 1</u> in the above paragraph?
    A. Though uncertain of the definite reasons for this behavior, scientists believe the birds digest the clay in order to counteract toxins contained in the seeds of certain fruits that are eaten by macaws.
    B. The macaw's intelligence has led to intense study by scientists, who have discovered some macaw behaviors that have not yet been explained.
    C. It is believed that macaws are forced to resort to these toxic fruits during the dry season, when foods are more scarce.
    D. Scientists have studied their intelligence for many years.

24.____

25. *Because they were some of the first explorers to venture into the western frontier of North America, the French were responsible for the naming of several native tribes. Perhaps the most poorly-conceived French name for an Indian tribe is Eskimo, the name for the natives of the far North which translates roughly as "eaters of raw flesh."*
Which of the following would be MOST suitable for concluding the above paragraph?
    A. Some of these names were actually just nicknames that stuck; the Gros Ventre ("Big Bellies") and Nez Perce ("Pierced Noses") were two of the large tribes that were named in this way.
    B. A smaller tribe, the Sans Arcs ("No Bows") were so named because the French believed the tribe had not yet discovered the bow and arrow.
    C. The French explorers enjoyed granting French names to people and places they had discovered.
    D. The name is incorrect; these people have always cooked their fish and game, and they now call themselves the Inuit, a native term that means "the people."

25.____

KEY (CORRECT ANSWERS)

1.	C	11.	A
2.	B	12.	D
3.	D	13.	B
4.	A	14.	A
5.	C	15.	C
6.	B	16.	C
7.	A	17.	A
8.	D	18.	D
9.	B	19.	B
10.	C	20.	C

21.	B
22.	D
23.	A
24.	B
25.	D

EXAMINATION SECTION
TEST 1

DIRECTIONS: Each question or incomplete statement is followed by several suggested answers or completions. Select the one that BEST answers the question or completes the statement. *PRINT THE LETTER OF THE CORRECT ANSWER IN THE SPACE AT THE RIGHT.*

1. The phrase "an incremental adjustment to meet a new stimulus level" (i.e., an increase in military strength) is an example of

    A. gobbledygook to make the idea seem more impressive
    B. propaganda for foreign consumption
    C. ambiguity to confuse foreign analysts
    D. distortion of the actual truth

    1.____

2. Which word is spoken with the same stress both as a noun and as a verb?

    A. Permit   B. Desert
    C. Convert   D. Resort

    2.____

3. Which term has become *least* specific in meaning because of excessive use?

    A. Happy   B. Nice
    C. Intelligent D. Careless

    3.____

4. Which level of language usage is illustrated in the sentences below?
    "Hula hoops used to be a hot item in toy stores."
    "The crook was driving a hot car."

    A. Specialized B. Archaic
    C. Standard   D. Colloquial

    4.____

5. Which prefix can be used to mean "artificial"?

    A. Quad   B. Tri
    C. Pseudo D. Circum

    5.____

6. Which word is *most* abstract?

    A. Sympathy B. Ship
    C. Soil   D. Smudge

    6.____

7. Which pair of prefixes has the same meaning?

    A. Sub and ultra   B. Ante and pre
    C. Intra and circum D. Hyper and tele

    7.____

8. Which of the following is the *most* specific in meaning?

    A. Athlete   B. Girl
    C. Tracy Austin D. Student

    8.____

9. A writer's expressions of approval or disapproval of something are BEST regarded as

    A. inferences B. reports
    C. allusions D. judgments

    9.____

67

QUESTIONS 10-24

In questions 10-24, the same idea is expressed in four different ways. Select the way that is BEST and print the corresponding letter in the space at the right.

10.
- A. Each time one of her cubs was threatened, the mother lion was ready to attack.
- B. Each time one of her cubs were threatened, the mother lion got ready to attack.
- C. Ready to attack, the cubs were protected from every threat by the mother lion.
- D. Protected from every threat, the mother lion was ready to defend her cubs every time one of them were threatened.

10.____

11.
- A. Seatbelts, while unquestionably a good idea, it's sometimes a nuisance to use them.
- B. Seatbelts, while unquestionably a good idea, are sometimes a nuisance.
- C. Seatbelts are unquestionably a good idea and also they are sometimes a nuisance.
- D. Seatbelts, while it's unquestionably a good idea to have them, it's sometimes a nuisance to have them.

11.____

12.
- A. While trimming the hedges, a bird's nest was discovered.
- B. He discovered a bird's nest trimming the hedges.
- C. Trimming the hedges, a bird's nest was discovered.
- D. As he was trimming the hedges, he discovered a bird's nest.

12.____

13.
- A. Each person applying for a job must fill out a card listing his or her previous places of employment.
- B. Applying for a job, each person must fill out a card listing their previous places of employment.
- C. Listing his or her previous places of employment on a card, each person must do this when applying for a job.
- D. Each person, by filling out a card on which they list their previous places of employment, can apply for a job.

13.____

14.
- A. A man, who's successful sets reasonable goals for himself.
- B. A man whose successful sets reasonable goals for himself.
- C. A man who's successful sets reasonable goals for himself.
- D. A man, whose successful sets reasonable goals for himself.

14.____

15.
- A. I don't like hiking as much as I like cross-country skiing.
- B. I don't like to hike as much as I like cross-country skiing.
- C. I don't like hiking as much as I like to ski crosscountry.
- D. I don't like to hike as much as I like going crosscountry skiing.

15.____

16.
- A. I wouldn't of gone if I had known about Emily.
- B. I wouldn't have gone if I had known about Emily.
- C. I wouldn't have went if I had known about Emily.
- D. I wouldn't of went if I had known about Emily.

16.____

17. A. She planned a trip to the beach, a visit with her grandmother, and to take a long walk with her cousin.
     B. She planned to go to the beach, a visit with her grandmother, and a long walk with her cousin.
     C. She planned a trip to the beach, a visit with her grandmother, and a long walk with her cousin.
     D. She planned a trip to the beach, visiting with her grandmother, and to take a long walk with her cousin.

17.____

18. A. It is better to, I think, tell the truth than to lie.
     B. It is better to, I think, tell the truth than lying.
     C. Telling the truth, I think, is better than to lie.
     D. It is better, I think, to tell the truth than to lie.

18.____

19. A. He was not only a fine student but also a superior athlete.
     B. Not only was he a fine student but a superior athlete, also.
     C. He was not only a fine student but a superior athlete also.
     D. Also, he was not only a superior athlete, but a fine student.

19.____

20. A. Either Janice wanted to be student council president or valedictorian of her class.
     B. Janice either wanted to be student council president or class valedictorian.
     C. Janice wanted either to be president of student council or class valedictorian.
     D. Janice wanted to be either student council president or class valedictorian.

20.____

21. A. John having left school was without his father's permission.
     B. John left school without his fathers' permission.
     C. John left school without his father's permission.
     D. John having left school was without his father's permission.

21.____

22. A. Jane is the girl, who's purse was stolen.
     B. Jane is the girl whose purse was stolen.
     C. Jane is the girl who's purse was stolen.
     D. Jane is the girl, whose purse was stolen.

22.____

23. A. It's too bad that people are not more compassionate.
     B. Its to bad that people are not more compassionate.
     C. Its too bad that people are not more compassionate.
     D. It's to bad that people are not more compassionate.

23.____

24. A. The character who suffered the most was Laura.
     B. The character, which suffered the most, was Laura.
     C. The character which suffered the most was Laura.
     D. The character, who suffered the most, was Laura.

24.____

QUESTIONS 25-30
Questions 25-30 are based on the dictionary entry below.

of-fi' cious (o-fis h' us), adj. (F. or L. ; F. officieux; fr. L. officious.) 1. Obs. Kind; obliging; dutiful. 2. Volunteering one's services where they are neither asked nor needed; meddlesome. 3. Of an informal or unauthorized nature; unofficial; as, an officious conversation. of·fi'cious·ly adv.

of·fi'cious·ness , n. Syn. Impertinent, imprudent, saucy, pert, cool

25. The expression "1., *Obs*.Kind; obliging; dutiful" means that 25._____

    A. at one time "officious" meant "kind"
    B. "officious" has a slang meaning
    C. a common meaning of "officious" is "kind"
    D. an important meaning of "officious" is "impertinent"

26. The vowel sound of the last syllable in "officious" is the same as the vowel sound in 26._____

    A. cute B. loot C. rub D. ought

27. The expression "2. Volunteering one's services where they are neither asked nor needed; meddlesome" gives 27._____

    A. a meaning of "officious" as a verb
    B. a second meaning of "officious"
    C. an unusual meaning of "officious"
    D. an unauthorized meaning of "officious"

28. The expression "3. *Diplomacy.* Of an informal or unauthorized nature; unofficial ; as, an *officious* conversation" gives a meaning of "officious" which is 28._____

    A. authoritative   B. colloquial
    C. official   D. specialized

29. This entry suggests that today "officious" 29._____

    A. has a positive connotation
    B. can be used to mean "official"
    C. has almost no shades of meaning
    D. has a negative connotation

30. Which sentence BEST makes clear to a reader a current meaning of "officious"? 30._____

    A. How can you be so officious?
    B. He is a very officious person.
    C. Only an officious person would be so concerned with others' business.
    D. His kindness stamps him as one of the most officious people I know.

KEY (CORRECT ANSWERS)

1.	A	16.	B
2.	D	17.	C
3.	B	18.	D
4.	D	19.	A
5.	C	20.	D
6.	A	21.	C
7.	B	22.	B
8.	C	23.	A
9.	D	24.	A
10.	A	25.	A
11.	B	26.	C
12.	D	27.	B
13.	A	28.	D
14.	C	29.	D
15.	A	30.	C

EXAMINATION SECTION
TEST 1

DIRECTIONS: Each question or incomplete statement is followed by several suggested answers or completions. Select the one that BEST answers the question or completes the statement. *PRINT THE LETTER OF THE CORRECT ANSWER IN THE SPACE AT THE RIGHT.*

Questions 1-13.

DIRECTIONS: Questions 1 through 13 are to be answered on the basis of the following passage. Read the passage carefully before you choose your answers. (This passage was first published in 1935.)

I was glad when somebody told me, "You may go and collect Negro folk-lore."
In a way it would not be a new experience for me. When pitched headforemost into the world I landed in a crib of negroism. From the earliest rocking of my cradle, I had known about the capers Brer Rabbit is apt to cut and what the Squinch Owl says from the house
(5) top. But it was fitting me like a tight chemise. I couldn't see it for wearing it. It was only when I was off in college, away from my native surroundings, that I could see myself like somebody else and stand off and look at my garment. Then I had to have the spyglass of Anthropology to look through at that.
Dr. Boas asked me where I wanted to work and I said, "Florida," and gave, as my big
(10) reason, that "Florida is a place that draws people - white people from all over the world, and Negroes from every Southern state surely and some from the North and West." So I knew that it was possible for me to get a cross section of the Negro South in the one state. And then I realized that I was new myself, so it looked sensible for me to choose familiar ground.
First place I aimed to stop to collect material was Eatonville,
(15) Florida.
And now, I'm going to tell you why I decided to go to my native village first. I didn't go back there so that the home folks could make admiration over me because I had been up North to college and come back with a diploma and a Chevrolet. I knew they were not going to pay either one of these items too much mind. I was just Lucy Hurston's daughter,
(20) Zora, and even if I had - to use one of our down-home expressions - had a Kaiser baby, and that's something that hasn't been done in this Country yet, I' d still be just Zora to the neighbors. If I had exalted myself to impress the town, some body would have sent me word in a match-box that I had been up North there and had rubbed the hair off of my head against some college wall, and then come back there with a lot of form and fashion and outside
(25) show to the world. But they'd stand flat-footed and tell me that they didn't have me, neither my sham-polish, to study 'bout. And that would have been that.
I hurried back to Eatonville because I knew that the town was full of material and that I could get it without hurt, harm or danger. As early as I could remember it was the habit of the men folks particularly to gather on the store porch of evenings and swap stories. Even
(30) the women folks would stop and break a breath with them at times. As a child when I was sent down to Joe Clarke's store, I'd drag out my leaving as long as possible in order to hear more.
Folk-lore is not as easy to collect as it sounds. The best source is where there are the least outside influences and these people, being usually under-privileged, are the shyest.
(35) They are most reluctant at times to reveal that which the soul lives by.

1. It can be inferred from the passage that the speaker was glad when she was told, *You may go and collect Negro folk-lore* (lines 1) because

    A. she did not like the university she was attending
    B. she had asked many times before but had always been turned down
    C. it was something she had had little success at
    D. it was something she had been doing informally all her life
    E. she knew that folklore was easy to collect

2. In the second paragraph (lines 2-7), the speaker employs the metaphor of a close-fitting garment to express

    A. her struggle to learn about anthropology in college
    B. the difficulty of viewing her cultural heritage objectively
    C. her impression of imagery typical in stories of Brer Rabbit and the Squinch Owl
    D. the circumstances surrounding her birth and childhood
    E. the experience of attending a college far away from her native surroundings

3. In the second paragraph, the images of seeing and looking all refer to the speaker's experience of

    A. becoming aware of new modes of fashion
    B. seeking to improve herself through travel
    C. hearing stories about Brer Rabbit
    D. trying to fit into old clothes
    E. recognizing her early exposure to folklore

4. In the third paragraph (lines 9-12), the speaker's description of her research strategy includes all of the following EXCEPT a(n)

    A. apparently objective defense of her choice
    B. realization that personal concerns affected her choice
    C. tone that reflects both confidence and uncertainty
    D. sense of anxiety about being a pioneer in her profession
    E. understanding of the importance of gathering diverse information

5. In lines 14, the phrase *And then I realized that I was new myself* can BEST be interpreted as a reference to the speaker's

    A. regret that it has been so long since she last visited in Florida
    B. awareness of her inexperience in the role of anthropologist
    C. skepticism about whether she has matured since she left her hometown
    D. view of herself as a maverick in a very narrow field
    E. anticipation of returning to the area where she grew up

6. In the context of the passage as a whole, the fifth paragraph (lines 16-26) functions as an
    I. introduction to the values that predominated in Eatonville
    II. expansion of biographical information about the speaker
    III. overview of the speaker's planned research

    The CORRECT answer is:

    A. I only
    B. III only
    C. I, II
    D. II, III
    E. I, II, III

7. Which of the following BEST describes the tone of the speaker's voice in lines 21-22 when she says, *I'd still be just Zora to the neighbors*?

   A. Brash
   B. Sarcastic
   C. Arrogant
   D. Accepting
   E. Disappointed

8. The phrase *they'd stand flat-footed* (line 25) suggests that the

   A. townspeople would not be impressed by her fashionable ways
   B. townspeople would not be ready for what she has to say
   C. townspeople would not be able to understand why she wanted to leave
   D. speaker and her former neighbors are not on friendly terms
   E. speaker and her former neighbors are stubborn people

9. The shift in tone from the sixth paragraph (lines 27-32) to the seventh paragraph (lines 33-35) can be BEST described as a shift from _____ to _____.

   A. personal reminiscence; objective exposition
   B. poetic rhapsody; minute description
   C. philosophical logic; scientific rigor
   D. speculation; generalization
   E. profound meditation; cold reasoning

10. In context, the phrase *that which the soul lives by* (line 35) is probably intended to

    A. suggest that the most powerful folktales are never revealed
    B. give value to the folklore tradition
    C. arouse skepticism about the speaker's objectivity
    D. stimulate our curiosity about the future of the characters
    E. characterize folklore as old-fashioned

11. Of the following, the speaker's attitude in the passage toward the townspeople of Eatonville is BEST described as, she

    A. feels inadequate in their presence
    B. resents the fact that they do not admire her
    C. appreciates their approach to life
    D. believes they deserve better rewards in their lives
    E. understands them but does not take them seriously

12. The speaker apparently assumes that the audience she addresses is

    A. well informed about folklore
    B. fascinated by Southern traditions
    C. not interested in factual information
    D. obsessed with scientific methodology
    E. not composed only of professional anthropologists

13. The various roles taken by the speaker in the passage reflect PRIMARILY the speaker's

    A. uncertainty about her audience
    B. process of self-discovery
    C. stated belief in presenting multiple viewpoints

D. changing ambitions
E. effort to impress the scientific community

Questions 14-25.

DIRECTIONS: Questions 14 through 25 are to be answered on the basis of the following passage. Read the passage carefully before you choose your answers.

How easy is it to call rogue and villain, and that wittily! But how hard to make a man appear a fool, a blockhead, or a knave without using any of thos opprobrious terms! To spare the gross-ness of the names, and to do the thing yet more severely, is to draw a full face, and to make the nose and cheeks stand out, and yet not to employ any depth of
(5) shadowing. This is the mystery of that noble trade, which yet no master can teach to his apprentice; he may give the rules, but the scholar is never the nearer in his practice. Neither is it true that this fineness of raillery is offensive. A witty man is tickled while he is hurt in this manner, and a fool feels it not. The occasion of an offense may possibly be given, but he cannot take it. If it be granted that in effect this way does more mischief;
(10) that a man is secretly wounded, and though he be not sensible himself, yet the malicious world will find it out for him; yet there is still a vast difference betwixt the slovenly butchering of a man, and the fineness of a stroke that separates the head from the body, and leaves it standing in its place. A man may be capable, as Jack Ketch's wife said of his servant, of a plain piece of work, a bare hanging; but to make a malefactor die sweetly
(15) was only belonging to her husband. I wish I could apply it to myself, if the reader would be kind enough to think it belongs to me.

[1]A notorious public executioner

14. In the first two sentences of the passage (lines 1), the speaker draws a distinction between

A. obvious invective and indirect satire
B. esoteric knowledge and common understanding
C. coarse speaking and inferior painting
D. speaking and writing
E. wit and humor

14._____

15. In the sentence beginning *To spare* (lines 2-3), the speaker makes use of

A. understatement B. hyperbole C. a syllogism
D. an allegory   E. an analogy

15._____

16. In line 5, *that noble trade* refers to which of the following?

A. *to call rogue and villain* (line 1)
B. *to employ any depth of shadowing* (line 4)
C. *the scholar* (line 6)
D. *fineness of raillery* (line 9)
E. *The occasion of an offense* (line 8)

16._____

17. The sentence *Neither... offensive* (lines 6-7) does which of the following?

    A. Undercuts a point made previously
    B. Contradicts the thesis of the passage
    C. Answers a possible objection
    D. Offers an opposing point of view
    E. Presents an authoritative example

18. The contrast drawn between the witty man and the fool (lines 7-8) emphasizes the witty man's _____ and the fool's _____.

    A. self-confidence; lack of self-knowledge
    B. appreciation; lack of comprehension
    C. justified anger; innocence
    D. sense of humor; resentment
    E. ability to retaliate; lack of wit

19. In the sentence *If...place* (lines 9-13), the author does which of the following?

    A. Distinguishes an explanation of a timeworn idea from a common occurrence
    B. Raises an objection and then overrides it with an assertion
    C. Presents a dilemma and then explains its difficulties
    D. Offers a contrasting example and then dismisses it
    E. Cites an exaggeration and then minimizes it

20. Which of the following BEST describes the speaker's professed attitude toward the reputation of Jack Ketch?

    A. Admiration verging on envy
    B. Thinly veiled contempt
    C. Sympathy bordering on pity
    D. Respect tinged with impatience
    E. Repugnance combined with jealousy

21. In the context of the passage, the author probably intends the reader to find the words of Jack Ketch's wife

    A. sobering   B. deceptive   C. horrifying
    D. humorous   E. compassionate

22. The speaker draws on contrasts between all of the following EXCEPT

    A. wit and dullness
    B. ordinariness and excellence
    C. maliciousness and compassion
    D. coarseness and refinement
    E. skill and ineptitude

23. In lines 11, the speaker describes the *vast difference* between subtle satire and scurrilous speech using a(n)

    A. metaphor   B. simile   C. idiom
    D. personification   E. colloquialism

24. In the sentence *This is the mystery of the noble trade... practice* (lines 5-6), the speaker suggests that

    A. obvious invective is a superior art
    B. the scholarly profession is more noble than the satirist's trade
    C. the subtle technique of satire cannot be taught
    D. opprobrious terms are more effective than sophisticated sarcasm
    E. satire is always derogatory in nature

25. In the phrase *Yet there is still a vast difference betwixt the slovenly butchering of a man* (lines 11-12), the word *betwixt* is BEST described as a(n)

    A. understatement   B. interjection   C. innuendo
    D. analogy   E. archaism

KEY (CORRECT ANSWERS)

1.	D	11.	C
2.	B	12.	E
3.	E	13.	B
4.	D	14.	A
5.	B	15.	E
6.	C	16.	D
7.	D	17.	C
8.	A	18.	B
9.	A	19.	B
10.	B	20.	A

21. D
22. C
23. A
24. C
25. E

TEST 2

DIRECTIONS: Each question or incomplete statement is followed by several suggested answers or completions. Select the one that BEST answers the question or completes the statement. *PRINT THE LETTER OF THE CORRECT ANSWER IN THE SPACE AT THE RIGHT.*

Questions 1-17.

DIRECTIONS: Questions 1 through 17 are to be answered on the basis of the following passage. Read the passage carefully before you choose your answers.

It was not a union which seemed likely to prosper, since its chief characteristics were imprudence, youth and extreme good looks. But the narried life of the young Brudenells unexpectedly turned out a rustic idyll. They chose to live quietly in the country at the Manor, Hableden, Buckinghamshire, a Jacobean house set on gently rising ground and
(5) framed in chestnut trees. The rector of Hambleden at the time has left letters in which are glimpses of an amiable, charitable and democratic pair. They preferred not to use their title and, even after Robert had succeeded his uncle as Earl of Cardigan, they were known in Hambleden as Mr. and Mrs. Brudenell. They were much given to good works, and Robert, "ever a good friend to Hambleden," bought two and a half acres of land and
(10) presented it to the village for cottagers' gardens; "these gardens are a great benefit and much prized." Penelope interested herself in the village women and the school. "She is a sweet woman, possessing a temper both mild and engaging," wrote the rector.

And at the Manor on October 16th, 1797, their second child and only male infant was born and christened James Thomas.
(15) The circumstances surrounding his arrival were impressive. It was three generations since the succession of the Earls of Cardigan had gone direct from father to son. The much desired heir was of almost mystic importance, and, as he lay in his cradle, wealth, rank, power and honours gathered round his head.

It was unfortunate that he was destined to grow up in a world that was almost entirely
(20) feminine. He already had an elder sister, and seven more girls followed his birth, of whom six survived. He remained the only son, the only boy among seven girls, unique, unchallenged, and the effect on his character was decisive. He was brought up at home among his sisters, and he grew up as such boys do, spoilt, domineering and headstrong. No arm was stronger than his. No rude voice contradicted him, no rough shoulder
(25) pushed him. From his earliest consciousness he was the most important, the most interesting, the most influential person in the world. He retained, however, from these early years a liking for the society of women and a softness in his manner towards them which, having regard to his manner with men, struck his contemporaries with surprise. For a woman, a pretty woman, above all a pretty woman in distress, James Brudenell, later
(30) Lord Cardigan, had an almost medieval deference, a chivalrous turn of phrase, a sometimes embarrassing readiness to protect and defend, which, though productive of astonishment and mirth, were nevertheless rooted in a genuine sympathy.

It was to be expected that his parents and sisters should be passionately attached to him, and natural affection and pride were immensely heightened by the circumstance of
(35) his extraordinary good looks. In him the Brudenell beauty had come to flower. He was tall, with wide shoulders tapering to a narrow waist, his hair was golden, his eyes flashing sapphire blue, his nose aristocratic, his bearing proud. If there were a fault it was that the lower part of his face was oddly long and narrow so that sometimes one was surprised to

catch an obstinate, almost a foxy look. But the boy had a dash and gallantry that were
(40) irresistible. He did not know what fear was. A superb and reckless horseman, he risked
his neck on the most dangerous brutes. No tree was too tall for him to climb, no tower too
high to scale. He excelled in swordsmanship and promised to be a first-class shot. He
had in addition to courage another characteristic which impressed itself on all who met
him. He was, alas, unusually stupid; in fact, as Greville pronounced later, an ass. The
(45) melancholy truth was that his glorious golden head had nothing in it.

1. The speaker's PRIMARY purpose in the passage is to

    A. describe a series of unprecedented events
    B. characterize an idyllic era
    C. portray an unusual character
    D. depict an inequitable situation
    E. comment on a popular assumption

2. The speaker's perspective in the passage is that of a(n)

    A. acquaintance of James Brudenell
    B. chronicler of past events
    C. uninvolved eyewitness
    D. commentator on social trends
    E. defender of an unpopular figure

3. In the first sentence of the passage, the speaker's attitude toward the material is that of a person who is

    A. fearful of finding a flaw in those who have been regarded as ideals
    B. fascinated by the unique capabilities of individual characters
    C. so familiar with the realm described as to be somewhat cynical
    D. coolly assessing random data in search of a possible pattern
    E. overtly sympathetic toward the subjects of the discussion

4. The word *democratic* in line 6 is BEST understood to mean

    A. enterprising   B. conscientious   C. lenient
    D. law-abiding   E. unpretentious

5. The citations from the rector of Hambleden's letters do all of the following EXCEPT

    A. document the speaker's sketch of the Brudenells
    B. illustrate the rector's influence over the Brudenells
    C. characterize the simplicity of life in Hambleden
    D. provide evidence of the Brudenells' philanthropy
    E. enliven the speaker's descriptions with present-tense commentary

6. Which of the following BEST describes the words *wealth, rank, power and honours* as they are used in lines 17-18 ?

    A. Allusions to members of James Brudenell's family
    B. Euphemisms for the heavy burdens placed on the child
    C. Personifications of the inordinate blessings of the child
    D. Ambiguous references to previous earls of Cardigan
    E. Exaggerations of James Brudenell's later accomplishments

7. In lines 23-24, the phrase *as such boys do* functions PRIMARILY as a(n)

   A. caution to the reader that the material presented is based on hearsay
   B. characterization of the speaker as a close acquaintance of the Brudenells
   C. reminder to the reader about the era in which the events described took place
   D. means of underscoring through generalization the viciousness of the faults described
   E. emphasis on the inevitability of a particular environment producing a particular effect

8. The speaker uses the images of *No arm, No rude voice,* and *no rough shoulder* in lines 24 to emphasize that James Brudenell lacked

   A. parental guidance
   B. the competition of male siblings
   C. adversaries in adult life
   D. sensitivity toward his sisters
   E. skill in fighting and arguing

9. Of the following, the phrase that could BEST be substituted for the phrase *he was* in line 25 to make the meaning more explicit would be, he

   A. proved himself to be
   B. might have become
   C. aspired to be
   D. was treated as
   E. was fated to be

10. In context, the phrase *having regard to his manner with men* (lines 28) indicates that James Brudenell

    A. enjoyed enormous popularity
    B. relied heavily on the advice of others
    C. respected the criticism of his peers
    D. was often rude and arrogant
    E. was widely known for his courage

11. The phrase *productive of astonishment and mirth* (lines 31-32) is BEST described as a(n)

    A. deliberately puzzling paradox
    B. circumlocution for *appearing ridiculous*
    C. intentional shift in the level of diction
    D. sarcastic interpretation of *embarrassing* (line 39)
    E. authorial aside directed at the speaker's opponents

12. In lines 35-36, the speaker creates the impression that James Brudenell was a(n)

    A. extraordinary figure with minor imperfections
    B. representative of an ideal that the world no longer admires
    C. prime example of the effect of a nurturing environment on human character
    D. amusing oddity in an otherwise dull world
    E. man doomed to be misunderstood by his contemporaries

13. Which of the following contribute(s) to the effect of the last three sentences of the passage (lines 42-45)?

    I. The appending of stupidity to a list of positive attributes
    II. The speaker's earlier description of James Brudenell
    III. The speaker's admiring tone in lines 39-42

    The CORRECT answer is:

    A. I only   B. I, II   C. I, III
    D. II, III   E. I, II, III

14. The interjection *alas* (line 44) emphasizes the speaker's

    A. willingness to defend James Brudenell
    B. shock on encountering the unexpected
    C. awareness of a central irony
    D. repudiation of Greville's accusation
    E. apologetic attitude toward the subject

15. The reference to Greville's pronouncement (lines 43-45) serves PRIMARILY to

    A. reveal the speaker's naivete
    B. arouse sympathy for James Brudenell
    C. provide an opinion contrary to that of the speaker
    D. introduce the primary source of the speaker's information
    E. reinforce what the speaker has said about James Brudenell's intellect

16. In the concluding sentence of the passage, the speaker's attitude toward James Brudenell is CHIEFLY one of

    A. wry detachment   B. embarrassed apology
    C. inquisitive perplexity   D. strong resentment
    E. surprised confusion

17. In the last paragraph, a PRIMARY rhetorical strategy of the speaker is to

    A. use the events of one individual's life to generalize about other individuals
    B. stimulate the reader's interest by progressively expanding the focus of attention
    C. arouse expectations about a character which are proved to be false
    D. convince the reader *of* the speaker's wisdom by disproving opposing viewpoints
    E. appear initially uncertain about matters on which a firm stand is later taken

Questions 18-30.

DIRECTIONS: Questions 18 through 30 are to be answered on the basis of the following passage. Read the passage carefully before you choose your answers. (This passage is a translation into English of material written in the nineteenth century.)

Fetters and headsmen were the coarse instruments that tyranny formerly employed; but the civilization of our age has perfected despotism itself, though it seemed to have nothing to learn. Monarchs had, so to speak, materialized oppression; the democratic (5) republics of the present day have rendered it as entirely an affair of the mind as the will

(5) which it is intended to coerce. Under the absolute sway of one man the body was attacked in order to subdue the soul; but the soul escaped the blows which were directed against it and rose proudly superior. Such is not the course adopted by tyranny in democratic republics; there the body is left free, and the soul is enslaved. The master no longer says: "You shall think as I do or you shall die"; but he says: "You are free to think

(10) differently from me and to retain your life, your property, and all that you possess; but you are henceforth a stranger among your people. You may retain your civil rights, but they will be useless to you, for you will never be chosen by your fellow citizens if you solicit their votes; and they will affect to scorn you if you ask for their esteem. You will remain among men, but you will be deprived of the rights of mankind. Your fellow creatures will

(15) shun you like an impure being; and even those who believe in your innocence will abandon you, lest they should be shunned in their turn. Go in peace! I have given you your life, but it is an existence worse than death."

Absolute monarchies had dishonored despotism; let us beware lest democratic republics should reinstate it and render it less odious and degrading in the eyes of the

(20) many by making it still more onerous to the few.

Works have been published in the proudest nations of the Old World expressly intended to censure the vices and the follies of the times: La Bruy?re inhabited the palace of Louis XIV when he composed his chapter upon the Great, and Moli?re criticized the courtiers in the plays that were acted before the court. But the ruling power in the

(25) United States is not to be made game of. The smallest reproach irritates its sensibility, and the slightest joke that has any foundation in truth renders it indignant; from the forms of its language up to the solid virtues of its character, everything must be made the subject of encomium. No writer, whatever be his eminence, can escape paying this tribute of adulation to his fellow citizens. The majority lives in the perpetual utterance of

(30) self-applause, and there are certain truths which the Americans can learn only from strangers or from experience.

18. In context, *headsmen* (line 1) is BEST understood to mean

    A. censors   B. courtiers   C. monarchs
    D. executioners E. philosophers

19. In the context of the passage, *coarse* (line 1) is BEST interpreted as

    A. cruel   B. crude   C. improper
    D. common   E. ribald

20. All of the following are evident in lines 1-8 EXCEPT

    A. overstatement
    B. generalization
    C. parallel construction
    D. balanced sentence structure
    E. citations from well-known authorities

21. The *master* quoted in lines 8-9 refers to

   A. an appointed judge
   B. a modern headsman
   C. a contemporary absolute monarch
   D. the ruling power of a democratic republic
   E. the benevolent despot in an ideal society

22. The tone of lines 16-17 *(Go in peace!...worse than death)* is BEST described as

   A. skeptical   B. remorseful   C. ominous
   D. empathetic   E. resigned

23. In can be inferred that the *existence* mentioned in line 17 will be characterized PRIMARILY by

   A. corruption   B. triviality
   C. alienation   D. self-doubt
   E. physical hardship

24. The function of the quoted sentences (lines 8-17) is to

   A. illustrate an assertion
   B. characterize rulers in general
   C. contrast the ideal with the historical
   D. depict a view that contradicts the speaker's view
   E. portray historical background in a colorful manner

25. The phrase *let us beware* (line 18) helps establish the speaker as

   A. critical of monarchical political systems
   B. defensive about newly formed democratic republics
   C. concerned about potential abuses of power within democratic republics
   D. skeptical of the ability of a democratic republic to control the individual
   E. respectful of the power inherent in absolute monarchies

26. It can be inferred that *the few* (line 20) refers MOST specifically to

   A. tyrants   B. courtiers
   C. monarchs   D. dissenters
   E. foreign observers

27. The PRIMARY function of the second paragraph is to

   A. introduce exceptions to earlier generalizations
   B. caution the reader that statements in the first paragraph may be misleading
   C. recapitulate ideas in the first paragraph and provide a transition to the third paragraph
   D. shift the focus from personal experience to objective analysis
   E. expand the generalizations introduced in paragraph one to include various other forms of government

28. The speaker cites La Bruyère and Molière as evidence that writers in powerful European monarchies

    A. were able to stimulate reforms in the regimes they served
    B. had traditionally assumed that their primary function was to expose corruption
    C. were able to condemn the foolishness that they discovered within their societies
    D. had more substantive ideas than do writers in democratic republics
    E. justified in their commentaries the magnificence of their courts

29. By *the ruling power in the United States* (lines 24-25), the speaker means the

    A. majority of voters
    B. legal system
    C. influential writers
    D. critics of the government
    E. wealthiest landowners

30. The use of the phrase *certain truths* (line 30) has the effect of

    A. characterizing the speaker as intentionally deceptive
    B. forcing the reader to infer from earlier material what the phrase means
    C. repeating the earlier references to *encomium* (line 28) and *adulation* (line 29)
    D. clarifying the meaning of *self-applause* (line 30)
    E. exposing the speaker's uncertainty about his judgment of the American political system

KEY (CORRECT ANSWERS)

1.	C	16.	A
2.	B	17.	C
3.	C	18.	D
4.	E	19.	B
5.	B	20.	E
6.	C	21.	D
7.	E	22.	C
8.	B	23.	C
9.	D	24.	A
10.	D	25.	C
11.	B	26.	D
12.	A	27.	C
13.	E	28.	C
14.	C	29.	A
15.	E	30.	B

EXAMINATION SECTION
TEST 1

DIRECTIONS: Each question or incomplete statement is followed by several suggested answers or completions. Select the one that BEST answers the question or completes the statement. *PRINT THE LETTER OF THE CORRECT ANSWER IN THE SPACE AT THE RIGHT.*

1. The items in a bibliography are arranged in

    A. alphabetical order according to the author's last name
    B. chronological order according to date of publication
    C. alphabetical order according to the first word in the title
    D. alphabetical order according to name of publisher

2. Which reference source would contain the MOST complete information on the British game of cricket?

    A. THE WORLD ALMANAC
    B. SKEAT'S ETYMOLOGICAL DICTIONARY
    C. READERS' GUIDE TO PERIODICAL LITERATURE
    D. ENCYCLOPEDIA BRITANNICA

3. How are novels arranged on a library shelf?

    A. Alphabetically by subject
    B. Alphabetically by author's last name
    C. Numerically by Dewey Decimal number
    D. Alphabetically by title

4. In the card catalog, cross reference cards are used PRIMARILY to

    A. locate a book on the shelves
    B. determine the author of a certain work
    C. locate additional information on a subject
    D. find other books by an author

5. Which would NOT be likely to appear on the editorial page of a newspaper?

    A. Readers' reactions
    B. Masthead
    C. Syndicated columns
    D. Classified ads

Questions 6-10.

DIRECTIONS: Questions 6 through 10 are based on the entry below from the READERS' GUIDE TO PERIODICAL LITERATURE. For each question, select the word or expression that BEST completes the statement or answers the question, and write its letter in the space at the right.

LITERARY prizes
   Added attraction; Seal Novel Awards for a first novel by a
     Canadian. P. S. Nathan. Pub W 216:26 D 3 '79
   Case of the two first novels: the Hemingway Award reexamined.
     S. Dong. Pub W 215:40+ Je 25 '79
   Consolation Prize; awarding of the Austrian State Prize for
     Literature to S. de Beauvoir. E. M. von Kuehnelt-Leddihn.
     Nat R 31:1040 Ag 17 '79
   Hasen wins Hemingway Award; figures suggest 1979 rise in
     published first novels. S. Dong. Pub W 215:17-18 Je 11 '79
   National Jewish Book Awards. Pub W 215:17 Je 11 '79
   1978: the year in review; literary prizes and awards.
     il Pub W 215:47-52 F 19 '79
   Tenth anniversary of the Freedley Memorial Award. D. B. Wilmeth.
     USA Today 108:66 Jl '79
   Three groups found awards for African heritage books.
     M. Reuter. Pub W 215:26+ Ap 2 '79
    See also
American Book Awards
Carey-Thomas Awards
National Book Awards
National Book Critics Circle Awards
Nobel prizes
Poetry-Awards
Pulitzer prizes
Scientific literature for children-Awards

6. In this entry on literary prizes, how are authors' names given?

   A. Last name only
   B. Last name and then first name
   C. First name and then last name
   D. Initials and then last name

7. According to this entry on literary prizes, which abbreviation does READERS' GUIDE use for *June*?

   A. J   B. Je   C. Jn   D. Ju

8. Under the heading *Literary prizes,* the entry *1978: the year in review* is listed

   A. chronologically
   B. alphabetically
   C. by subject
   D. by degree of importance

9. In the entry titled *Three groups found awards for African heritage books,* Ap 2 '79 refers to the date the

   A. magazine was published
   B. award was given
   C. article was written
   D. groups established the award

10. Which other article appears in the same issue of PUBLISHERS WEEKLY as *Hasen Wins Hemingway Award?*

   A. Added attraction
   B. Case of the two first novels
   C. National Jewish Book Awards
   D. 1978: the year in review

Questions 11-25.

DIRECTIONS: Listed below are some types of information you might want to locate together with several books in which you might look. For each write the letter of the BEST answer in the space at the right.

11. The officers and addresses of the regional and district officers of the Office of Price Administration may be found in 11.____

    A. CONGRESSIONAL DIRECTORY
    B. ENCYCLOPEDIA AMERICANA
    C. STATESMAN'S YEARBOOK
    D. GOVERNMENT MANUAL
    E. LARNED'S NEW HISTORY FOR READY REFERENCE

12. The current membership of the standing committees of the Senate may be found in 12.____

    A. CONGRESSIONAL DIRECTORY
    B. WORLD ALMANAC
    C. GOVERNMENTAL MANUAL
    D. STATESMAN'S YEARBOOK

13. The Washington addresses of the members of Congress may be found in 13.____

    A. WORLD ALMANAC   B. ENCYCLOPEDIA AMERICANA
    C. CONGRESSIONAL DIRECTORY D. GOVERNMENT MANUAL
    E. STATESMAN'S YEARBOOK

14. To locate summaries of Franklin D. Roosevelt's speeches in 1942, one should consult 14.____

    A. WORLD ALMANAC   B. ENCYCLOPEDIA AMERICANA
    C. READERS' GUIDE   D. CURRENT BIOGRAPHY
    E. WHO'S WHO IN AMERICA

15. The definition of *Grossmann's law* may be found in Webster's NEW INTERNATIONAL DICTIONARY in 15.____

    A. new words section
    B. below the line in the main alphabet
    C. main alphabet
    D. Gazetteer
    E. biographical dictionary

16. The provisions and benefits of the New Zealand Social Security legislation of 1938 may be found in 16.____

    A. STATESMAN'S YEARBOOK
    B. LARNED'S NEW HISTORY FOR READY REFERENCE
    C. ENCYCLOPEDIA AMERICANA
    D. WORLD ALMANAC
    E. GOVERNMENT MANUAL

17. To find the location of the poem THE HIGHWAYMAN by Alfred Noyes, one would look in   17.___

    A. BARTLETT'S FAMILIAR QUOTATIONS
    B. COMPTON'S PICTURED ENCYCLOPEDIA
    C. ENCYCLOPEDIA AMERICANA
    D. THE WORLD BOOK
    E. GRANGER'S INDEX TO POETRY AND RECITATIONS

18. The biography of the Prime Minister of Great Britain may be found in   18.___

    A. WHO'S WHO IN AMERICA
    B. GRANGER'S INDEX TO POETRY AND RECITATIONS
    C. CURRENT BIOGRAPHY
    D. GROVE'S DICTIONARY OF MUSIC AND MUSICIANS

19. An account of Antarctic exploration featuring excerpts from scientific books and journals: 19.___

    A. LARNED'S NEW HISTORY FOR READY REFERENCE
    B. ENCYCLOPEDIA AMERICANA
    C. STATESMAN'S YEARBOOK
    D. GOVERNMENT MANUAL
    E. WORLD ALMANAC

20. The dates of Ash Wednesday and Easter Sunday from the year 1801 through 2000 may be found in   20.___

    A. COMPTON'S PICTURED ENCYCLOPEDIA
    B. LARNED'S NEW HISTORY FOR READY REFERENCE
    C. NEW INTERNATIONAL DICTIONARY
    D. WORLD ALMANAC
    E. STATESMAN'S YEARBOOK

21. The meaning of the letters D.A.G. may be found in the NEW STANDARD DICTIONARY in   21.___

    A. Key to abbreviations
    B. Statistics of population
    C. main alphabet
    D. Foreign words and phrases
    E. disputed pronunciations

22. To find the author of the poem beginning *"Thou are not lovelier than lilacs"*, look in   22.___

    A. GRANGER'S INDEX TO POETRY AND RECITATIONS
    B. COMPTON'S PICTURED ENCYCLOPEDIA
    C. BARTLETT'S FAMILIAR QUOTATIONS
    D. THE WORLD BOOK
    E. ENCYCLOPEDIA AMERICANA

23. The BOSTON MASSACRE may be found in WEBSTER'S NEW INTERNATIONAL DICTIONARY, 2nd ed. in the

    A. main alphabet
    B. Gazetteer
    C. new words section
    D. main alphabet below the line
    E. biographical dictionary

24. A table showing the rank in population of the largest cities of the United States is the

    A. GOVERNMENT MANUAL
    B. CONGRESSIONAL DICTIONARY
    C. WORLD ALMANAC
    D. WEBSTER'S NEW INTERNATIONAL DICTIONARY

25. The definition of *coup d'etat* may be found in WEBSTER'S NEW INTERNATIONAL DICTIONARY in the

    A. Gazetteer
    B. new words
    C. pronouncing biographical dictionary
    D. WORLD ALMANAC
    E. main alphabet

KEY (CORRECT ANSWERS)

1.	A	11.	D
2.	D	12.	B
3.	B	13.	C
4.	C	14.	C
5.	D	15.	C
6.	D	16.	A
7.	B	17.	E
8.	B	18.	C
9.	A	19.	A
10.	C	20.	D

21. C
22. A
23. A
24. C
25. E

TEST 2

Questions 1-10.

DIRECTIONS: Listed below are some of the main headings of the Dewey decimal classification such as might appear on the library book shelves. Below the headings are ten topics on which you might want information. If you know under which heading each topic belongs, you could go *directly* to the shelf for the book you want. In the space at the right of each topic, write the number of the heading that BEST covers the topic. Use ONE number only for each topic and use *no* number more than once.

220	Bible	640	Home economics
290	Non-Christian religion	720	Architecture
320	Political science	730	Sculpture
330	Economics	750	Painting
350	Administration	760	Engraving
390	Customs and folklore	770	Photography
53	Physics	780	Music
540	Chemistry	800	Literature
550	Geology	910	Geography
580	Botany	913	Archaeology
590	Zoology	930	Ancient history
620	Engineering	942	English history
630	Agriculture	970	North American histor

1. Hunting with a camera 1.____

2. Interior decoration 2.____

3. Excavations in the pyramids 3.____

4. A survey predicting the probability of oil 4.____

5. The poems of Robert Browning 5.____

6. The spread of representative government 6.____

7. A discussion of longitude and latitude 7.____

8. Classification of plants 8.____

9. A discussion of the technical points of bridge building 9.____

10. A copy of the picture, Moria Lisa, by Leonardo da Vinci 10.____

Questions 11-25.

DIRECTIONS: Each of the following statements lists a topic on which you might wish to find a book, together with the *possible* word under which to look for it in the card catalog. For each, write the letter of the BEST answer in the space at the right.

2 (#2)

11. French revolution   11._____

    A. Napoleonic wars   B. Reign of terror
    C. France-Revolution   D. Revolution, French
    E. Terror, Reign of

12. North American Indians   12._____

    A. Indians of North America
    B. Aborigines
    C. American aborigines
    D. American Indians
    E. Mounds and mound builders

13. Democracy   13._____

    A. Democracy   B. Free institutions
    C. Popular government   D. Federal government
    E. Politics

14. Soap carving   14._____

    A. Sculpture   B. Soap sculpture
    C. Arts and crafts   D. Fine Arts
    E. Handicrafts

15. Business depressions   15._____

    A. Business cycles   B. Economic cycles
    C. Stabilization in industry   D. Economic conditions
    E. Depressions, Business

16. Applied art   16._____

    A. Art industry and trade   B. Decorative arts
    C. Industrial arts   D. Arts and crafts movement
    E. Commercial art

17. Prehistoric antiquities   17._____

    A. Antiquities
    B. Excavations
    C. Lake dwellers and lake dwellings
    D. Archaeology
    E. Ruins

18. Conduits   18._____

    A. Aqueducts   B. Water conduits
    C. Civil engineering   D. Hydraulic engineering
    E. Water supply

19. Actresses   19._____

    A. Actors and actresses   B. Drama
    C. Theater   D. Stage
    E. Acting

20. Abolition of slavery

    A. American history
    B. Southern states
    C. Civil war
    D. Slavery
    E. Negroes

21. The 1984 platforms of both the Republican and Democratic political parties may be found in

    A. GOVERNMENT MANUAL
    B. CURRENT BIOGRAPHY
    C. ENCYCLOPEDIA AMERICANA
    D. LINCOLN LIBRARY
    E. WORLD ALMANAC

22. An authoritative bibliography for each country described is given in the

    A. WORLD ALMANAC
    B. GOVERNMENT MANUAL
    C. STATESMAN'S YEARBOOK
    D. CONGRESSIONAL DIRECTORY
    E. CURRENT BIOGRAPHY

23. To find the author and title of the poem beginning *"Dear charming, nymph, neglected and dearied"*, look in

    A. COMPTON'S PICTURED ENCYCLOPEDIA
    B. BARTLETT'S FAMILIAR QUOTATIONS
    C. GRANGER'S INDEX TO POETRY AND RECITATION
    D. THE WORLD BOOK
    E. ENCYCLOPEDIA AMERICANA

24. A history of Alaska told by quotations (excerpts) from the writings of several historians may be found in

    A. STATESMAN'S YEARBOOK
    B. ENCYCLOPEDIA AMERICANA
    C. LARNED'S NEW HISTORY FOR READY REFERENCE
    D. WORLD ALMANAC
    E. CONGRESSIONAL DIRECTORY

25. A biographical note on Jane Addams may be found in the NEW STANDARD DICTIONARY in the

    A. main alphabet
    B. foreign words and phrases
    C. biographical section
    D. statistics of population
    E. rules for simplification of spelling

KEY (CORRECT ANSWERS

1. 770
2. 640
3. 913
4. 550
5. 800

6. 320
7. 910
8. 580
9. 620
10. 750

11. C
12. A
13. A
14. B
15. A

16. A
17. D
18. A
19. A
20. D

21. E
22. C
23. C
24. C
25. A

TEST 3

Questions 1-20.

DIRECTIONS: Each question consists of a statement. You are to indicate whether the statement is TRUE (T) or FALSE (F). *PRINT THE LETTER OF THE CORRECT ANSWER IN THE SPACE AT THE RIGHT.*

1. Biographies of poets may be found in GRANGER'S INDEX TO POETRY AND RECITATIONS.   1.__

2. To use THE LINCOLN LIBRARY OF ESSENTIAL INFORMATION, one should consult the index.   2.__

3. The words at the top of each page in the dictionary indicate the inclusive contents of the page.   3.__

4. THE STATESMAN'S YEARBOOK is published biennially.   4.__

5. The index is a valuable aid in the use of the ENCYCLOPAEDIA BRITANNICA.   5.__

6. The arrangement of BARTLETT'S FAMILIAR QUOTATIONS is chronological by author.   6.__

7. CURRENT BIOGRAPHY is arranged alphabetically.   7.__

8. The ENCYCLOPEDIA AMERICANA is arranged in large subject groups with an index.   8.__

9. WEBSTER'S NEW INTERNATIONAL DICTIONARY arranges all kinds of words in the English language in one alphabetical list.   9.__

10. Names of government officials may be found in the U.S. GOVERNMENT MANUAL.   10.__

11. WHO'S WHO IN AMERICA contains biographies of important people both living and dead.   11.__

12. COMPTON'S PICTURED ENCYCLOPEDIA is particularly good for children in the intermediate grades.   12.__

13. The articles in both the ENCYCLOPAEDIA BRITANNICA and the ENCYCLOPEDIA AMERICANA are signed.   13.__

14. A feature of the NEW STANDARD DICTIONARY is the divided page by which obsolete words are given below the line.   14.__

15. The U.S. GOVERNMENT MANUAL contains biographies of government officials.   15.__

16. BARTLETT'S FAMILIAR QUOTATIONS contains complete poems.   16.__

17. CURRENT BIOGRAPHY is published monthly and then cumulated.   17.__

18. CURRENT BIOGRAPHY contains biographies of persons in the news.   18.__

19. A description of the duties of the departments of the United States government will be found in the GOVERNMENT MANUAL.   19.__

20. An encyclopedia should be consulted for the pronunciation of words. 20._____

Questions 21-25.

DIRECTIONS: Listed below are some types of information you might want to locate, together with several books in which you might look. For each, write the letter of the BEST answer in the space at the right.

21. To find a list of magazine articles published in 1919 on the Versailles Treaty, you would consult 21._____

    A. the ENCYCLOPAEDIA BRITANNICA
    B. THE READER'S GUIDE
    C. LARNED'S NEW HISTORY FOR READY REFERENCE
    D. the card catalog
    E. WEBSTER'S NEW INTERNATIONAL DICTIONARY

22. The purposes, powers, and personnel of the United States Government War Agencies of World War II may be found in the 22._____

    A. CONGRESSIONAL DIRECTORY   B. GOVERNMENT MANUAL
    C. STATESMAN'S YEARBOOK   D. ENCYCLOPAEDIA BRITANNICA
    E. WORLD ALMANAC

23. A list of representative publications of departments and agencies of the federal government may be found in 23._____

    A. LARNED'S NEW HISTORY FOR READY REFERENCE
    B. STATESMAN'S YEARBOOK
    C. GOVERNMENT MANUAL
    D. AMERICAN ENCYCLOPEDIA
    E. CONGRESSIONAL DIRECTORY

24. For a discussion of the life and works of Beethoven, one should consult 24._____

    A. CURRENT BIOGRAPHY
    B. a daily newspaper
    C. GRANGER'S INDEX TO POETRY AND RECITATIONS
    D. GROVE'S DICTIONARY OF MUSIC AND MUSICIANS
    E. WHO'S WHO

25. The population of Topeka, Kansas, may be found in the NEW STANDARD DICTIONARY in the 25._____

    A. main alphabet
    B. foreign words and phrases
    C. disputed pronunciations
    D. key to abbreviations
    E. statistics of population

KEY (CORRECT ANSWERS)

1.	F	11.	F
2.	T	12.	T
3.	T	13.	T
4.	F	14.	F
5.	T	15.	F
6.	T	16.	F
7.	T	17.	T
8.	F	18.	T
9.	F	19.	T
10.	T	20.	F

21. B
22. B
23. C
24. D
25. E

ENGLISH GRAMMAR AND USAGE
EXAMINATION SECTION
TEST 1

DIRECTIONS: In the passages that follow, certain words and phrases are underlined and numbered. In each question, you will find alternatives for each underlined part. You are to choose the one that BEST expresses the idea, makes the statement appropriate for standard written English, or is worded MOST consistently with the style and tone of the passage as a whole. Choose the alternative you consider BEST and write the letter in the space at the right. If you think the original version is BEST, choose NO CHANGE. Read each passage through once before you begin to answer the questions that accompany it. You cannot determine most answers without reading several sentences beyond the phrase in question. Be sure that you have read far enough ahead each time you choose an alternative.

Questions 1-14.

DIRECTIONS: Questions 1 through 14 are based on the following passage.

Modern filmmaking <u>had began</u> in Paris in 1895 with the work of the Lumiere brothers.
                     1
Using their <u>invention, the Cinématographe,</u> the Lumières were able to photograph, print,
              2
and project moving pictures onto a screen. Their films showed <u>actual occurrences. A</u> train
                                                                      3
approaching a station, people a factory, workers demolishing a wall.

These early films had neither plot nor sound. But another Frenchman, Georges Méliès,
soon incorporated plot lines <u>into</u> his films. And with his attempts to draw upon the potential of
                                 4
film to create fantasy <u>worlds.</u> Méliès also <u>was an early pioneer from</u> special film effects. Edwin
                          5   6
Porter, an American filmmaker, took Méliès emphasis on narrative one step further. Believing
<u>that, continuity of shots</u> was of primary importance in filmmaking, Porter connected
       7
<u>images to present,</u> a sustained action. His GREAT TRAIN ROBBERY of 1903 opened a new
     8
era in film.

<u>Because</u> film was still considered <u>as</u> low entertainment in early twentieth century America,
    9   10
it was on its way to becoming a respected art form. Beginning in 1908, the American director
D.W. Griffith discovered and explored techniques to make film a more expressive medium.

2 (#1)

With his technical contributions, <u>as well as</u> his attempts to develop the intellectual and moral
                                    11
potential of film, Griffith helped build a solid foundation for the industry.

<u>Thirty</u> years after the Lumière brothers' first show, sound <u>had yet been</u> added to the
  12   13
movies. Finally, in 1927, Hollywood produced its first *talkie*, THE JAZZ SINGER. With sound,

modern film <u>coming</u> of age.
              14

1. A. NO CHANGE   B. begun   1._____
    C. began   D. had some beginnings

2. A. NO CHANGE   B. invention—the Cinématographe   2._____
    C. invention, the Cinématgraphe— D. invention, the Cinématographe

3. A. NO CHANGE   B. actually occurrences, a   3._____
    C. actually occurrences—a   D. actual occurrences: a

4. A. NO CHANGE   B. about   4._____
    C. with   D. to

5. A. NO CHANGE   B. worlds   5._____
    C. worlds' and   D. worlds and

6. A. NO CHANGE   B. pioneered   6._____
    C. pioneered the beginnings of   D. pioneered the early beginnings of

7. A. NO CHANGE   B. that continuity of shots   7._____
    C. that, continuity of shots,   D. that continuity of shots

8. A. NO CHANGE   B. images to present   8._____
    C. that, continuity of shots   D. that continuity of shots

9. A. NO CHANGE   9._____
    B. (Begin new paragraph) in view of the fact that
    C. (Begin new paragraph) Although
    D. Do NOT begin new paragraph) Since

10. A. NO CHANGE   B. as if it were   10._____
    C. like it was   D. OMIT the underlined portion

11. A. NO CHANGE   B. similar to   11._____
    C. similar with   D. like with

3 (#1)

12. A. NO CHANGE
    B. (Begin new paragraph) Consequently, thirty
    C. (Do NOT begin new paragraph) Therefore, thirty
    D. (Do NOT begin new paragraph) As a consequence, thirty

    12.____

13. A. NO CHANGE
    B. (Begin new paragraph) Consequently, thirty
    C. (No NOT begin new paragraph) Therefore, thirty
    D. (Do NOT begin new paragraph As a consequence, thirty

    13.____

14. A. NO CHANGE   B. comes
    C. came   D. had came

    14.____

Questions 15-22.

DIRECTIONS: Questions 15 through 22 are based on the following passage.

One of the most awesome forces in nature is the tsunami, or tidal wave. A tsunami—the word is Japanese for harbor wave, can generate the destructive power of many atomic bombs.
                        15

Tsunamis usually appear in a series of four or five waves about fifteen minutes apart.
         16
They begin deep in the ocean, gather remarkable speed as they travel, and cover great instances. The wave triggered by the explosion of Krakatoa in 1883 circled the world in three days.

Tsunamis being known to sink large ships at sea, they are most dangerous when they
         17
reach land. Close to shore, an oncoming tsunami is forced upward and skyward, perhaps as
                                                             18
high as 100 feet. This combination of height and speed accounts for the tsunami's great power.

That *tsunami* is a Japanese word is no accident, due to the fact that no nation
                                                  19
frequently has been so visited by giant waves as Japan. Tsunamis reach that country regularly,
   20   21
and with devastating consequences. One Japanese tsunami flattened several towns in
1896, also killed 27,000 people. The 2011 tsunami caused similar loss of life as well as untold
         22
damage from nuclear radiation.

101

15. A. NO CHANGE
    B. tsunami, the word is Japanese for harbor wave—
    C. tsunami—the word is Japanese for harbor wave—
    D. tsunami—the word being Japanese for harbor wave,

16. A. NO CHANGE
    B. (Begin new paragraph) Consequently, tsunamis
    C. (Do NOT begin new paragraph) Tsunamis consequently
    D. (Do NOT begin new paragraph) Yet, tsunamis

17. A. NO CHANGE
    B. Because tsunamis have been
    C. Although tsunamis have been
    D. Tsunamis have been

18. A. NO CHANGE
    B. upward to the sky,
    C. upward in the sky
    D. upward,

19. A. NO CHANGE
    B. when one takes into consideration the fact that
    C. seeing as how
    D. for

20. A. NO CHANGE
    B. (Place after *has*)
    C. (Place after *so*)
    D. (Place after *visited*)

21. A. NO CHANGE
    B. Moreover, tsunamis
    C. However, tsunamis
    D. Because tsunamis

22. A. NO CHANGE
    B. 1896 and killed 27,000 people
    C. 1896 and killing 27,000 people
    D. 1896, and 27,000 people as well

Questions 23-33.

DIRECTIONS: Questions 23 through 33 are based on the following passage.

I was <u>married one</u> August on a farm in Maine. The <u>ceremony, itself, taking</u> place in an
              23   24
arbor of pine boughs <u>we had built and constructed</u> in the yard next to the house. On the morning
                           25
of the wedding day, we parked the tractors behind the shed, <u>have tied</u> the dogs to an oak tree to
                                                 26
keep them from chasing the guests, and put the cows out to pasture. <u>Thus</u> we had thought of
                                                      27
everything, it seemed. we had forgotten how interested a cow can be in what is going on

<u>around them.</u> During the ceremony, my sister <u>(who has taken several years of lessons)</u> was to
    28   29
play a flute solo. We were all listening intently when she <u>had began</u> to play. As the first notes
                                                                30
reached us, we were surprised to hear a bass line under the flute's treble melody. Looking

around, the source was quickly discovered. There was Star, my pet Guernsey, her head hanging
              31
over the pasture fence, mooing along with the delicate strains of Bach.

Star took our laughter as being like a compliment, and we took her contribution that way,
                                 32
too. It was a sign of approval—the kind you would find only at a farm wedding.

23. A. NO CHANGE
    B. married, one
    C. married on an
    D. married, in an

24. A. NO CHANGE
    B. ceremony itself taking
    C. ceremony itself took
    D. ceremony, itself took

25. A. NO CHANGE
    B. which had been built and constructed
    C. we had built and constructed it
    D. we had built

26. A. NO CHANGE
    B. tie
    C. tied
    D. tying

27. A. NO CHANGE
    B. (Do NOT begin new paragraph) And
    C. (Begin new paragraph) But
    D. (Begin new paragraph (Moreover,

28. A. NO CHANGE
    B. around her
    C. in her own vicinity
    D. in their immediate area

29. A. NO CHANGE
    B. (whom has taken many years of lessons)
    C. (who has been trained in music)
    D. OMIT the underlined portion

30. A. NO CHANGE
    B. begun
    C. began
    D. would begin

31. A. NO CHANGE
    B. the discovery of the source was quick
    C. the discovery of the source was quickly made.
    D. we quickly discovered the source.

32. A. NO CHANGE
    A. as
    C. just as
    D. as if

33. A. NO CHANGE B. Yet it was
    C. But it was D. Being

Questions 34-42.

DIRECTIONS: Questions 34 through 42 are based on the following passage,

Riding a bicycle in Great Britain is not the same as riding a bicycle in the United States. Americans bicycling in Britain will find some <u>basic fundamental</u> differences in the rules of the
                                                                    34
road and in the attitudes of motorists.

<u>Probably</u> most difficult for the American cyclist is adjusting <u>with</u> British traffic patterns.
  35   36
<u>Knowing that traffic</u> in Britain moves on the left-hand side of the road, bicycling <u>once</u> there is the
  37   38
mirror image of what it is in the United States.

The problem of adjusting to traffic patterns is somewhat lessened, <u>however</u> by the respect
                                                                      39
with which British motorists treat bicyclists. A cyclist in a traffic circle, for example, is given the same right-of-way <u>with</u> the driver of any other vehicle. However, the cyclist is expected to obey
                      40
the rules of the road. <u>This difference in the American and British attitudes toward bicyclists</u> may
                                                        41
stem from differing attitudes toward the bicycle itself. Whereas Americans frequently view bicycles as <u>toys, but</u> the British treat them primarily as vehicles.
              42

34. A. NO CHANGE   B. basic and fundamental
    C. basically fundamental D. basic

35. A. NO CHANGE   B. Even so, probably
    C. Therefore, probably D. As a result, probably

36. A. NO CHANGE   B. upon
    C. on   D. to

37. A. NO CHANGE   B. Seeing that traffic
    C. Because traffic   D. Traffic

38. A. NO CHANGE   B. once you are
    C. once one is   D. OMIT the underlined portion

39. A. NO CHANGE B. also, C. moreover, D. therefore,

40. A. NO CHANGE B. as C. as if D. as with

41. A. NO CHANGE
    B. difference in the American and British attitudes toward bicyclists
    C. difference, in the American and British attitudes toward bicyclists
    D. difference in the American, and British, attitudes toward bicyclists

42. A. NO CHANGE B. toy; C. toys, D. toys; but

Questions 43-51.

DIRECTIONS: Questions 43 through 51 are based on the following passage.

People have always believed that supernatural powers <u>tend toward some influence on</u>
                                                         43
lives for good or for ill. Superstition originated with the idea that individuals <u>could in turn,</u> exert
                                                                                    44
influence <u>at</u> spirits. Certain superstitions are <u>so deeply embedded</u> in our culture that intelligent
          45   46
people sometimes act in accordance with them.

One common superstitious act is knocking on wood after boasting of good fortune. People once believed that gods inhabited trees and, therefore, were present in the wood used to build houses. Fearing that speaking of good luck within the gods' hearing might anger <u>them, people</u>
                                                                                                47
knocked on wood to deafen the gods and avoid their displeasure.

Another superstitious <u>custom and practice</u> is throwing salt over the left shoulder.
                       48
<u>Considering</u> salt was once considered sacred, people thought that spilling it brought bad
 49
luck. Since right and left represented good and evil, the believers used their right hands, which symbolized good, to throw a pinch of salt over their left shoulders into the eyes of the evil gods.

<u>Because of this</u>, people attempted to avert misfortune.
 50
Without realizing the origin of superstitions, many people exhibit superstitious behavior.

<u>Others avoid</u> walking under ladders and stepping on cracks in sidewalks, without having any
 51
idea why they are doing so.

8 (#1)

43. A. NO CHANGE
     C. tend to influence on
     C. can influence
     D. are having some influence on
     43.____

44. A. NO CHANGE.
     C. could, in turn
     B. could, turning
     D. could, in turn,
     44.____

45. A. NO CHANGE
     C. toward
     C. of
     D. on
     45.____

46. A. NO CHANGE
     C. deepest embedded
     B. deepest embedded
     D. embedded deepest
     46.____

47. A. NO CHANGE
     C. them: some people
     B. them; some people
     D. them, they
     47.____

48. A. NO CHANGE
     C traditional custom
     B. Custom
     D. customary habit
     48.____

49. A. NO CHANGE
     C. Because
     B. Although
     D. Keeping in mind that
     49.____

50. A. NO CHANGE
     C. Consequently
     B. As a result of this,
     D. In this way,
     50.____

51. A. NO CHANGE
     C. Avoiding
     B. Often avoiding
     D. They avoid
     51.____

Questions 52-66.

DIRECTIONS: Questions 52 through 65 are based on the following passage.

In the 1920s, the Y.M.C.A. sponsored one of the first programs <u>in order to promote</u>
$\qquad\qquad\qquad\qquad\qquad\qquad\qquad\qquad\qquad\qquad\qquad\qquad\qquad\qquad\qquad$ 52
more enlightened public opinion on racial matters; the organization started special university classes <u>in which</u> young people could study race relations. Among the guest speakers invited to
$\qquad\quad$ 53
conduct the sessions, one of the most popular was George Washington Carver, the scientist from Tuskegee Institute.

As a student, Carver himself had been active in the Y.M.C.A. <u>He shared</u> its evangelical
$\qquad\qquad\qquad\qquad\qquad\qquad\qquad\qquad\qquad\qquad\qquad\qquad\qquad\qquad\qquad$ 54
and educational philosophy. However, in <u>1923,</u> the Y.M.C.A. arranged <u>Carver's first initial</u>
$\qquad\qquad\qquad\qquad\qquad\qquad\qquad\qquad$ 55 $\qquad\qquad\qquad\qquad\qquad\qquad$ 56
speaking tour, the scientist accepted with apprehension. He was to speak at several white colleges, most of whose students had never seen, let alone heard, an educated black man.

9 (#1)

Although Carver's appearances did sometimes cause occasional controversy, but
                                    57   58
his quiet dedication prevailed, and his humor quickly won over his audiences. Nevertheless, for
                                                                                59
the next decade, Carver toured the Northeast, Midwest, and South under Y.M.C.A.

sponsorship. Speaking at places never before open to blacks. On these tours Carver
        60
befriended thousands of students, many of whom subsequently corresponded with his
                                        61
afterwards. The tours, unfortunately were not without discomfort for Carver. There were
  62   63
the indignities of *Jim Crow* accommodations and racial insults from strangers. As a result,
                                                                                 64
the scientist's enthusiasm never faltered. Avoiding any discussion of the political and social
                                              65
aspects of racial injustice; instead, Carver conducted his whole life as an indirect attack to
                                                                                         66
prejudice. This, as much as his science, is his legacy to humankind.

52. A. NO CHANGE   B. to promote   52.____
    C. for the promoting of what is D. for the promotion of what are

53. A. NO CHANGE   C. from which   53.____
    C. that   D. by which

54. A. NO CHANGE   B. Sharing.   54.____
    C. Having Shared   D. Because He Shared

55. A. NO CHANGE   B. 1923   55.____
    C. 1923, and   D. 1923, when

56. A. NO CHANGE   B. Carvers' first, initial   56.____
    C. Carvers first initial   D. Carver's first

57. A. NO CHANGE   B. sometimes did   57.____
    C. did   D. OMIT the underlined portion

58. A. NO CHANGE   B. controversy and   58.____
    C. controversy   D. controversy, however

59. A. NO CHANGE   B. However, for   59.____
    C. However, from   D. For

60. A. NO CHANGE   B. sponsorship and spoke   60.____
    C. sponsorship; and spoke   D. sponsorship, and speaking

61. A. NO CHANGE
    B. who
    C. them
    D. those

62. A. NO CHANGE
    B. later
    C. sometimes later.
    D. OMIT the underlined portion and end the sentence with a period

63. A. NO CHANGE
    B. tours, unfortunately, were
    C. tours unfortunately, were
    D. tours, unfortunately, are

64. A. NO CHANGE
    B. So
    C. But
    D. Therefore,

65. A. NO CHANGE
    B. He avoided discussing
    C. Having avoided discussing
    D. Upon avoiding the discussion of

66. A. NO CHANGE
    B. over
    C. on
    D. of

Questions 67-75.

DIRECTIONS: Questions 67 through 75 are based on the following passage.

Shooting rapids is not the only way to experience the thrill of canoeing. An ordinary-
                                                                                67
looking stream, innocent of rocks and white water, can provide adventure, as long as it has

three essential features; a swift current, close banks, and has plenty of twists and turns.
              68   69
A powerful current causes tension, for canoeists know they will have only seconds for
70
executing the maneuvers necessary to prevent crashing into the threes lining the narrow

streams banks. Of course, the narrowness, itself, being crucial in creating the tension. On a
    71   72
broad stream, canoeists can pause frequently, catch their breath, and get their bearings.

However to a narrow stream, where every minute you run the risk of being knocked down by a
         73   74
low-hanging tree limb, they be constantly alert. Yet even the fast current and close banks would

be manageable if the stream were fairly straight. The expenditure of energy required to paddle

furiously, first on one side of the canoe and then on the other, wearies both the nerves as well
                                                                          75
as the body.

11 (#1)

67.
- A. NO CHANGE
- B. They say that for adventure an
- C. Many finding that an
- D. The old saying that an

67._____

68.
- A. NO CHANGE
- B. features
- C. features,
- D. features; these being

68._____

69.
- A. NO CHANGE
- B. there must be
- C. with
- D. OMIT the underlined portion

69._____

70.
- A. NO CHANGE
- B. Thus, a
- C. Therefore, a
- D. Furthermore, a

70._____

71.
- A. NO CHANGE
- B. stream's banks.
- C. streams bank's
- D. banks of the streams

71._____

72.
- A. NO CHANGE
- B. narrowness, itself is
- C. narrowness itself is
- D. narrowness in itself being

72._____

73.
- A. NO CHANGE
- B. near
- C. on
- D. with

73._____

74.
- A. NO CHANGE
- B. the canoer runs
- C. one runs
- D. they run

74._____

75.
- A. NO CHANGE
- B. the nerves as well as the body
- C. the nerves, also, as well as the body
- D. not only the body but also the nerves as well

75._____

KEY (CORRECT ANSWERS)

1.	C	21.	A	41.	A	61.	A
2.	A	22.	B	42.	C	62.	D
3.	D	23.	A	43.	B	63.	B
4.	A	24.	C	44.	C	64.	C
5.	B	25.	D	45.	D	65.	B
6.	B	26.	C	46.	A	66.	C
7.	D	27.	C	47.	A	67.	A
8.	B	28.	B	48.	B	68.	B
9.	C	29.	D	49.	C	69.	D
10.	D	30.	C	50.	D	70.	A
11.	A	31.	D	51.	D	71.	B
12.	A	32.	B	52.	B	72.	C
13.	B	33.	A	53.	A	73.	C
14.	C	34.	D	54.	A	74.	D
15.	C	35.	A	55.	D	75.	B
16.	A	36.	D	56.	D		
17.	C	37.	C	57.	C		
18.	D	38.	D	58.	C		
19.	D	39.	A	59.	D		
20.	C	40.	B	60.	B		

EXAMINATION SECTION
TEST 1

DIRECTIONS: In each of the following groups, one of the four sentences contains an error in grammar, usage, diction, or punctuation. Indicate the INCORRECT sentence. *PRINT THE LETTER OF THE CORRECT ANSWER IN THE SPACE AT THE RIGHT.*

1.
   A. If I were you, he should not be allowed to regret having befriended the child.
   B. Deserted, surrounded and outnumbered, and with everything at stake, their refusal to surrender took great courage.
   C. Considering all his efforts in our behalf, our warmest thanks were clearly merited by him.
   D. He enjoyed, in his mountain retreat, not only skimming over the ice on his skates, but also feeling the danger of a mad rush down perilous slopes on his bobsled.

1._____

2.
   A. A young author is apt to run into a confusion of mixed metaphors which leaves the sense disjointed and the imagination distracted.
   B. We do not intend, in enforcing this rule, to guarantee your safety under all conditions; however, under ordinary circumstances, you will find you are adequately protected.
   C. When John entered the room, he shouted, "Run for your lives!" and then sat down quietly at the piano.
   D. My friend Eldridge has bought a plot of ground and intends to build a small house upon it within the year.

2._____

3.
   A. The students in the dormitories were forbidden, unless they had special passes, from staying out after 11:00 P.M.
   B. The Student Court rendered a decision satisfactory to both the defendant and the accuser.
   C. Margarine is being substituted for butter to a considerable extent.
   D. In this school there are at least fifteen minor accidents a year which are due to this traffic violation.

3._____

4.
   A. Everyone at camp must have his medical certificate on file before participating in competitive sports.
   B. A crate of oranges were sent from Florida for all the children in Cabin Six.
   C. John and Danny's room looks as if they were prepared for inspection.
   D. Three miles is too far for a young child to walk.

4._____

5.
   A. Sailing along New England's craggy coastline, you will relive a bygone era of far-roving whalers and graceful clipper ships.
   B. The march of history is reenacted in folk festivals, outdoor pageants, and fiestas local in theme, but national in import.
   C. Visiting the scenes of the past, our interest in American history is renewed and enlivened.
   D. What remained was a few unrecognizable fragments.

5._____

6. A. The game over, the spectators rushed out on the field and tore down the goalposts.
    B. The situation was aggravated by disputes over the captaincy of the team.
    C. Yesterday they lay their uniforms aside with the usual end-of-the season regret.
    D. It is sometimes thought that politics is not for the high-minded.

7. A. Sandburg's autobiography, as well as his poems, are familiar to many readers.
    B. A series of authentic records of the American Indian tribes is being published.
    C. The Smokies are the home of the decendants of this brave tribe.
    D. Five dollars is really not too much to pay for a book of this type.

8. A. No one but her could have recognized him.
    B. She knew the stranger to be him whom she had given up as lost.
    C. He looked like he had been in some strange land where age advanced at a double pace.
    D. It is impossible to include that item; the agenda have already been mimeographed.

9. A. You have probably heard of the new innovation in the regular morning broadcast.
    B. During the broadcast you are expected to stand, to salute, and to sing the fourth stanza of "America."
    C. None of the rocks which form the solid crust of our planet is more than two billions years old.
    D. "I have finished my assignment," said the pupil. "May I go home now?"

10. A. The text makes the process of developing and sustaining a successful home zoo appear to be a pleasant profitable one.
    B. The warmth and humor, the clear characterization of the Walmsey family, which includes three children, two dogs, and two cats, is such fun to read that this reviewer found herself reading it all over again.
    C. You will be glad, I am sure, to give the book to whoever among your young friends has displayed an interest in animals.
    D. The consensus among critics of children's literature is that the book is well worth the purchase price.

11. A. Participation in active sports produces both release from tension as well as physical well-being.
    B. The problem of taxes is still with them.
    C. Every boy and every girl in the auditorium was thrilled when the color guard appeared.
    D. At length our club decided to send two representatives to the meeting, you and me.

12. A. B. Nelson & Co. has a sale of dacron shirts today.
    B. Venetian blinds-called that although they probably did not originate in Venice-are no longer used as extensively as they were at one time.
    C. He determined to be guided by the opinion of whoever spoke first.
    D. There is often disagreement as to whom is the better Shakespearean action, Evans or Gielgud.

13. A. Remains of an ancient civilization were found near Mexico City.
    B. It is interesting to compare the interior of one of the pyramids in Mexico to the interior of one of the pyramids in Egypt.
    C. In two days' journey you will be reminded of political upheavals comparable to the volcanic eruptions still visible and audible in parts of Mexico.
    D. There is little danger of the law's being broken, so drastic is the penalty.

    13._____

14. A. It did not take him long to develop an interest in the great American pastime - baseball.
    B. If you had made your way to the Whipsnade Zoo, you would have had an opportunity of seeing wild animals in more or less natural habitats.
    C. How I should have liked to have spent a few more days in Paris!
    D. Neither baseball pools nor any other form of gambling is allowed in or near the school.

    14._____

15. A. If the bill were introduced, it would provoke endless debate.
    B. Since George, with his two dogs, is to be with us, it might be better to rent a cabin.
    C. He, not I, is the one to decide.
    D. He is, however, one of those restless people who never seems content in his present environment.

    15._____

16. A. Instead of looking disdainfully at London grime, think of it as a mantle of tradition.
    B. Nobody but the pilot and the co-pilot was permitted to handle the mysterious package.
    C. Not only is industry anxious to hire all available engineers, but they are being offered commissions by the armed forces.
    D. For immediate service go direct to the store manager.

    16._____

17. A. The delegates alighted and started off in a taxi, their baggage having been taken care of.
    B. That kind of potatoes is grown in Idaho.
    C. Besides Alan Stevens, there were eight officers of the organization on the dais.
    D. As the delegates reached the convention hall late, they blamed their tardiness on the taxi driver.

    17._____

18. A. The new system is superior from every point of view to the inefficient system in use until now.
    B. The reason for the strike, you may recall, was because the union demanded a closed shop.
    C. Who's to decide whether it is to be installed?
    D. To suit Mr. Knolls, the new device will have to save time, money, and the dispositions of the employees.

    18._____

19. A. Everyone can have a wonderful time in New York if they will just not try to see the entire city in one week.
    B. Being a stranger in town myself, I know how you feel.
    C. New York City is a city of man-made wonders awe-inspiring as those found in nature.
    D. He felt deep despair (as who has not?) at the evidence of man's inhumanity to man.

    19._____

20.
A. In the recipe for custard, two cupfuls of milk will be enough.
B. In the home economics classroom two tubs of clothes showed that it was not a day for cooking.
C. It was 4:00 P.M. before the dishes were cleared away, washed, and put back into the closet.
D. If only I had a fairy godmother like Cinderella!

20.____

21.
A. The zinnia has the more vivid color, but the violet is the sweeter-smelling.
B. About three-fourths of the review I read was merely a summary of the story; the rest, criticism.
C. I shall insist that he not be accepted as a member, since he is very bad-tempered.
D. No sooner had he begun to speak when his auditors started to boo and hiss.

21.____

22.
A. The children's determination to find their dog almost resulted in tragedy.
B. They spent the first night in a house that was unlocked and with no one at home.
C. "What he asked me," said the boy, "was, 'Where can I find your father?'"
D. It was the whimpering of a younger child and the comforting words of her brother that a member of the search-party heard about ten feet off the road.

22.____

23.
A. If I would have known how extraordinarily conscientious these visitors would be, I would have prepared a more elaborate trip.
B. Enormous purchases of millinery are not warranted by business conditions in the large cities of this country.
C. Joan studies English, physics, history, French, and algebra.
D. I was asked which of the two books I liked better.

23.____

24.
A. When I reached the station, I discovered that I forgot my billfold.
B. If Brutus had taken Cassius's advice, he would not have given Antony permission to speak.
C. If John fails to help his mother, he will regret his selfishness.
D. My father plans to visit the Philippines Islands in the fall, provided he can get accommodations on a steamer.

24.____

25.
A. There was something surreptitious and sacrilegious about his conduct: I didn't care for his personality at all.
B. Since it is liable to rain, be sure to take your umbrella with you to the game.
C. If he could ever remember consistently where he had laid important papers, he would assume that the millenium had arrived.
D. There is no need to engage in self-flagellation each time you make an error; to err is human.

25.____

26.
A. In this cool room, neither the rose nor the gardenia will lose their freshness.
B. Unless his persistent asceticism gets immediate psychiatric attention, the patient is very likely to find himself in a sanitarium.
C. He has doubtless fully proven his innocence.
D. Whether the Korean War has seriously affected the home front or not is a matter that needs further discussion.

26.____

27.   A. Confectioner's sugar is frequently used in baking.
       B. What happens when an immovable object meets an irrestible force?
       C. The principle reason for his objecting to any propitiatory gestures was that he was not a person who forgets an insult easily.
       D. He was operated upon for appendicitis.

28.   A. I read where the weather forecaster said a snow storm was coming.
       B. The thunder, not the flashes of lightning, frightens Janet.
       C. Harold doesn't study as I do.
       D. Thomas prefers that kind of grapes to any other on the market.

29.   A. From the position of the fingerprints, the detective inferred that the man who had fired the shot was left-handed.
       B. Do you know the name of the boy who sits next to you in our music class?
       C. He spared himself much embarrassment by returning back home.
       D. How serious a matter it is to try to resist, I have had ample opportunity to observe.

30.   A. My old friend and adviser is sick, I am sorry to say.
       B. Can you recall my telling you the story?
       C. He used a ten-foot pole in the pole vault, and very nearly broke the record.
       D. Obviously pleased, the assemblyman told the senator that he had been elected.

31.   A. His indifferent attitude and phlegmatic temperament contributed to the candidate's defeat in the plebiscite.
       B. We reached home, but the house was completely dark and we opened the door and saw Buster wagging his tail.
       C. With leaden feet Time creeps along.
       D. Jerry asked this question: "How should the ghost be represented on the stage?"

32.   A. The entire list of names of candidates was printed in the evening papers.
       B. If I should miss the train heaven forbid! I'll telephone you at once.
       C. During the current year, I have bought a new book every month.
       D. Since the bell did not ring yet, I plan to remain in the room for a while longer.

33.   A. I gave a folder to everybody present, not omitting myself.
       B. I was pleased delighted, I should say to hear your excellent report.
       C. The reason I have no pen is that I lent it to my assistant.
       D. Can you ever be sure that the person whom you know is a friend of yours today will be your friend tomorrow?

34.   A. Many colleges report that war veterans do work equal in quality to that of other students, or even better.
       B. I intend to be a lawyer because it is interesting work.
       C. Today the news is very disturbing, and we hear it through many avenues.
       D. How different he is from his younger brother!

35.
  A. In one aspect of the situation, Sam was better than any of the other men in his group; he could endure long hours, cold winds, and get drenched all day.
  B. No sooner had he entered the room than pandemonium broke loose.
  C. As a young man, I was incorrigible with respect to order; now that I am grown old, I feel very sensibly the want of it.
  D. If my father were as young as I, he would have a very different outlook on life.

36.
  A. Dickens' A TALE OF TWO CITIES is widely read in English classes.
  B. Give the book to whoever appeared first on line.
  C. Having borrowed over a thousand dollars, he was able to attend college for a year.
  D. 30 scientists listened in rapt attention to a succinct explanation of the function of chlorophyll.

37.
  A. These are the criteria for judging the merit of this composition.
  B. Aside from this error in punctuation, your composition is excellent.
  C. The sign on the road cautioned him to drive slow and to watch for children.
  D. The pupils asked permission to partake in the assembly program; however, they were refused.

38.
  A. He determined to enter and win the race.
  B. I find it difficult even to imagine a good excuse for his absence.
  C. Do you object to him joining us?
  D. If I were only there now, perhaps I might be able to help.

39.
  A. See that you attribute to no word a meaning different from the one it had a hundred years ago.
  B. No one could say for sure whether the scurrilous attack in the newspaper had brought on the cerebral hemorrhage.
  C. There were less pupils in the auditorium during the rehearsal for the school pageant than we had expected.
  D. When I saw that he wasn't working today, I realized fully the seriousness of his ailment.

40.
  A. When the President had finished his speech, everybody cheered; he lifted his hand in acknowledgment to them as he took his seat.
  B. I never heard of a woman's being offended by flattery.
  C. Some who have participated in military trials say it is not designed to promote justice for the defendant.
  D. Officers serving on court martial should peruse the documents with the utmost care.

41.
  A. Within his huge area is produced two-thirds the oats, more than half the corn, and half the wheat, wool and cotton.
  B. We can send you the refrigerator today, or we can keep it in the factory for a few days, if it is necessary to do so.
  C. Since his car is headed west, he'll not reach Maryland on that road.
  D. Never underestimate the value of a high school education.

42.
   A. All my friends were waiting when I arrived, and, despite my lateness, they greeted me courteously.
   B. He worked silently and swiftly, hoping to end his patient's discomfort quickly.
   C. Born in Salzburg, Mozart spent his childhood touring the cities of Europe.
   D. Please note the difference between "wither," "weather," "Whether," and "Whither."

43.
   A. Who did they say won?
   B. The man whom I thought was my friend deceived me.
   C. Send whoever will do the work.
   D. The question of who should be leader arose.

44.
   A. I will not go unless I receive a special invitation.
   B. The pilot shouted orders to his assistant as the plane burst into flames.
   C. She acts as though her feelings were hurt.
   D. Please come here and try and help me finish this piece of work.

45.
   A. Choose an author as you choose a friend.
   B. Home is home, be it ever so humble.
   C. You always look well in that sort of clothes.
   D. We had no sooner entered the room when the bell rung.

46.
   A. Never before, to the best of my recollection, have there been such promising students.
   B. It is only because your manners are so objectionable that you are not invited to the party.
   C. I fully expected that the children would be at their desks and to find them ready to begin work.
   D. A complete system of railroads covers the entire country.

47.
   A. The remainder of the time was spent in prayer.
   B. Immigration is when people come into a foreign country to live.
   C. He coughed continually last winter.
   D. The method is different from the one that was formerly used.

48.
   A. She is not nearly so clever as her older sister.
   B. In some ways our immediate ancestors differed but slightly from our primitive forebears.
   C. You had better pay close attention to the directions.
   D. This young cartoonist can draw as well or even better than a veteran artist.

49.
   A. Had the warden been more alert, the desperado would not have escaped so easily.
   B. "Come into my parlor," he said, "and make yourself at home."
   C. If we would have held out another week, the strike would have ended in our favor.
   D. The embattled troops rallied around that famous cry, "They shall not pass!"

50.
   A. Stroking his beard thoughtfully, an idea suddenly came to him.
   B. I read recently in an encyclopedia that Izaak Walton lived to the age of ninety.
   C. There are many reasons given for his success, his wit being most frequently mentioned.
   D. Having heard all the testimony in the case, the jury was charged by the judge.

KEY (CORRECT ANSWERS)

1. B	11. A	21. D	31. B	41. A
2. A	12. D	22. B	32. D	42. D
3. A	13. B	23. A	33. D	43. B
4. B	14. C	24. A	34. B	44. D
5. C	15. D	25. B	35. A	45. D
6. C	16. C	26. A	36. D	46. C
7. A	17. D	27. C	37. D	47. B
8. C	18. B	28. A	38. C	48. D
9. A	19. A	29. C	39. C	49. C
10. B	20. D	30. D	40. C	50. A

TEST 2

DIRECTIONS: In each of the following groups, one of the four sentences contains an error in grammar, usage, diction, or punctuation. Indicate the INCORRECT sentence. *PRINT THE LETTER OF THE CORRECT ANSWER IN THE SPACE AT THE RIGHT.*

1. A. In recent years, the metals in many articles have been substituted by plastics.
   B. They are not in Boston now, but I think they're going to that city next week.
   C. The bag of peanuts was lost.
   D. His decision was firmly stated: there would be no more excursions.

   1._____

2. A. There is, in these manifestations of distrust and suspicion, the very germ of dissension which may sprout into war.
   B. Whenever I read Somerset Maugham's OF HUMAN BONDAGE, I take a renewed interest in El Greco's art.
   C. The newest model of gun, as well as all previous models, have been made obsolete by atomic power.
   D. Neither machines nor manpower is lacking for the peaceful tasks that lie ahead.

   2._____

3. A. There was, in the first place, no indication that a crime had been committed.
   B. She is taller than any other member of her class.
   C. She decided to leave the book lay on the table.
   D. Haven't you any film in stock at the present time?

   3._____

4. A. The boys at camp liked swimming, boating, and to go on long hikes.
   B. The news of the victory was broadcast to all the soldiers in the field.
   C. He dived into the pool and swam to the opposite end.
   D. There were half a dozen people present who were attending the club's meeting for the first time.

   4._____

5. A. Located on a mountainside with a babbling brook beside the door, it was a dream palace.
   B. Blessed are they who have not seen and yet have believed.
   C. The customs in that part of the country are much different than I expected.
   D. Politics, even in towns of small population, has always attracted ambitious young lawyers.

   5._____

6. A. If John were here, he would help you solve the problem.
   B. Your statement that the report was not complete has aroused our suspicions.
   C. Every time I see you, you act like you're angry about something.
   D. Had he been your friend, he would have told you the plan.

   6._____

7. A. I'm not feeling so good, may I lie down for a few minutes?
   B. Although the second attempt was somewhat better than the first, it was far from satisfactory.
   C. I wish I could play golf as well as he.
   D. We plan to meet my brother and her at the church.

   7._____

119

8.
  A. Baseball games, which are generally noisy, should not be played on the sand lot near the hospital.
  B. Boys, who work their way through school find it difficult to visit the library.
  C. They offered the prize to the girl who had the highest average for the term.
  D. This tall, anemic girl, who is considerably younger than she appears, has been undernourished since babyhood.

9.
  A. She is somewhat disagreeable at home, but is always pleasant at school.
  B. During the entire night, we heard the mournful sound of the fog horn.
  C. Anyone can read the huge warning sign at the turn in the road, if they want to.
  D. The United States is a great country; its citizens should cherish its ideals of democracy.

10.
  A. If everyone does his duty, the plan will not fail.
  B. In the present situation, no one but I can help you.
  C. The sick man lay in bed all day, but rose in the evening to eat his dinner.
  D. I had begun to think I had lost my way, when suddenly I saw the paved highway.

11.
  A. Our vacation is over, I am sorry to say.
  B. It is so dark that I can't hardly see.
  C. Either you or I am right; we cannot both be right.
  D. After it had lain in the rain all night, it was not fit for use again.

12.
  A. The climate of New York is colder than California.
  B. I shall wait for you on the corner opposite the drug store.
  C. Here come my father and mother.
  D. Being a very modest person, John seldom talks about his invention.

13.
  A. My visit to Africa was fraught with untold perils.
  B. Visiting Montmartre is always an exciting adventure.
  C. Will there be a chance of you visiting Europe next year?
  D. Visiting me the other day, she explained why she had failed to leave them.

14.
  A. Do you remember when the late President Roosevelt said that "We have nothing to fear but fear itself?"
  B. Alas, how soon we grow forgetful of those rows of little white crosses all over the world!
  C. Mosquitoes have many larvae in stagnant pools; the best way to destroy them is to suffocate them by means of a film of oil spread over the water.
  D. "Please tell me," he politely interrupted, "whether you can spell 'Mississippi'."

15.
  A. If he were wealthy, he would build a hospital for the poor.
  B. I shall insist that he obey you.
  C. They believe it to be she who sent me the warning.
  D. What kind of cactus is this one?

16.
  A. When you go to the library tomorrow, please bring this book to the librarian in the reference room.
  B. His speech is so precise as to seem affected.
  C. I had sooner serve overseas than remain inactive at home.
  D. We read each other's letters.

17. A. John, a popular boy with many friends, was invited to spend a week at the camp.   17._____
     B. My failure was due to the poor method of study I employed at that time.
     C. When I graduated high school, I was only fifteen years old.
     D. We have a right to infer from your remarks that you think him guilty.

18. A. Ladies' hats are more expensive now than ever.   18._____
     B. They were frightened by his shrieking.
     C. They were grateful to whomever would help them.
     D. Large groups of persons visit the shrine every day.

19. A. On one side was a swamp, on the other a river.   19._____
     B. Take those books next door.
     C. Jack was running for our team when suddenly he drops the ball.
     D. The data which were used had been supplied by the agents.

20. A. Such consideration as you can give us will be appreciated.   20._____
     B. It looks to me like another World War will break out any minute.
     C. The boat sank at noon, but it was early evening before the first rescuers arrived on the spot.
     D. Microscopy is, with him, more than a fad.

21. A. Such participation, under wise leadership, has developed a sense of security and happiness in many citizens.   21._____
     B. He is here using the word "esquire" in the British sense of country gentlemen.
     C. We were sure, knowing him, that of the two alternatives, he would choose the one that was most difficult.
     D. It is true of Jim; it is true of Bill; it is true of Mary.

22. A. Neither opportunity nor ability has been absent from his career.   22._____
     B. The new era was brought about by us younger women.
     C. New York City is larger than any other city in the country.
     D. Anybody can sell this magazine in their neighborhood.

23. A. I am neither a villain, as has been alleged, or a coward.   23._____
     B. I wish I had been there when the incident occurred.
     C. He asked, "Shall you be twenty on your next birthday?"
     D. They went through all the formalities of a diplomatic function.

24. A. I can't understand Helen's making that mistake.   24._____
     B. He has lain there so long that he feels stiff all over.
     C. I don't know that we can go along.
     D. The reason why he had always avoided the honor of the Garter was because he knew that it cost a thousand pounds.

25. A. My brother detected the cause of the fire himself.   25._____
     B. Every sheet of white paper has been torn across the middle.
     C. The word "concurred" has been deleted and substituted by the word "dissented."
     D. This is a plain statement of fact endorsed by every diplomat now in Paris.

26. A. After all, consistency is the one important thing in business letter copy. 26.____
    B. I urged her to come down from off her high horse.
    C. A tattered flag hung all day from an attic window.
    D. There is nothing to puzzle you, because you don't have to send one penny or promise anything.

27. A. You are entirely right in your opinion about trespassing. 27.____
    B. He accepted the invitation because he enjoyed both fishing and to swim.
    C. All the sample books have thrilled countless readers.
    D. Getting down to brass tacks is difficult for my chief.

28. A. She objected to me reading so many novels and mystery stories. 28.____
    B. She is younger by many years than I.
    C. The ornateness of the paintings and the furnishings was not pleasing to my aesthetic sense.
    D. If you hadn't laid the book in the drawer, I should have had no difficulty in locating it.

29. A. Among the Bible stories that interest most people is the one about the battle between David and the giant, Goliath. 29.____
    B. They all arrived on time except you and I.
    C. She is so much taller than I, that I feel like a pigmy alongside her.
    D. I have always heard that the four years at college are the happiest years in a man's life.

30. A. We trusted to the sound of our footsteps on the gravel to keep us on the path. 30.____
    B. I have never been partial to those kind of newspapers.
    C. All suggestions pertaining to the improvement of conditions were considered from the standpoint of their practicability.
    D. My brother, with two of his friends, has joined the World Federalist movement.

31. A. While I was there I had many unpleasant experiences, some of which I shall never forget. 31.____
    B. Because he was independent of any political affiliation, his was a one-man campaign.
    C. The people cheered as soldier after soldier made their appearance.
    D. It is every citizen's duty first to register, and then to vote for the candidate best qualified.

32. A. The chairman, elected unanimously by the committee, has resigned. 32.____
    B. I shall give a copy of this pamphlet to whoever would like one.
    C. The boy should of completed his work the day before yesterday.
    D. Through all my troubles, I depended upon my roommate, than whom no stauncher friend exists.

33. A. Any of them is eligible to compete for the scholarship. 33.____
    B. Irregardless of your opinion, I feel inclined to be guided by my intuition.
    C. I should like everyone who I believe is capable to undertake this task.
    D. He was intent upon what he was doing and could not be distracted,

34.
  A. At the school at which she registered she will learn painting, dancing and to sing.
  B. Far out on the last jagged rock we could detect what appeared to be a wreck.
  C. She had, as those with strong natures always have, an unbounded confidence in her luck.
  D. Shaw made his first plunge into controversy: he rose to his feet, shaking with excitement, and heard himself speaking.

35.
  A. Neither the salary nor the work offers any great inducement to him.
  B. This property of my sister's is going to be sold soon.
  C. The temperature in Bermuda is almost never higher than Arizona or New Mexico.
  D. His satire on the corrupt society of the seventeenth century is subtly drawn.

36.
  A. Having eaten their lunch, the boat was quickly loaded and the picknickers departed.
  B. The materials were distributed among the four applicants.
  C. The man who was really responsible, the accountant, was arrested.
  D. "When did you arrive?" he asked.

37.
  A. The broiled fish looked good but tasted bad.
  B. The woman whom I believed to be his sister is his daughter.
  C. The last suggestion is more suitable than all that have been offered up to this point.
  D. The person who I always thought was my most dependable friend proved a great disappointment.

38.
  A. The scholarship was offered to whoever could show need of financial assistance.
  B. By applying himself diligently to the task, it was finally whipped into shape.
  C. This book has apparently lain undisturbed on the library shelf for many years.
  D. Weather prediction is based on data which are ascertained by means of sensitive instruments.

39.
  A. No answer having been received, it was assumed that Farley was no longer interested in the project.
  B. Neither the teachers nor the principal was discouraged by the results of the test.
  C. When engaged in reading, I do not like to be disturbed.
  D. Reading a few books thoughtfully is better than to skim many books superficially.

40.
  A. The pupil whom the faculty believed would win the essay contest failed to submit a paper.
  B. Bats are unable to see in the dark, yet avoid obstacles in a lightless cave.
  C. Luckily, none of the passengers in the wrecked plane was killed.
  D. None of Joan's class can draw more sensitively than she.

41.
  A. The rapid growth of television cannot but affect other media of mass entertainment.
  B. As a health resort, the high, dry air of the Rockies is always recommended for people suffering from lung trouble.
  C. Each of the children was given two teaspoonfuls of cod liver oil.
  D. "Ask Mr. Esposito," said Tom; "perhaps he can tell you."

42. A. The results of his investigations he embodied in three of the most brilliant essays he or any other Harvard graduate ever wrote.
    B. Whatever the consequences, my decision is irrevocable.
    C. If Barbara would have thought twice, she would not have spoken as she did.
    D. I think that you'll agree with me that CHARLOTTE'S WEB is one of the best children's books that have been published this year.

43. A. Mozart's chamber music, as well as his operas, are delightful to hear.
    B. The producer reported that he had recently read the revised third act and thought it excellent.
    C. Nobody but James and him was able to go to the Planetarium.
    D. The chimes rang true and sweet and gladdened the hearts of the listeners.

44. A. "Why," asked the magistrate, "did you pass the red light?"
    B. Respect for others, loyalty, integrity—these are the essential ingredients of good character.
    C. Be only satisfied with the best.
    D. If I were able to play a musical instrument, I should be very happy.

45. A. Doctors say that certain throat conditions are aggravated by smoking.
    B. When I hear someone speak of their thirteenth year as an unlucky year, I am irritated by the persistence of superstition.
    C. There are no words in English in which two c's follow the prefix re.
    D. Sir Toby Belch—he is the clown in TWELFTH NIGHT—is one of Shakespeare's most vivid characters.

46. A. The men's department is on the fifth floor, while the boys' is on the fourth.
    B. It was she whom the policeman had warned to remain on the sidewalk.
    C. Into every life come both joy and sorrow.
    D. The carton contained these items; a loaf of bread, a compass, a tattered diary, and a pair of muddy shoes.

47. A. The fact that Jones and Company reduced the amount of it's employees is no indication that there is a slump.
    B. I saw Mrs. Brown, her whom you pointed out at the meeting.
    C. John, that suit looks unusually good on you.
    D. We know the culprits to be them.

48. A. I don't see why he should feel so bad about his loss; its not as though he were impoverished.
    B. If he was honest, he would return the money.
    C. But for his uncle's intervention he would have been discharged.
    D. think they, on the average, are much heavier than we.

49. A. Conditions here are much better than Europe.
    B. The study of the changes that have taken place and the reasons for them is fascinating.
    C. I found the play exciting (and frightening), but the audience seemed unmoved by it.
    D. Neither of the boys was willing to go.

50. A. The lazy pupil, of course, will tend to write the minimum amount of words acceptable.
    B. The proposal that we should all go together was accepted enthusiastically.
    C. Had you heard the argument, you would be ready to excuse his anger.
    D. Dickens wrote DAVID COPPERFIELD; Thackeray, VANITY FAIR.

50.____

KEY (CORRECT ANSWERS)

1. A	11. B	21. C	31. C	41. B
2. C	12. A	22. D	32. C	42. C
3. C	13. C	23. A	33. B	43. A
4. A	14. A	24. D	34. A	44. C
5. C	15. C	25. C	35. C	45. B
6. C	16. A	26. B	36. A	46. D
7. A	17. C	27. B	37. C	47. A
8. B	18. C	28. A	38. B	48. B
9. C	19. C	29. B	39. D	49. A
10. B	20. B	30. B	40. A	50. A

WRITTEN ENGLISH EXPRESSION
EXAMINATION SECTION
TEST 1

DIRECTIONS: The following questions are designed to test your knowledge of grammar, sentence structure, correct usage, and punctuation. In each group there is one sentence that contains no errors. Select the letter of the CORRECT sentence. *PRINT THE LETTER OF THE CORRECT ANSWER IN THE SPACE AT THE RIGHT.*

1.
   A. A low ceiling is when the atmospheric conditions make flying inadvisable.
   B. They couldn't tell who the card was from.
   C. No one but you and I are to help him.
   D. What kind of a teacher would you like to be?
   E. To him fall the duties of foster parent.

   1.____

2.
   A. They couldn't tell whom the cable was from.
   B. We like these better than those kind.
   C. It is a test of you more than I.
   D. The person in charge being him, there can be no change in policy.
   E. Chicago is larger than any city in Illinois.

   2.____

3.
   A. Do as we do for the celebration.
   B. Do either of you care to join us?
   C. A child's food requirements differ from the adult.
   D. A large family including two uncles and four grandparents live at the hotel.
   E. Due to bad weather, the game was postponed.

   3.____

4.
   A. If they would have done that they might have succeeded.
   B. Neither the hot days or the humid nights annoy our Southern visitor.
   C. Some people do not gain favor because they are kind of tactless.
   D. No sooner had the turning point come than a new issue arose.
   E. I wish that I was in Florida now.

   4.____

5.
   A. We haven't hardly enough tine.
   B. Immigration is when people come into a foreign country to live.
   C. After each side gave their version, the affair was over with.
   D. Every one of the cars were tagged by the police.
   E. He either will fail in his attempt or will seek other employment.

   5.____

6.
   A. They can't seem to see it when I explain the theory.
   B. It is difficult to find the genuine signature between all those submitted.
   C. She can't understand why they don't remember who to give the letter to
   D. Every man and woman in America is interested in his tax bill.
   E. Honor as well as profit are to be gained by these studies.

   6.____

127

7.
A. He arrived safe.
B. I do not have any faith in John running for office.
C. The musicians began to play tunefully and keeping the proper tempo indicated for the selection.
D. Mary's maid of honor bought the kind of an outfit suitable for an afternoon wedding.
E. If you would have studied the problem carefully you would have found the solution more quickly.

8.
A. The new plant is to be electric lighted.
B. The reason the speaker was offended was that the audience was inattentive.
C. There appears to be conditions that govern his behavior.
D. Either of the men are influential enough to control the situation.
E. The gallery with all its pictures were destroyed.

9.
A. If you would have listened more carefully, you would have heard your name called.
B. Did you inquire if your brother were returning soon?
C. We are likely to have rain before nightfall.
D. Let's you and I plan next summer's vacation together.
E. The man whom I thought was my friend deceived me.

10.
A. There's a man and his wife waiting for the doctor since early this morning.
B. The owner of the market with his assistants is applying the most modern principles of merchandise display.
C. Every one of the players on both of the competing teams were awarded a gold watch.
D. The records of the trial indicated that, even before attaining manhood, the murderer's parents were both dead.
E. We had no sooner entered the room when the bell rang.

11.
A. Why don't you start the play like I told you?
B. I didn't find the construction of the second house much different from that of the first one I saw.
C. "When", inquired the child, "Will we begin celebrating my birthday?"
D. There isn't nothing left to do but not to see him anymore.
E. There goes the last piece of cake and the last spoonful of ice cream.

12.
A. The child could find neither the shoe or the stocking.
B. The musicians began to play tunefully and keeping the proper tempo indicated for the selection.
C. The amount of curious people who turned out for Opening Night was beyond calculation.
D. I fully expected that the children would be at their desks and to find them ready to begin work,
E. "Indeed," mused the poll-taker, "the winning candidate is much happier than I."

13. A. Just as you said, I find myself gaining weight.
    B. A teacher should leave the capable pupils engage in creative activities.
    C. The teacher spoke continually during the entire lesson, which, of course, was poor procedure.
    D. We saw him steal into the room, pick up the letter, and tear it's contents to shreds.
    E. It is so dark that I can't hardly see.

    13.____

14. A. The new schedule of working hours and rates was satis factory to both employees and employer.
    B. Many common people feel keenly about the injustices of Power Politics.
    C. Mr. and Mrs. Burns felt that their grandchild was awfully cute when he waved good-bye.
    D. The tallest of the twins was also the most intelligent,
    E. Please come here and try and help me finish this piece of work.

    14.____

15. A. My younger brother insists that he is as tall as me.
    B. Suffering from a severe headache all day, one dose of the prescribed medicine relieved me,
    C. "Please let my brothers and I help you with your packages," said Frank to Mrs. Powers.
    D. Every one of the rooms we visited had displays of pupils' work in them.
    E. Do you intend bringing most of the refreshments yourself?

    15.____

16. A. The telephone linesmen, working steadily at their task during the severe storm, the telephones soon began to ring again.
    B. Meat, as well as fruits and vegetables, is considered essential to a proper diet.
    C. He looked like a real good boxer that night in the ring.
    D. The man has worked steadily for fifteen years before he decided to open his own business.
    E. The winters were hard and dreary, nothing could live without shelter.

    16.____

17. A. No one can foretell when I will have another opportunity like that one again.
    B. The last group of paintings shown appear really to have captured the most modern techniques,
    C. We searched high and low, both in the attic and cellar, but were unsuccessful in locating mementos.
    D. None of the guests was able to give the rules of the game accurately.
    E. When you go to the library tomorrow, please bring this book to the librarian in the reference room.

    17.____

18. A. After the debate, every one of the speakers realized that, given another chance, he could have done better.
    B. The reason given by the physician for the patient's trouble was because of his poor eating habits.
    C. The fog was so thick that the driver couldn't hardly see more than ten feet ahead.
    D. I suggest that you present the medal to who you think best.
    E. I don't approve of him going along.

    18.____

19. A. A decision made by a man without much deliberation is sometimes no different than a slow one.
     B. By the time Mr. Brown's son will graduate Dental School, he will be twenty-six years of age.
     C. Who did you predict would win the election?
     D. The auctioneer had less stamps to sell this year than last year.
     E. Being that he is occupied, I shall not disturb him.

20. A. Having pranced into the arena with little grace and unsteady hoof for the jumps ahead, the driver reined his horse.
     B. Once the dog wagged it's tail, you knew it was a friendly animal.
     C. Like a great many artists, his life was a tragedy.
     D. When asked to choose corn, cabbage, or potatoes, the diner selected the latter.
     E. The record of the winning team was among the most noteworthy of the season.

21. A. The maid wasn't so small that she couldn't reach the top window for cleaning.
     B. Many people feel that powdered coffee produces a really good flavor.
     C. Would you mind me trying that coat on for size?
     D. This chair looks much different than the chair we selected in the store.
     E. I wish that he would have talked to me about the lesson before he presented it.

22. A. After trying unsuccessfully to land a job in the city, Will located in the country on a farm.
     B. On the last attempt, the pole-vaulter came nearly to getting hurt.
     C. The observance of Armistice Day throughout the world offers an opportunity to reflect on the horrors of war.
     D. Outside of the mistakes in spelling, the child's letter was a very good one.
     E. The annual income of New York is far greater than Florida.

23. A. Scissors is always dangerous for a child to handle.
     B. I assure you that I will not yield to pressure to sell my interest.
     C. Ask him if he has recall of the incident which took place at our first meeting.
     D. The manager felt like as not to order his usher-captain to surrender his uniform,
     E. Everyone on the boat said their prayers when the storm grew worse.

24. A. The mother of the bride climaxed the occasion by exclaiming, "I want my children should be happy forever."
     B. We read in the papers where the prospects for peace are improving.
     C. "Can I share the cab with you?" was frequently heard during the period of gas rationing.
     D. The man was enamored with his friend"s sister.
     E. Had the police suspected the ruse, they would have taken proper precautions.

25. A. The teacher admonished the other students neither to speak to John, nor should they annoy him.
     B. Fortunately we had been told that there was but one service station in that area.
     C. An usher seldom rises above a theatre manager.
     D. The epic, "Gone With the Wind," is supposed to have taken place during the Civil War Era.
     E. Now that she has been graduated she should be encouraged to make her own choice as to the career she is to follow.

KEY (CORRECT ANSWERS)

1. E
2. A
3. A
4. D
5. E

6. D
7. A
8. B
9. C
10. B

11. B
12. E
13. A
14. A
15. E

16. B
17. D
18. A
19. C
20. E

21. B
22. C
23. B
24. E
25. B

TEST 2

DIRECTIONS: The following questions are designed to test your knowledge of grammar, sentence structure, correct usage, and punctuation. In each group, there is one sentence that contains no errors. Select the letter of the CORRECT sentence. *PRINT THE LETTER OF THE CORRECT ANSWER IN THE SPACE AT THE RIGHT.*

1.
   A. Shall you be at home, let us say, on Sunday at two o'clock?
   B. We see Mr. Lewis take his car out of the garage daily, newly polished always.
   C. We have no place to keep our rubbers, only in the hall closet.
   D. Isn't it true what you told me about the best way to prepare for an examination?
   E. Mathematics is among my favorite subjects.

   1.____

2.
   A. The host thought the guests were of the hungry kinds so he prepared much food.
   B. The museum is often visited by students who are fond of early inventions, and especially patent attorneys.
   C. I rose to nominate the man who most of us felt was the most diligent worker in the group.
   D. The child was sent to the store to purchase a bottle of milk, and brought home fresh rolls, too.
   E. Hidden away in the closet, I found the long-lost purse.

   2.____

3.
   A. The garden tool was sent to be sharpened, and a new handle to be put on.
   B. At the end of her vacation, Joan came home with little money, but which systematic thrift soon overcame.
   C. We people have opportunities to show the rest of the world how real democracy functions.
   D. The guide paddled along, then fell in a reverie which he related the history of the region.
   E. No sooner had the curtain dropped when the audience shouted its approval in chorus.

   3.____

4.
   A. The data you need is to be made available shortly.
   B. The first few strokes of the brush were enough to convince me that Tom could paint much better than me.
   C. We inquired if we could see the owner of the store, after we waited for one hour.
   D. The highly-strung parent was aggravated by the slightest noise that the baby made.
   E. We should have investigated the cause of the noise by bringing the car to a halt.

   4.____

5.
   A. The police, investigating the crime, were successful in discovering only one possibly valuable clue.
   B. Due to an unexpected change in plans, the violin soloist did not perform.
   C. Besides being awarded a Bachelor's degree at college, the scientist has since received many honorary degrees.
   D. The data offered in advance of the recent Presidential election seems to have possessed elements of inaccuracy.
   E. I don't believe your the only one who has been asked to come here.

   5.____

6.
  A. I don't quite see that I will be able to completely finish the job in time.
  B. By my statement, I infer that you are guilty of the offense as charged.
  C. Wasn't it strange that they wouldn't let no one see the body?
  D. I hope that this is the kind of rolls you requested me to buy.
  E. The storekeeper distributed cigars as bonuses between his many customers.

7.
  A. He said he preferred the climate of Florida to California.
  B. Because of the excessive heat, a great amount of fruit juice was drunk by the guests.
  C. This week's dramatic presentation was neither as lively nor as entertaining as last week.
  D. The fashion expert believed that no one could develop new creations more successfully than him.
  E. A collection of Dicken's works is a "must" for every library.

8.
  A. There was such a large amount of books on the floor that I couldn't find a place for my rocking chair.
  B. Walking up the rickety stairs, the bottle slipped from his hands and smashed.
  C. The reason they granted his request was because he had a good record.
  D. Little Tommy was proud that the teacher always asked him to bring messages to the office.
  E. That kind of orange is grown only in Florida.

9.
  A. The new mayor is a resident of this city for thirty years.
  B. Do you mean to imply that had he not missed that shot he would have won?
  C. Next term I shall be studying French and history.
  D. I read in last night's paper where the sales tax is going to be abolished.
  E. In order to prevent breakage, she placed a sheet of paper between each of the plates when she packed them.

10.
  A. To have children vie against one another is psychologically unsound.
  B. Would anyone else care to discuss his baby?
  C. He was interested and aware of the problem.
  D. I sure would like to discover if he is motivating the lesson properly.
  E. The cloth was first lain on a flat surface; then it was pressed with a hot iron.

11.
  A. She graduated Barnard College twenty-five years ago.
  B. He studied the violin since he was seven.
  C. She is not so diligent a researcher as her classmate.
  D. He discovered that the new data corresponds with the facts disclosed by Werner.
  E. How could he enjoy the television program; the dog was barking and the baby was crying.

12.
  A. You have three alternatives: law, dentistry, or teaching.
  B. If I would have worked harder, I would have accomplished my purpose.
  C. He affected a rapid change of pace and his opponents were outdistanced.
  D. He looked prosperous, although he had been unemployed for a year.
  E. The engine not only furnishes power but light and heat as well.

13.
 A. The children shared one anothers toys and seemed quite happy.
 B. They lay in the sun for many hours, getting tanned.
 C. The reproduction arrived, and had been hung in the living room.
 D. First begin by calling the roll.
 E. Tell me where you hid it; no one shall ever find it.

14.
 A. Deliver these things to whomever arrives first.
 B. Everybody but she and me is going to the conference.
 C. If the number of patrons is small, we can serve them.
 D. When each of the contestants find their book, the debate may begin.
 E. Some people, farmers in particular, lament the substitution of butter by margarine.

15.
 A. After his illness, he stood in the country three weeks.
 B. If you wish to effect a change, submit your suggestions.
 C. It is silly to leave children play with knives.
 D. Play a trick on her by spilling water down her neck.
 E. There was such a crowd of people at the crossing we couldn't hardly get on the bus.

16.
 A. This is a time when all of us must show our faith and devotion to our country.
 B. Either you or I are certain to be elected president of the new club.
 C. The interpellation of the Minister of Finance forced him to explain his policies.
 D. After hoisting the anchor and removing the binnacle, the ship was ready to set sail.
 E. Please bring me a drink of cold water from the refrigerator.

17.
 A. Mistakes in English, when due to carelessness or haste, can easily be rectified.
 B. Mr. Jones is one of those persons who will try to keep a promise and usually does.
 C. Being very disturbed by what he had heard, Fred decided to postpone his decision.
 D. There is a telephone at the other end of the corridor which is constantly in use.
 E. In his teaching, he always kept the childrens' interests and needs in mind.

18.
 A. The lazy pupil, of course, will tend to write the minimum amount of words acceptable.
 B. His success as a political leader consisted mainly of his ability to utter platitudes in a firm and convincing manner.
 C. To be cognizant of current affairs, a person must not only read newspapers and magazines but also recent books by recognized authorities.
 D. Although we intended to have gone fishing, the sudden outbreak of a storm caused us to change our plans.
 E. It is the colleges that must take the responsibility for encouraging greater flexibility in the high-school curriculum.

19. A. "I am sorry," he said, "but John's answer was 'No'."
    B. A spirited argument followed between those who favored and opposed Marie's expulsion from the club.
    C. Whether a forward child should be humored or punished often depends upon the circumstances.
    D. Excessive alcoholism is certainly not conducive with efficient performance of one's work.
    E. Stroking his beard thoughtfully, an idea suddenly came to him.

    19._____

20. A. "Take care, my children," he said sadly, "lest you not be deceived."
    B. Those continuous telephone calls are preventing Betty from completing her homework.
    C. They dug deep into the earth at the spot indicated on the map, but they found nothing.
    D. We petted and cozened the little girl until she finally stopped weeping.
    E. There was, in the mail, an inquiry for a house by a young couple with two or three bedrooms.

    20._____

21. A. Please fill in the required information on the application form and return same by April 15.
    B. Tom was sitting there idly, watching the clouds scud across the sky.
    C. We started for home so that our parents would not suspect that anything out of the ordinary took place.
    D. The sudden abatement from the storm enabled the ladies to resume their journey.
    E. Each of the twelve members were agreed that the accused man was innocent.

    21._____

22. A. The number of gifted students not continuing their education beyond secondary school present a nationwide problem.
    B. A man's animadversions against those he considers his enemies are usually reflections of his own inadequacies.
    C. The alembic of his fevered imagination produced some of the greatest romantic poetry of his era.
    D. The first case of smallpox dates back more than 3000 years and has gone unchecked until recently.
    E. He promised to go irregardless of the rain or snow.

    22._____

23. A. The child picked up several of the coracles, which he had seen glittering in the sand, and brought them to his mother.
    B. He muttered in dejected tones – and no one contradicted him – "We have failed."
    C. A girl whom I believed to be she waved cheerily to me from a passing automobile.
    D. We discovered that she was a former resident of our own neighborhood who eloped some years ago with a milkman.
    E. It looks now like he will not be promoted after all.

    23._____

24. A. Mary is the kind of a person on whom you can depend in any emergency.
    B. I am sure that either applicant can fill the job you offer competently and efficiently.
    C. Although we searched the entire room, the scissors was not to be found.
    D. Being that you are here, we can proceed with the discussion.
    E. In spite of our warning whistle, the huge ship continued to sail athwart our course.

25. A. The salaries earned by college graduates vary as much if not more than those earned by high school graduates.
    B. The apothegms that he felt to be so witty were all too often either trite or platitudinous.
    C. She read the letter carefully, took out one of the pages, and tore it into small pieces.
    D. A young man, who hopes to succeed, must be diligent in his work and alert to his opportunities.
    E. No one should plan a long journey for pleasure in these days.

KEY (CORRECT ANSWERS)

1.	A	11.	C
2.	C	12.	D
3.	C	13.	E
4.	E	14.	C
5.	A	15.	B
6.	D	16.	C
7.	B	17.	A
8.	E	18.	E
9.	B	19.	C
10.	B	20.	C
21.	B		
22.	C		
23.	B		
24.	E		
25.	B		

EXAMINATION SECTION
TEST 1

DIRECTIONS: The questions that follow the paragraphs below are designed to test your appreciation of correctness and effectiveness of expression in English. The paragraphs are presented first in full so that you may read it through for sense. Disregard the errors you find as you will be asked to correct them in the questions that follow. The paragraphs are then presented sentence by sentence with portions underlined and numbered. At the end of this material, you will find numbers corresponding to those below the underlined portions, each followed by five alternatives lettered A, B, C, D, and E. In every case, the usage in the alternative lettered A is the same as that in the original paragraph and is followed by four possible usages. Choose the usage that you consider BEST in each case. *PRINT THE LETTER OF THE CORRECT ANSWER IN THE SPACE AT THE RIGHT.*

The use of the machine produced up to the present time outstanding changes in our modern world. One of the most significant of these changes have been the marked decreases in the length of the working day and the working week. The fourteen-hour day not only has been reduced to one of ten hours but also, in some lines of work, to one of eight or even six. The trend toward a decrease is further evidenced in the longer weekend already given to employees in many business establishment. There seems also to be a trend toward shorter working weeks and longer summer vacations. An important feature of this development is that leisure is no longer the privilege of the wealthy few,—it has become the common right of most people. Using it wisely, leisure promotes health, efficiency and happiness, for there is time for each individual to live their own "more abundant life" and having opportunities for needed recreation.

Recreation, like the name implies, is a process of revitalization. In giving expression to the play instincts of the human race, new vigor and effectiveness are afforded by recreation to the body and to the mind. Of course not all forms of amusement, by no means constitute recreation. Furthermore, an activity that provides recreation for one person may prove exhausting for another. Today, however, play among adults, as well as children, is regarded as a vital necessity of modern life. Play being recognized as an important factor in improving mental and physical health and thereby reducing human misery and poverty.

Among the most important form of amusement available at the present time are the automobile, the moving picture, the radio, television, and organized sports. The automobile, especially, has been a boon to the American people, since it has been the chief means of them getting out into the open. The motion picture, the radio and television have tremendous opportunities to supply whole-some recreation and to promote cultural advancement. A criticism often leveled against organized sports as a means of recreation is because they make passive spectators of too many people. It has been said "that the American public is afflicted with "spectatoritis," but there is some recreational advantages to be gained even from being a spectator at organized games. Such sports afford a release from the monotony of daily toil, get people outdoors and also provide an exhilaration that is tonic in its effect.

2 (#1)

The chief concern, of course, should be to eliminate those forms of amusement that are socially undesirable. There are, however, far too many people who, we know, do not use their leisure to the best advantage. Sometime leisure leads to idleness, and idleness may lead to demoralization. The value of leisure both to the individual and to society will depend on the uses made of it.

The use of the machine <u>produced</u> up to the
                                       1

1. A. produced   B. produces   C. has produced   1.____
    D. had produced   E. will have produced

present time many outstanding changes in our modern world. One of the most significant of these changes <u>have been</u> the marked
                                                                     2

2. A. have been   B. was   C. were   2.____
    D. has been   E. will be

decreases in the length of the working day and the working week. <u>The fourteen-hour day not only has been reduced</u> to one of ten hours but also, in some lines of work, to one of eight or
            3
even six.

3. A. The fourteen-hour day not only has been reduced   3.____
    B. Not only the fourteen-hour day has been reduced
    C. Not the fourteen-hour day only has been reduced
    D. The fourteen-hour day has not only been reduced

The trend toward a decrease is further evidenced in the longer week-end <u>already</u> given

4. A. already   B. all ready   C. allready   4.____
    D. ready   E. all in all

to employees in many business establishments. There seems also to be a trend toward shorter working weeks and longer summer vacations. An important feature of this development is that leisure is no longer the privilege of the wealthy few<u>, —it</u> has become the common right of most people.

5. A. , —it   B. : it   C. ; it   5.____
    D. ...it   E. omit punctuation

<u>Using it wisely,</u> leisure promotes health, efficiency, and happiness, for there is time for each
      6
individual to live <u>their</u> own "more abundant life" and <u>having</u> opportunities for needed recreation
                            7   8

6. A. Using it wisely   B. If used wisely   6.____
    C. Having used it wisely   D. Because of its wise use
    E. Because of usefulness

3 (#1)

7. A. their   B. his   C. its   D. our   E. your   7._____

8. A. having   B. having had   C. to have   8._____
    D. to have had   E. had

Recreation, <u>like</u> the name implies, is a
               9

9. A. like   B. since   C. through   D. for   E. as   9._____

process of revitalization. In giving expression to the play instincts of the human race, <u>new vigor and effectiveness are afforded by creation to the body and to the mind.</u>
                                                                                            10

10. A. new vigor and effectiveness are afforded by recreation to the body and to   10._____
       the mind
    B. recreation affords new vigor and effectiveness to the body and to the mind
    C. there are afforded new vigor and effectiveness to the body and to the mind
    D. by recreation the body and mind are afforded new vigor and effectiveness
    E. the body and the mind afford new vigor and effectiveness to themselves by
       recreation

Of course not all forms of amusement, <u>by no means,</u> constitute recreation. Furthermore, an
                                          11
activity that provides recreation for one person may prove exhausting for another. Today, however, play among adults, as well as children is regarded as a vital necessity of modern life.

11. A. by no means   B. by those means   C. by some means   11._____
    D. by every means   E. by any means

<u>Play being recognized</u> as an important factor in improving mental and physical health and
        12
thereby reducing human misery and poverty.

12. A. . Play being recognized as   B. , by their recognizing play as   12._____
    C. . They recognizing play as   D. . Recognition of it being
    E. , for play is recognized as

Among the most important forms of amusement available at the present time are the automobile, the moving picture, the radio, television, and organized sports. The automobile, especially, has been a boon to the American people, since it has been the chief means of <u>them</u>
                                                                                                  13
getting out into the open. The motion picture, the radio and television have tremendous opportunities to supply wholesome recreation and to promote cultural advancement. A criticism often leveled against organized

13. A. them   B. their   C. his   D. our   E. the people   13._____

141

sports as a means of recreation is <u>because</u> they make passive spectators of too many people.
                                                        14

14. A. because   B. since   C. as   D. that   E. why   14.____

it has been said "<u>that</u> the American public is afflicted with "spectatoritis," but there <u>is</u> some
                        15   16
recreational advantages to be gained even from being a spectator at organized games.

15. A. "that   B. "that"   C. that"   D. 'that   E. that   15.____

16. A. is   B. was   C. are   D. were   E. will be   16.____

Such sports afford a release from the monotony of daily toil, get people outdoors and also provide an exhilaration that is tonic in its effect. The chief concern, of course, should be to eliminate those forms of amusement that are socially undesirable. There are, however, far too many people <u>who,</u> we know, do not use their leisure to the best advantage. Sometimes leisure
                      17
leads to idleness, and idleness may lead to demoralization. The value of leisure both to the individual and to society will depend on the uses made of it.

17. A. who   B. whom   C. which   D. such as   E. that which   17.____

KEY (CORRECT ANSWERS)

1.	C	11.	E
2.	D	12.	E
3.	E	13.	B
4.	A	14.	D
5.	C	15.	E
6.	B	16.	C
7.	B	17.	A
8.	C		
9.	E		
10.	B		

TEST 2

DIRECTIONS: The questions that follow the paragraphs below are designed to test your appreciation of correctness and effectiveness of expression in English. The paragraphs are presented first in full so that you may read it through for sense. Disregard the errors you find as you will be asked to correct them in the questions that follow. The paragraphs are then presented sentence by sentence with portions underlined and numbered. At the end of this material, you will find numbers corresponding to those below the underlined portions, each followed by five alternatives lettered A, B, C, D, and E. In every case, the usage in the alternative lettered A is the same as that in the original paragraph and is followed by four possible usages. Choose the usage that you consider BEST in each case. *PRINT THE LETTER OF THE CORRECT ANSWER IN THE SPACE AT THE RIGHT.*

    When this war is over, no nation will either be isolated in war or peace. Each will be within trading distance of all the others and will be able to strike them. Every nation will be most as dependent on the rest for the maintainance of peace as is any of our own American states on all the others. The world that we have known was a world made up of individual nations, each of which had the privilege of doing about as they pleased without being embarassed by outside interference. The world has dissolved before the impact of an invention, the airplane has done to our world what gunpowder did to the feudal world. Whether the coming century will be a period of further tragedy or one of peace and progress depend very largely on the wisdom and skill with which the present generation adjusts their thinking to the problems immediately at hand. Examining the principal movements sweeping through the world, it can be seen that they are being accelerated by the war. There is undoubtedly many of these whose courses will be affected for good or ill by the settlements that will follow the war. The United States will share the responsibility of these settlements with Russia, England and China. The influence of the United States, however, will be great. This country is likely to emerge from the war stronger than any other nation. Having benefitted by the absence of actual hostilities on our own soil, we shall probably be less exhausted that our allies and better able than them to help restore the devastated areas. However many mistakes have been made in our past, the tradition of America, not only the champion of freedom but also fair play, still lives among millions who can see light and hope scarcely nowhere else.

When this war is over, no nation will <u>either be isolated in war or peace.</u>
                                                                           1

1.   A. either be isolated in war or peace   1.____
      B. be either isolated in war or peace
      C. be isolated in neither war nor peace
      D. be isolated either in war or in peace
      E. be isolated neither in war or peace

<u>Each</u> will be
 2

2.   A. Each   B. It   C. Some   D. They   E. A nation   2.____

143

2 (#2)

<u>within trading distance of all others and will be able to strike them.</u>
                            3

3.   A. within trading distance of all the others and will be able to strike them   3.____
       B. near enough to trade with and strike all the others
       C. trading and striking the others
       D. within trading and striking distance of all the others
       E. able to strike and trade with all the others

Every nation will be <u>most</u> as dependent on

4.   A. most   B. wholly   C. much   D. mostly   E. almost   4.____

the rest for the <u>maintainance</u> of peace as is
                    5

5.   A. maintainance   B. maintainence   C. maintenence   5.____
       D. maintenance   E. maintanence

any of our own American states on all the others. The world that we have known as a world made up of individual <u>nations, each</u>
                                                 6

6.   A. nations, each   B. nations. Each   C. nations: each   6.____
       D. nations; each   E. nations each

of which had the <u>priviledge</u> of doing about as
                      7

7.   A. priviledge   B. priveledge   C. privelege   7.____
       D. privalege   E. privilege

<u>they</u> pleased without being
 8

8.   A. they   B. it   C. they individually   8.____
       D. he   E. the nations

<u>embarassed</u> by outside interference. That
      9

9.   A. embarassed   B. embarrassed   C. embaressed   9.____
       D. embarrased   E. embarrassed

world has dissolved before the impact of an <u>invention, the</u> airplane has done to our world what
                                                                    10

gunpowder did to the feudal world. Whether the coming century will be a period of further tragedy or one of peace and

3 (#2)

10. A. invention, the   B. invention but the   C. invention: the   10.____
    D. invention. The   E. invention and the

progress <u>depend</u> very largely on the wisdom and skill with which the present generation
         11

11. A. depend   B. will have depended   C. depends   11.____
    D. depended   E. shall depend

<u>adjusts their</u> thinking to the problems immediately at hand.
    12

12. A. adjusts their   B. adjusts there   C. adjusts its   12.____
    D. adjust our   E. adjust it's

<u>Examining the principal movements sweeping through the world, it can be seen</u>
                                13

13. A. Examining the principal movements sweeping through the world, it can be seen   13.____
    B. Having examined the principal movements sweeping through the world, it can be seen
    C. Examining the principal movements sweeping through the world can be seen
    D. Examining the principal movements sweeping through the world, we can see
    E. It can be seen examining the principal movements sweeping through the world

that they are being <u>accelerated</u> by the war.
                         14

14. A. accelerated   B. acelerated   C. accelerated   14.____
    D. acellerated   E. accelerated

There <u>is</u> undoubtedly many of these whose courses will be affected for good or ill by the
      15
settlements that will follow the war. The United States will share the responsibility of these
settlements with Russia, England and China. The influence of the United

15. A. is   B. were   C. was   D. are   E. might be

States, <u>however,</u> will be great. This country is likely to emerge from the war stronger than any
         16
other nation.

16. A. , however,   B. however,   C. , however   16.____
    D. however   E. ; however,

145

4 (#2)

Having <u>benefitted</u> by the absence of actual hostilities on our own soil, we shall probably be
        17
less exhausted

17. A. benefitted   B. beniffited   C. benefited   17.____
     D. benifited   E. benafitted

than our allies and better able than <u>them</u> to help restore the devastated areas. However many
                                             18
mistakes have been made in our past, the tradition of America,

18. A. them   B. themselves   C. they   18.____
     D. the world   E. the nations

<u>not only the champion of freedom but also fair play,</u> still lives among millions who can
                        19

19. A. not only the champion of freedom but also fair play,   19.____
     B. the champion of not only freedom but also of fair play,
     C. the champion not only of freedom but also of fair play,
     D. not only the champion but also freedom and fair play,
     E. not the champion of freedom only, but also fair play,

see light and hope <u>scarcely nowhere else.</u>
                      20
20. A. scarcely nowhere else   B. elsewhere   20.____
     C. nowhere   D. scarcely anywhere else
     E. anywhere

KEY (CORRECT ANSWERS)

1.	D	11.	C
2.	A	12.	C
3.	D	13.	D
4.	E	14.	A
5.	D	15.	D
6.	A	16.	A
7.	E	17.	C
8.	B	18.	C
9.	B	19.	C
10.	D	20.	D

WRITTEN ENGLISH EXPRESSION
EXAMINATION SECTION
TEST 1

DIRECTIONS: In each of the sentences below, four portions are underlined and lettered. Read each sentence and decide whether any of the UNDERLINED parts contains an error in spelling, punctuation, or capitalization, or employs grammatical usage which would be inappropriate for carefully written English. If so, note the letter printed under the unacceptable form and indicate this choice in the space at the right. If all four of the underlined portions are acceptable as they stand, select the answer E. (No sentence contains more than ONE unacceptable form.)

1. The revised <u>procedure</u> was <u>quite</u> different <u>than</u> the one which <u>was</u> employed up to that time. <u>No error</u>
             A   B   C   D   E

    1.____

2. <u>Blinded</u> by the storm that <u>surrounded</u> him, his plane <u>kept going</u> in <u>circles</u>. <u>No error</u>
   A   B   C   D   E

    2.____

3. They <u>should</u> give the book to <u>whoever</u> <u>they</u> think deserves <u>it</u>. <u>No error</u>
       A   B   C   D   E

    3.____

4. The <u>government</u> will not consent to your <u>firm</u> <u>sending</u> that package as <u>second class</u> matter. <u>No error</u>
       A   B C   D   E

    4.____

5. She <u>would have</u> avoided all the trouble <u>that</u> followed if she <u>would have</u> waited ten minutes <u>longer</u>. <u>No error</u>
      A   B   C   D   E

    5.____

6. <u>His</u> poetry, <u>when</u> it was carefully examined, showed <u>characteristics</u> not unlike <u>Wordsworth</u>. <u>No error</u>
  A   B   C   D   E

    6.____

7. <u>In my opinion</u>, based upon long years of research, <u>I think</u> the plan offered by my opponent is <u>unsound</u>, because it is not <u>founded</u> on true facts. <u>No error</u>
    A   B   C   D   E

    7.____

8. The soldiers of <u>Washington's</u> army at Valley Forge <u>were</u> men ragged in
                     A   B
   <u>appearance</u> but <u>who were</u> noble in character. <u>No error</u>
      C   D   E

   8._____

9. Rabbits <u>have a distrust</u> of man <u>due to</u> the fact <u>that</u> they are <u>so often</u> shot.
            A   B   C   D
   <u>No error</u>
    E

   9._____

10. <u>This</u> is the man <u>who</u> I believe <u>is</u> best <u>qualified</u> for the position. <u>No error</u>
     A   B   C   D   E

    10._____

11. Her voice was <u>not only</u> <u>good</u>, but <u>she</u> also very clearly <u>enunciated</u>.
                      A   B   C   D
    <u>No error</u>
    E

    11._____

12. <u>Today he</u> is wearing a <u>different</u> suit <u>than</u> the <u>one</u> he wore yesterday. <u>No error</u>
        A   B   C   D   E

    12._____

13. Our work <u>is</u> to improve the club; if anybody <u>must</u> resign, let it <u>not</u> be you or <u>I</u>.
               A   B   C   D
    <u>No error</u>
    E

    13._____

14. There was so much talking <u>in back of</u> me <u>as</u> I <u>could</u> not <u>enjoy</u> the music.
                                    A   B   C   D
    <u>No error</u>
    E

    14._____

15. <u>Being that</u> he is that <u>kind of</u> <u>boy</u>, he cannot be blamed <u>for</u> the mistake.
       A   B   C   D
    <u>No error</u>
    E

    15._____

16. <u>The king, having read</u> the speech, <u>he</u> and the <u>queen</u> <u>departed</u>. <u>No error</u>
               A   B   C   D   E

    16._____

17. I <u>am</u> <u>so tired</u> I <u>can't</u> <u>scarcely</u> stand. <u>No error</u>
       A   B   C   D   E

    17._____

18. We are <u>mailing bills</u> to our customers <u>in Canada</u>, and, <u>being</u> eager to
                    A   B   C
    clear our books before the new season opens, it is <u>to be hoped</u> they will
                                                                   D
    send their remittances promptly. <u>No error</u>
                                             E

    18._____

3 (#1)

19. I reluctantly acquiesced to the proposal. No error   19.____
    A   B   C   D   E

20. It had lain out in the rain all night. No error   20.____
    A B   C   D   E

21. If he would have gone there, he would have seen a marvelous sight. 21.____
          A   B   C   D
    No error
    E

22. The climate of Asia Minor is somewhat like Utah. No error   22.____
                 A   B   C   D   E

23. If everybody did unto others as they would wish others to do unto them, this 23.____
       A   B   C   D
    world would be a paradise. No error
                                E

24. This was the jockey whom I saw was most likely to win the race. No error   24.____
    A   B   C   D   E

25. The only food the general demanded was potatoes. No error   25.____
        A   B   C   D   E

KEY (CORRECT ANSWERS)

1.	C	11.	C
2.	A	12.	C
3.	B	13.	D
4.	B	14.	B
5.	C	15.	A
6.	D	16.	A
7.	B	17.	C
8.	D	18.	C
9.	B	19.	E
10.	E	20.	E

21. A
22. D
23. D
24. B
25. E

TEST 2

DIRECTIONS: In each of the sentences below, four portions are underlined and lettered. Read each sentence and decide whether any of the UNDERLINED parts contains an error in spelling, punctuation, or capitalization, or employs grammatical usage which would be inappropriate for carefully written English. If so, note the letter printed under the unacceptable form and indicate this choice in the space at the right. If all four of the underlined portions are acceptable as they stand, select the answer E. (No sentence contains more than ONE unacceptable form.)

1. A party <u>like</u> <u>that</u> <u>only</u> <u>comes</u> once a year. <u>No error</u>
         A   B   C   D   E
1.____

2. <u>Our's</u> <u>is</u> <u>a</u> <u>swift moving</u> age. <u>No error</u>
    A   B C   D   E
2.____

3. The <u>healthy</u> climate soon <u>restored</u> him <u>to</u> his <u>accustomed</u> vigor. <u>No error</u>
       A   B   C   D   E
3.____

4. <u>They</u> needed six typists and hoped that <u>only</u> that <u>many</u> <u>would</u> apply for the
    A   B   C   D
position. <u>No error</u>
           E
4.____

5. He <u>interviewed</u> people <u>whom</u> he thought had <u>something</u> <u>to impart</u>. <u>No error</u>
         A   B   C   D   E
5.____

6. <u>Neither</u> of his three sisters <u>is</u> older <u>than</u> <u>he</u>. <u>No error</u>
    A   B   C D   E
6.____

7. <u>Since</u> he is <u>that</u> <u>kind</u> of <u>a</u> boy, he cannot be expected to cooperate with us.
    A   B   C   D
<u>No error</u>
  E
7.____

8. When <u>passing</u> <u>through</u> the tunnel, the air pressure <u>affected</u> <u>our</u> years. <u>No error</u>
          A   B   C   D   E
8.____

9. <u>The story having</u> a sad ending, <u>it</u> never <u>achieved</u> popularity <u>among</u> the
         A   B   C   D
students. <u>No error</u>
             E
9.____

10. <u>Since</u> we are both hungry, <u>shall</u> we go <u>somewhere</u> for lunch? <u>No error</u>
     A   B   C   D E
10.____

11. Will you please bring this book down to the library and give it to my friend, who is waiting for it? No error
    A   B   C   D
                                                                                                    E

12. You may have the book; I am finished with it. No error
         A   B   C   D   E

13. I don't know if I should mention it to her or not. No error
        A   B   C   D   E

14. Philosophy is not a subject which has to do with philosophers and mathematics only. No error
                      A   B   C   D   E

15. The thoughts of the scholar in his library are little different than the old woman who first said, "It's no use crying over spilt milk." No error
                                  A   B   C   D   E

16. A complete system of philosophical ideas are implied in many simple utterances. No error
               A   B   C   D   E

17. Even if one has never put them into words, his ideas compose a kind of a philosophy. No error
         A   B   C   D   E

18. Perhaps it is well enough that most people do not attempt this formulation. No error
              A   B   C   D   E

19. Leading their ordered lives, this confused body of ideas and feelings is sufficient. No error
    A   B   C   D   E

20. Why should we insist upon them formulating it? No error
         A   B   C   D   E

21. Since it includes something of the wisdom of the ages, it is adequate for the purposes of ordinary life. No error
        A   B   C   D   E

22. Therefore, I <u>have sought</u> to make a pattern <u>of mine,</u> <u>and so</u> there were, early
                   A   B   C
    moments of <u>my trying</u> to find out what were the elements with which I had to
                D
    deal. <u>No error</u>
           E   22.____

23. I <u>wanted</u> <u>to get</u> <u>what</u> knowledge I <u>could</u> about the general structure of the
       A   B   C   D
    universe. <u>No error</u>
               E   23.____

24. I wanted to <u>know</u> <u>if</u> life <u>per se</u> had any meaning or <u>whether</u> I must strive to give
               A B   C   D
    it one. <u>No error</u>
            E   24.____

25. <u>So,</u> in a <u>desultory</u> way, I <u>began</u> <u>to read.</u> <u>No error</u>
     A   B   C   D   E   25.____

KEY (CORRECT ANSWERS)

1.	C		11.	B
2.	A		12.	C
3.	A		13.	B
4.	C		14.	D
5.	B		15.	B
6.	A		16.	B
7.	D		17.	A
8.	A		18.	C
9.	A		19.	A
10.	E		20.	D

21. E
22. C
23. C
24. B
25. E

ENGLISH EXPRESSION
CHOICE OF EXPRESSION
COMMENTARY

One special form of the English Expression multiple-choice question in current use requires the candidate to select from among five (5) versions of a particular part of a sentence (or of an entire sentence), the one version that expresses the idea of the sentence most clearly, effectively, and accurately. Thus, the candidate is required not only to recognize errors, but also to choose the best way of phrasing a particular part of the sentence.

This is a test of choice of expression, which assays the candidate's ability to express himself correctly and effectively, including his sensitivity to the subtleties and nuances of the language.

SAMPLE QUESTIONS

DIRECTIONS: In each of the following sentences, some part of the sentence or the entire sentence is underlined. The underlined part presents a problem in the appropriate use of language. Beneath each sentence you will find five ways of writing the underlined part. The first of these indicates no change (that is, it repeats the original), but the other four are all different. If you think the original sentence is better than any of the suggested changes, you should choose answer A; otherwise you should mark one of the other choices. Select the BEST answer and print the letter in the space at the right.

This is a test of correctness and effectiveness of expression. In choosing answers, follow the requirements of standard written English; that is, pay attention to acceptable usage in grammar, diction (choice of words), sentence construction, and punctuation. Choose the answer that produces the most effective sentence—clear and exact, without awkwardness or ambiguity. Do not make a choice that changes the meaning of the original sentence.

SAMPLE QUESTION 1

Although these states now trade actively with the West, and although they are willing to exchange technological information, their arts and thoughts and social structure <u>remains substantially similar to what it has always been</u>.
    A. remains substantially similar to what it has always been
    B. remain substantially unchanged
    C. remains substantially unchanged
    D. remain substantially similar to what they have always been
    E. remain substantially without being changed

The purpose of questions of this type is to determine the candidate's ability to select the clearest and most effective means of expressing what the statement attempts to say. In this example, the phrasing in the statement, which is repeated in A, presents a problem of agreement between a subject and its verb (<u>their arts and thought and social structure</u> and <u>remains</u>), a problem of agreement between a pronoun and its antecedent (<u>their arts and thought and social structure</u> and <u>it</u>), an a problem of precise and concise phrasing (<u>remains</u>

substantially similar to what it has always been for remains substantially unchanged). Each of the four remaining choices in some way corrects one or more of the faults in the sentence, but only one deals with all three problems satisfactorily. Although C presents a more careful and concise wording of the phrasing of the statement and, in the process, eliminates the problem of agreement between pronoun and antecedent, it fails to correct the problem of agreement between the subject and its verb. In D, the subject agrees with its verb and the pronoun agrees with its antecedent, but the phrasing is not so accurate as it should be. The same difficulty persists in E. Only in B are all the problems presented corrected satisfactory. The question is not difficult.

SAMPLE QUESTION 2

Her latest novel is the largest in scope, the most accomplished in technique, and <u>it is more significant in theme than anything</u> she has written.
    A. it is more significant in theme than anything
    B. It is most significant in theme of anything
    C. more significant in theme than anything
    D. the most significant in theme than anything
    E. the most significant in theme of anything

This question is of greater difficulty than the preceding one. The problem posed in the sentence and repeated in A is essentially one of parallelism; Does the underlined portion of the sentence follow the pattern established by the first two elements of the series (<u>the largest</u>...<u>the most accomplished</u>)? It does not, for it introduces a pronoun and verb (<u>it is</u>) that the second term of the series indicates should be omitted and a degree of comparison (<u>more significant</u>) that is not in keeping with the superlatives used earlier in the sentence. B uses the superlative degree of <u>significant</u> but retains the unnecessary <u>it is</u>; C removes the <u>it is</u>, but retains the faulty comparative form of the adjective. D corrects both errors in parallelism, but introduces an error in idiom (<u>the most</u>...<u>than</u>). Only E corrects all the problems without introducing another fault.

SAMPLE QUESTION 3

Desiring to insure the continuity of their knowledge, <u>magical lore is transmitted by the chiefs</u> to their descendants.
    A. magical lore is transmitted by the chiefs
    B. transmission of magical lore is made by the chiefs
    C. the chiefs' magical lore is transmitted
    D. the chiefs transmit magical lore
    E. the chiefs make transmission of magical lore
The CORRECT answer is D.

SAMPLE QUESTION 4

<u>As Malcolm walks quickly and confident</u> into the purser's office, the rest of the crew wondered whether he would be charged with the theft.
    A. As Malcolm walks quickly and confident
    B. As Malcolm was walking quick and confident
    C. As Malcom walked quickly and confident

D. As Malcolm walked quickly and confidently
E. As Malcolm walks quickly and confidently
The CORRECT answer is D.

SAMPLE QUESTION 5

The chairman, <u>granted the power to assign any duties to whoever he</u> wished, was still unable to prevent bickering.
A. granted the power to assign any duties to whoever he wished
B. granting the power to assign any duties to whoever he wished
C. being granted the power to assign any duties to whoever he wished
D. having been granted the power to assign any duties to whosoever he wished
E. granted the power to assign any duties to whomever he wished
The CORRECT answer is E.

SAMPLE QUESTION 6

Certainly, well-seasoned products are more expensive, <u>but those kinds prove chaper</u> in the end.
A. but those kinds prove cheaper
B. but these kinds prove cheaper
C. but that kind proves cheaper
D. but those kind prove cheaper
E. but this kind proves cheaper
The CORRECT answer is A.

SAMPLE QUESTION 7

"We shall not," he shouted, "whatever the <u>difficulties." "lose faith in the success of our plan!!"</u>
A. difficulties," "lose faith in the success of our plan!"
B. difficulties, "lose faith in the success of our plan"!
C. "difficulties, lose faith in the success of our plan!"
D. difficulties, lose faith in the success of our plan"!
E. difficulties, lose faith in the success of our plan!"
The CORRECT answer is A.

SAMPLE QUESTION 8

<u>Climb up the tree</u>, the lush foliage obscured the chattering monkeys.
A. Climbing up the tree
B. Having climbed up the tree
C. Clambering up the tree
D. After we had climbed up the tree
E. As we climbed up the tree
The CORRECT answer is E.

EXAMINATION SECTION

TEST 1

DIRECTIONS: See DIRECTIONS for Sample Questions on Page 1. *PRINT THE LETTER OF THE CORRECT ANSWER IN THE SPACE AT THE RIGHT.*

1. At the opening of the story, Charles Gilbert <u>has just come</u> to make his home with his two unmarried aunts.
   A. No change
   B. hadn't hardly come
   C. has just came
   D. had just come
   E. has hardly came

   1.____

2. The sisters, who are no longer young, <u>are use to living</u> quiet lives.
   A. No change
   B. are used to live
   C. are use'd to living
   D. are used to living
   E. are use to live

   2.____

3. They <u>willingly except</u> the child.
   A. No change
   B. willingly eccepted
   C. willingly accepted
   D. willingly acepted
   E. willingly accept

   3.____

4. As the months pass, Charles' presence <u>affects many changes</u> in their household.
   A. No change
   B. affect many changes
   C. effects many changes
   D. effect many changes
   E. affected many changes

   4.____

5. These changes <u>is not all together</u> to their liking.
   A. No change
   B. is not altogether
   C. are not all together
   D. are not altogether
   E. is not alltogether

   5.____

6. In fact, they have some difficulty in adapting <u>theirselves</u> to these changes
   A. No change
   B. in adopting theirselves
   C. in adopting themselves
   D. in adapting theirselves
   E. in adapting themselves

   6.____

7. That is the man <u>whom I believe</u> was the driver of the car.
   A. No change
   B. who I believed
   C. whom I believed
   D. who to believe
   E. who I believe

   7.____

8. John's climb to fame was more rapid <u>than his brother's</u>.
   A. No change
   B. than his brother
   C. than that of his brother's
   D. than for his brother
   E. than the brother

   8.____

9. We knew that he had formerly swam on an Olympic team.
   A. No change
   B. has formerly swum
   C. did formerly swum
   D. had formerly swum
   E. has formerly swam

10. Not one of us loyal supporters ever get a pass to a game.
    A. No change
    B. ever did got a pass
    C. ever has get a pass
    D. ever had get a pass
    E. ever gets a pass

11. He was complemented on having done a fine job.
    A. No change
    B. was compliminted
    C. was compleminted
    D. was complemented
    E. did get complimented

12. This play is different from the one we had seen last night.
    A. No change
    B. have seen
    C. had saw
    D. have saw
    E. saw

13. A row of trees was planted in front of the house.
    A. No change
    B. was to be planted
    C. were planted
    D. were to be planted
    E. are planted

14. The house looked its age in spite of our attempts to beautify it.
    A. No change
    B. looks its age
    C. looked its' age
    D. looked it's age
    E. looked it age

15. I do not know what to council in this case.
    A. No change
    B. where to council
    C. when to councel
    D. what to counsel
    E. what to counsil

16. She is more capable than any other girl in the office.
    A. No change
    B. than any girl
    C. than any other girls
    D. than other girl
    E. than other girls

17. At the picnic the young children behaved very good.
    A. No change
    B. behave very good
    C. behaved better
    D. behave very well
    E. behaved very well

18. I resolved to go irregardless of the consequences.
    A. No change
    B. to depart irregardless of
    C. to go regarding of
    D. to go regardingly of
    E. to go regardless of

19. The new movie has a number of actors which have been famous on Broadway.   19.____
    A. No change
    B. which had been famous
    C. who had been famous
    D. that are famous
    E. who have been famous

20. I am certain that these books are not our's.   20.____
    A. No change
    B. have not been ours'
    C. have not been our's
    D. are not ours
    E. are not ours'

21. Each of your papers is filed for future reference.   21.____
    A. No change
    B. Each of your papers are filed
    C. Each of your papers have been filed
    D. Each of your papers are to be filed
    E. Each of your paper is filed

22. I wish that he would take his work more serious.   22.____
    A. No change
    B. he took his work more serious
    C. he will take his work more serious
    D. he shall take his work more seriously
    E. he would take his work more seriously

23. After the treasurer report had been read, the chairman called for the reports of the committees.   23.____
    A. No change
    B. After the treasure's report had been read
    C. After the treasurers' report had been read
    D. After the treasurerer's report had been read
    E. After the treasurer's report had been read

24. Last night the stranger lead us down the mountain.   24.____
    A. No change
    B. leaded us down the mountain
    C. let us down the mountain
    D. led us down the mountain
    E. had led us down the mountain

25. It would not be safe for either you or I to travel in Viet Nam.   25.____
    A. No change
    B. for either you or me
    C. for either I or you
    D. for either of you or I
    E. for either of I or you

KEY (CORRECT ANSWERS)

1.	A		11.	D
2.	D		12.	E
3.	E		13.	A
4.	C		14.	A
5.	D		15.	D
6.	E		16.	A
7.	E		17.	E
8.	A		18.	E
9.	D		19.	E
10.	E		20.	D

21.	A
22.	E
23.	E
24.	D
25.	B

TEST 2

DIRECTIONS: See DIRECTIONS for Sample Questions on Page 1. *PRINT THE LETTER OF THE CORRECT ANSWER IN THE SPACE AT THE RIGHT.*

1. Both the body and the mind <u>needs exercise</u>.
   A. No change
   B. have needs of exercise
   C. is needful of exercise
   D. needed exercise
   E. need exercise

   1._____

2. <u>It's paw injured</u>, the animal limped down the road.
   A. No change
   B. It's paw injured
   C. Its paw injured
   D. Its' paw injured
   E. Its paw injure

   2._____

3. The butter <u>tastes rancidly</u>.
   A. No change
   B. tastes rancid
   C. tasted rancidly
   D. taste rancidly
   E. taste rancid

   3._____

4. <u>Who do you think</u> has sent me a letter?
   A. No change
   B. Whom do you think
   C. Whome do you think
   D. Who did you think
   E. Whom can you think

   4._____

5. If more nations <u>would have fought</u> against tyranny, the course of history would have been different.
   A. No change
   B. would fight
   C. could have fought
   D. fought
   E. had fought

   5._____

6. Radio and television programs, along with other media of communication, <u>helps us to appreciate the arts and to keep informed</u>.
   A. No change
   B. helps us to appreciate the arts and to be informed
   C. helps us to be appreciative of the arts and to keep informed
   D. helps us to be appreciative of the arts and to be informed
   E. help us to appreciate the arts and to keep informed

   6._____

7. Music, <u>for example most always</u> has listening and viewing audiences numbering in the hundreds of thousands.
   A. No change
   B. for example, most always
   C. for example, almost always
   D. for example nearly always
   E. for example, near always

   7._____

8. When operas are performed on radio or television, <u>they effect the listener</u>.
   A. No change
   B. they inflict the listener
   C. these effect the listeners
   D. they affects the listeners
   E. they affect the listener

   8._____

9. After hearing then the listener wants to buy recordings of the music. 9._____
    A. No change
    B. After hearing them, the listener wants
    C. After hearing them, the listener want
    D. By hearing them the listener wants
    E. By hearing them, the listener wants

10. To we Americans the daily news program has become important. 10._____
    A. No change   B. To we the Americans
    C. To us Americans   D. To us the Americans
    E. To we and us Americans

11. This has resulted from it's coverage of a days' events. 11._____
    A. No change
    B. from its coverage of a days' events
    C. from it's coverage of a day's events
    D. from its' coverage of a day's events
    E. from its coverage of a day's events

12. In schools, teachers advice their students to listen to or to view certain programs. 12._____
    A. No change
    B. teachers advise there students
    C. teachers advise their students
    D. the teacher advises their students
    E. teachers advise his students

13. In these ways we are preceding toward the goal of an educated and an informed public. 13._____
    A. No change
    B. we are preeceding toward the goal
    C. we are proceeding toward the goal
    D. we are preceding toward the goal
    E. we are proceeding toward the goal

14. The cost of living is raising again. 14._____
    A. No change   B. are raising again
    C. is rising again   D. are rising again
    E. is risen again

15. We did not realize that the boys' father had forbidden them to keep there puppy. 15._____
    A. No change
    B. had forbade them to keep there puppy
    C. had forbade them to keep their puppy
    D. has forbidden them to keep their puppy
    E. had forbidden them to keep their puppy

16. Her willingness to help others' was her outstanding characteristic.
    A. No change
    B. Her willingness to help other's,
    C. Her willingness to help others's
    D. Her willingness to help others
    E. Her willingness to help each other

17. Because he did not have an invitation, the girls objected to him going.
    A. No change
    B. the girls object to him going
    C. the girls objected to him's going
    D. the girls objected to his going
    E. the girls object to his going

18. Weekly dances have become a popular accepted feature of the summer schedule.
    A. No change
    B. have become a popular accepted feature
    C. have become a popular excepted feature
    D. have become a popularly excepted feature
    E. have become a popularly accepted feature

19. I couldn't hardly believe that he would desert our party.
    A. No change
    B. would hardly believe
    C. didn't hardly believe
    D. should hardly believe
    E. could hardly believe

20. I found the place in the book more readily than she.
    A. No change
    B. more readily than her
    C. more ready than she
    D. more quickly than her
    E. more ready than her

21. A good example of American outdoor activities are sports.
    A. No change
    B. is sports
    C. are sport
    D. are sports events
    E. are to be found in sports

22. My point of view is much different from your's.
    A. No change
    B. much different from your's
    C. much different than yours
    D. much different from yours
    E. much different than yours'

23. The cook was suppose to use two spoonfuls of dressing for each serving.
    A. No change
    B. was supposed to use two spoonful
    C. was suppose to use two spoonful
    D. was supposed to use two spoonsfuls
    E. was supposed to use two spoonfuls

24. If anyone has any doubt about the values of the tour, refer him to me.
    A. No change
    B. refer him to I
    C. refer me to he
    D. refer them to me
    E. refer he to I

25. We expect that the affects of the trip will be neneficial.
    A. No change
    B. the effects of the trip will be beneficial
    C. the effects of the trip should be beneficial
    D. the affects of the trip would be beneficial
    E. the effects of the trip will be benificial

KEY (CORRECT ANSWERS)

1.	E	11.	E
2.	C	12.	C
3.	B	13.	E
4.	A	14.	C
5.	E	15.	E
6.	E	16.	D
7.	C	17.	D
8.	E	18.	E
9.	B	19.	E
10.	C	20.	A

21.	B
22.	D
23.	E
24.	A
25.	B

TEST 3

DIRECTIONS: See DIRECTIONS for Sample Questions on Page 1. *PRINT THE LETTER OF THE CORRECT ANSWER IN THE SPACE AT THE RIGHT.*

1. <u>That, my friend</u> is not the proper attitude. 1._____
   A. No change
   B. That my friend
   C. That my fried,
   D. That—my friend
   E. That, my friend,

2. The girl refused to admit <u>that the note was her's</u>. 2._____
   A. No change
   B. that the note were her's
   C. that the note was hers'
   D. that the note was hers
   E. that the note might be hers

3. There <u>were fewer candidates that we had been lead</u> to expect 3._____
   A. No change
   B. was fewer candidates than we had been lead
   C. were fewer candidates than we had been lead
   D. was fewer candidates than we had been led
   E. were fewer candidates than we had been led

4. When I first saw the car, <u>its steering wheel was broke</u>. 4._____
   A. No change
   B. its' steering wheel was broken
   C. it's steering wheel had been broken
   D. its steering wheel were broken
   E. its steering wheel was broken

5. I find that the essential spirit for <u>we beginners is missing</u>. 5._____
   A. No change
   B. we who begin are missing
   C. us beginners are missing
   D. us beginners is missing
   E. we beginners are missing

6. I believe that <u>you had ought</u> to study harder. 6._____
   A. No change
   B. you should have ought
   C. you had better
   D. you ought to have
   E. you ought

7. This is <u>Tom, whom I am sure</u>, will be glad to help you. 7._____
   A. No change
   B. Tom whom, I am sure,
   C. Tom, whom I am sure
   D. Tom who I am sure,
   E. Tom, who, I am sure,

8. His father or his mother <u>has read to him</u> every night since he was very small. 8._____
   A. No change
   B. did read to him
   C. have been reading to him
   D. had read to him
   E. have read to him

9. He become an authority
   A. No change
   B. becomed an authority
   C. become the authority
   D. became an authority
   E. becamed an authority

10. I know of no other reason in the club who is more kind-hearted than her.
    A. No change
    B. who are more kind-hearted than they
    C. who are more kind-hearted than them
    D. whom are more kind-hearted than she
    E. who is more kind-hearted than she

11. After Bill had ran the mile, he was breathless.
    A. No change
    B. had runned the mile
    C. has ran the mile
    D. had ranned the mile
    E. had run the mile

12. Wilson has scarcely no equal as a pitcher.
    A. No change
    B. has scarcely an equal
    C. has hardly no equal
    D. had scarcely no equal
    E. has scarcely any equals

13. It was the worse storm that the inhabitants of the island could remember.
    A. No change
    B. were the worse storm
    C. was the worst storm
    D. was the worsest storm
    E. was the most worse storm

14. If only we had began before it was too late.
    A. No change
    B. we had began
    C. we would have begun
    D. we had begun
    E. we had beginned

15. Lets evaluate our year's work.
    A. No change
    B. Let us' evaluate
    C. Lets' evaluate
    D. Lets' us evaluate
    E. Let's evaluate

16. This is an organization with which I wouldn't want to be associated with.
    A. No change
    B. with whom I wouldn't want to be associated with
    C. that I wouldn't want to be associated
    D. with which I would want not to be associated with
    E. with which I wouldn't want to be associated

17. The enemy fled in many directions, leaving there weapons on the field.
    A. No change
    B. leaving its weapons
    C. letting their weapons
    D. leaving alone there weapons
    E. leaving their weapons

18. I hoped that John could effect a compromise between the approved forces.
    A. No change
    B. could accept a compromise between
    C. could except a compromise between
    D. would have effected a compromise among
    E. could effect a compromise among

19. I was surprised to learn that he has not always spoke English fluently.
    A. No change
    B. that he had not always spoke English
    C. that he did not always speak English
    D. that he has not always spoken English
    E. that he could not always speak English

20. The lawyer promised to notify my father and I of his plans for a new trial.
    A. No change
    B. to notify I and my father
    C. to notify me and our father
    D. to notify my father and me
    E. to notify mine father and me

21. The most important feature of the series of tennis lessons were the large amount of strokes taught.
    A. No change
    B. were the large number
    C. was the large amount
    D. was the largeness of the amount
    E. was the large number

22. That the prize proved to be beyond her reach did not surprise him.
    A. No change
    B. has not surprised him
    C. had not ought to have surprised him
    D. should not surprise him
    E. would not have surprised him

23. I am not all together in agreement with the author's point of view.
    A. No change
    B. all together of agreement
    C. all together for agreement
    D. altogether with agreement
    E. altogether in agreement

24. Windstorms have recently established a record which meteorologists hope will not be equal for many years to come.
    A. No change
    B. will be equal
    C. will not be equalized
    D. will be equaled
    E. will not be equaled

25. A large number of Shakespeare's soliloquies must be considered as representing thought, not speech.   25.____
    A. No change
    B. as representative of speech, not thought
    C. as represented by thought, not speech
    D. as indicating thought, not speech
    E. as representative of thought, more than speech

KEY (CORRECT ANSWERS)

1.	E		11.	E
2.	D		12.	B
3.	E		13.	C
4.	E		14.	D
5.	D		15.	E
6.	E		16.	E
7.	E		17.	E
8.	A		18.	A
9.	D		19.	D
10.	E		20.	D

21. E
22. A
23. E
24. E
25. A

TEST 4

DIRECTIONS: See DIRECTIONS for Sample Questions on Page 1. *PRINT THE LETTER OF THE CORRECT ANSWER IN THE SPACE AT THE RIGHT.*

1. A sight to inspire fear <u>are wild animals on the lose</u>.
   A. No change
   B. are wild animals on the loose
   C. is wild animals on the loose
   D. is wild animals on the lose
   E. are wild animals loose

   1._____

2. For many years, the settlers <u>had been seeking to workship as they please</u>.
   A. No change
   B. had seeked to workship as they pleased
   C. sought to workship as they please
   D. sought to have worshiped as they pleased
   E. had been seeking to worship as they pleased

   2._____

3. The girls stated that the dresses were <u>their's</u>.
   A. No change   B. there's   C. theirs
   D. theirs'   E. there own

   3._____

4. <u>Please fellows</u> don't drop the ball.
   A. No change   B. Please, fellows
   C. Please fellows;   D. Please, fellows,
   E. Please! fellows

   4._____

5. Your sweater <u>has laid</u> on the floor for a week.
   A. No change   B. has been laying
   C. has been lying   D. laid
   E. has been lain

   5._____

6. I wonder whether <u>you're sure that scheme of yours'</u> will work.
   A. No change
   B. your sure that scheme of your's
   C. you're sure that scheme of yours
   D. your sure that scheme of yours
   E. you're sure that your scheme's

   6._____

7. Please let <u>her and me</u> do it.
   A. No change   B. she and I
   C. she and me   D. her and I
   E. her and him

   7._____

8. I expected him to be angry <u>and to scold</u> her.
   A. No change   B. and that he would scold
   C. and that he might scold D. and that he should scold
   E. , scolding

   8._____

169

9. Knowing little about algebra, it was difficult to solve the equation.
   A. No change
   B. the equation was difficult to solve
   C. the solution to the equation was difficult to find
   D. I found it difficult to solve the equation
   E. it being difficult to solve the equation

10. He worked more diligent now that he had become vice president of the company.
    A. No change
    B. works more diligent
    C. works more diligently
    D. began to work more diligent
    E. worked more diligently

11. Flinging himself at the barricade he pounded on it furiously.
    A. No change
    B. Flinging himself at the barricade: he
    C. Flinging himself at the barricade—he
    D. Flinging himself at the barricade; he
    E. Flinging himself at the barricade, he

12. When he begun to give us advise, we stopped listening.
    A. No change
    B. began to give us advise
    C. begun to give us advice
    D. began to give us advice
    E. begin to give us advice

13. John was only one of the boys whom as you know was not eligible.
    A. No change
    B. who as you know were
    C. whom as you know were
    D. who as you know was
    E. who as you know is

14. Why was Jane and he permitted to go?
    A. No change
    B. was Jane and him
    C. were Jane and he
    D. were Jane and him
    E. weren't Jane and he

15. Take courage Tom: we all make mistakes.
    A. No change
    B. Take courage Tom—we
    C. Take courage, Tom; we
    D. Take courage, Tom we
    E. Take courage! Tom: we

16. Henderson, the president of the class and who is also captain of the team, will lead the rally.
    A. No change
    B. since he is captain of the team
    C. captain of the team
    D. also being captain of the team
    E. who be also captain of the team

17. Our car has always run good on that kind of gasoline.
    A. No change
    B. run well
    C. ran good
    D. ran well
    E. done good

18. There was a serious difference of opinion among her and I. 18.____
    A. No change
    B. among she and I
    C. between her and I
    D. between her and me
    E. among her and me

19. "This is most unusual," said Helen, "the mailman has never been this late before." 19.____
    A. No change
    B. Helen, "The
    C. Helen—"The
    D. Helen; "The
    E. Helen." The

20. The three main characters in the story are Johnny Hobart a teenager, his mother a widow, and the local druggist. 20.____
    A. No change
    B. teenager; his mother, a widow; and
    C. teenager; his mother a widow; and
    D. teenager, his mother, a widow and
    E. teenager, his mother, a widow; and

21. How much has food costs raised during the past year? 21.____
    A. No change
    B. have food costs rose
    C. have food costs risen
    D. has food costs risen
    E. have food costs been raised

22. "Will you come too" she pleaded? 22.____
    A. No change
    B. too,?"she pleaded
    C. too?" she pleaded
    D. too," she pleaded?
    E. too, she pleaded?"

23. If he would have drank more milk, his health would have been better. 23.____
    A. No change
    B. would drink
    C. had drank
    D. had he drunk
    E. had drunk

24. Jack had no sooner laid down and fallen asleep when the alarm sounded. 24.____
    A. No change
    B. no sooner lain down and fallen asleep than
    C. no sooner lay down and fell asleep when
    D. no sooner laid down and fell asleep than
    E. no sooner lain down than he fell asleep when

25. Jackson is one of the few Sophomores, who has ever made the varsity team. 25.____
    A. No change
    B. one of the few Sophomores, who have
    C. one of the few sophomores, who has
    D. one of the few sophomores who have
    E. one of the few sophomores who has

KEY (CORRECT ANSWERS)

1.	C		11.	E
2.	E		12.	D
3.	C		13.	B
4.	D		14.	C
5.	C		15.	C
6.	C		16.	C
7.	A		17.	B
8.	A		18.	D
9.	D		19.	E
10.	E		20.	B

21. C
22. C
23. E
24. B
25. D

TEST 5

DIRECTIONS: See DIRECTIONS for Sample Questions on Page 1. *PRINT THE LETTER OF THE CORRECT ANSWER IN THE SPACE AT THE RIGHT.*

1. The lieutenant had ridden almost a kilometer when the scattering shells <u>begin landing</u> uncomfortably close.
    A. No change
    B. beginning to land
    C. began to land
    D. having begun to land
    E. begin to land

    1.____

2. <u>Having studied eight weeks</u>, he now feels sufficiently prepared for the examination.
    A. No change
    B. For eight weeks he studies so
    C. Due to eight weeks of study
    D. After eight weeks of studying
    E. Since he's been spending the last eight weeks in study

    2.____

3. <u>Coming from the Greek, and the word "democracy" means government by the people</u>.
    A. No change
    B. "Democracy," the word which comes from the Greek, means government by the people.
    C. Meaning government by the people, the word "democracy" comes from the Greek.
    D. Its meaning being government by the people in Greek, the word is "democracy."
    E. The word "democracy" comes from the Greek and means government by the people.

    3.____

4. Moslem universities were one of the chief agencies <u>in the development</u> and spreading Arabic civilization.
    A. No change
    B. in the development of
    C. to develop
    D. in developing
    E. for the developing of

    4.____

5. The water of Bering Strait <u>were closing</u> to navigation by ice early in the fall.
    A. No change
    B. has closed
    C. have closed
    D. had been closed
    E. closed

    5.____

6. The man, <u>since he grew up</u> on the block, felt sentimental when returning to it.
    A. No change
    B. having grown up
    C. growing up
    D. since he had grown up
    E. whose growth had been

    6.____

173

7. Jack and Jill watched the canoe to take their parents out of sight round the bend of the creek.
   A. No change
   B. The canoe, taking their parents out of sight, rounds the bend as Jack and Jill watch.
   C. Jack and Jill watched the canoe round the bend of the creek, taking their parents out of sight,
   D. The canoe rounded the bend of the creek as it took their parents out of sight, Jack and Jill watching.
   E. Jack and Jill watching, the canoe is rounding the bend of the creek to take their parents out of sight.

8. Chaucer's best-known work is THE CANTERBURY TALES, a collection of stories which he tells with a group of pilgrims as they travel to the town of Canterbury.
   A. No change
   B. which he tells through
   C. who tell
   D. told by
   E. told through

9. The Estates-General, the old feudal assembly of France, had not met for one hundred and seventy-five years when it convened in 1789.
   A. No change
   B. has not met
   C. has not been meeting
   D. had no meeting
   E. has no meeting

10. Just forty years ago, there had been fewer than one hundred symphony orchestras in the United States.
    A. No change
    B. there had
    C. there were
    D. there was
    E. there existed

11. Mrs. Smith complained that her son's temper tantrums aggravated her and caused her to have a headache.
    A. No change
    B. gave her aggravation
    C. were aggravating to her
    D. aggravated her condition
    E. instigated

12. A girl like I would never be seen in a place like that.
    A. No change
    B. as I
    C. as me
    D. like I am
    E. like me

13. Between you and me, my opinion is that this room is certainly nicer than the first one we saw.
    A. No change
    B. between you and I
    C. among you and me
    D. betwixt you and I
    E. between we

14. It is important to know for <u>what kind of a person you are working</u>. 14.____
    A. No change
    B. what kind of a person for whom you are working
    C. what kind of person you are working
    D. what kind of person you are working for
    E. what kind of a person you are working for

15. I had <u>all ready</u> finished the book before you came in. 15.____
    A. No change   B. already   C. previously
    D. allready   E. all

16. <u>Ask not for who the bell tolls, it tolls for thee</u>. 16.____
    A. No change
    B. Ask not for whom the bell tolls, it tolls for thee.
    C. Ask not whom the bell tolls for; it tolls for thee.
    D. Ask not for whom the bell tolls; it tolls for thee.
    E. As not who the bell tolls for: It tolls for thee.

17. It is a far better thing I do, than <u>ever I did</u> before. 17.____
    A. No change   B. never I did
    C. I have ever did   D. I have ever been done
    E. ever have I done

18. <u>Ending a sentence with a preposition is something up with which I will not put</u>. 18.____
    A. No change
    B. Ending a sentence with a preposition is something with which I will not put up.
    C. To end a sentence with a preposition is that which I will not put up with.
    D. Ending a sentence with a preposition is something of which I will not put up.
    E. Something I will not put up with is ending a sentence with a preposition.

19. Everyone <u>took off their hats and stand up</u> to sing the national anthem. 19.____
    A. No change
    B. took off their hats and stood up
    C. take off their hats and stand up
    D. took off his hat and stood up
    E. have taken off their hats and standing up

20. <u>She promised me that if she had the opportunity she would have came irregardless of the weather</u>. 20.____
    A. No change
    B. She promised me that if she had the opportunity she would have come regardless of the weather.
    C. She assured me that had she had the opportunity he would have come regardless of the weather.
    D. She assured me that if she would have had the opportunity she would have come regardless of the weather.

4 (#5)

    E. She promised me that if she had had the opportunity she would have came irregardless of the weather.

21. The man decided it would be advisable to marry a girl <u>somewhat younger than him</u>.
    A. No change
    B. somehow younger than him
    C. some younger than him
    D. somewhat younger from him
    E. somewhat younger than he

    21.____

22. Sitting near the campfire, the old man told <u>John and I about many exciting adventures he had had</u>.
    A. No change
    B. John and me about many exciting adventures he had,
    C. John and I about much exciting adventure which he'd had
    D. John and me about many exciting adventures he had had
    E. John and me about many exciting adventures he has had.

    22.____

23. <u>If you had stood at home and done your homework</u>, you would not have failed the course.
    A. No change
    B. If you had stood at home and done you're homework,
    C. If you had staid at home and done your homework,
    D. Had you stayed at home and done your homework,
    E. Had you stood at home and done your homework,

    23.____

24. The children didn't, as a rule, <u>do anything beyond</u> what they were told to do.
    A. No change
    B. do hardly anything beyond
    C. do anything except
    D. do hardly anything except for
    E. do nothing beyond

    24.____

25. <u>Either the girls or him is</u> right.
    A. No change
    B. Either the girls or he is
    C. Either the girls or him are
    D. Either the girls or he are
    E. Either the girls nor he is

    25.____

176

KEY (CORRECT ANSWERS)

1.	C	11.	D
2.	A	12.	E
3.	E	13.	A
4.	D	14.	C
5.	D	15.	B
6.	B	16.	D
7.	C	17.	E
8.	D	18.	E
9.	A	19.	D
10.	C	20.	C

21.	E
22.	D
23.	D
24.	A
25.	B

BASIC FUNDAMENTALS OF ENGLISH EXPRESSION

TABLE OF CONTENTS

		Page
A.	FUNCTIONAL INTRODUCTION TO GRAMMAR	1
	<u>Classification</u>	1
	1. Nominative Absolute ... 21. Verbals	1
	<u>Syntax</u>	1
	I. Uses of the Noun	1
	II. Uses of the Pronoun	2
	III. Uses of the Adjective	4
	IV. Uses of the Adverb	4
	V. Uses of Verbals	4
	VI. Uses of Phrases	5
	VII. Uses of Subordinate Clauses	6
	VIII. Uses of the Verb	6
	IX. Special Uses	7
B.	BASIC SYNTAX	8
	Rules 1-9	8
	Rules 10-21	9
	Rules 22-34	10
	Rules 35-38	11
C.	COMMON ERRORS IN USAGE	11

BASIC FUNDAMENTALS OF ENGLISH EXPRESSION

A. FUNCTIONAL INTRODUCTION TO GRAMMAR

For examination purposes, there are two clear-cut and yet related divisions in grammar: classification and syntax.

Classification refers to the required nomenclature for the proper identification and description of the uses of words or groups of words. Syntax refers to the relations of words and groups of words with one another in sentences.

The more usual terms of Classification are the following:

CLASSIFICATION

1. Nominative Absolute
2. Nominative of Direct Address
3. Nominative of Exclamation
4. Predicate Nominative
5. Predicate Adjective
6. Object of a Verb
7. Indirect Object
8. Object of a Preposition
9. Objective Complement
10. Adverbial Objective
11. Retained Object
12. Noun in Apposition
13. Auxiliary Verb
14. Copulative Verb
15. Progressive Forms of the Verb
16. Past Participle
17. Mood
18. Tense
19. Subject - complete subject, including modifiers
20. Predicate - verb and all modifiers and complements
21. Verbals

The more outstanding and the more frequently occurring types of syntactical relationships are defined in the illustrations appearing hereafter.

SYNTAX

I. Uses of the Noun
   A. Nominative Case:
      1. Subject of a verb: MARY bought a hat.
      2. Predicate Nominative: (Double Function)
         a. With a copulative verb: He became PRESIDENT. Is that the SORT of a person you take me for?
         b. With a verb in the passive voice: He was chosen PRESIDENT.
      3. Independent Constructions:
         a. Noun in Apposition with a noun in the nominative case: My sister, CLARA, is going with me.
         b. Nominative Absolute: The TRAIN having stopped, the passengers got out. James stood before me, his HANDS in his pocket
         c. Nominative of Direct Address: MARY, open the door.
         d. Nominative of Exclamation: What a MAN!

B. Possessive Case:
   1. To show ownership: MARY'S hat is brown.
   2. To indicate the relation of the doer to an act expressed in a particular noun: MARY'S having her homework saved the day. (See Predicate Complement of Copulative Verbal, below)
C. Objective Case: (Complements)
   1. Object of a
      a. Verb: The child ate the APPLE.
      b. Verbal:
         1. Infinitive: At times, it's a pleasure to eat an APPLE.
         2. Participle: Having lost the larger PART of his fortune, my friend found that economy was necessary.
         3. Participial Noun: Eating an APPLE is a pleasure.
      c. Preposition: She gave the book to CLARA.
      d. Cognate Object: He spoke his SPEECH well.
      e. Secondary Object of a Verb or Verbal: He told John the ANSWER. He asked John a QUESTION. He paid his workers good WAGES. (Differs from the indirect object because the secondary object can be dropped.)
   2. Indirect Object of a
      a. Verb: We gave JOHN our books.
      b. Verbal:
         1. Infinitive: He asked us to give CATHERINE the money.
         2. Participle: Giving my FRIEND the money I had borrowed, I heaved a sigh of relief.
         3. Participial Noun: Giving PEOPLE money makes most people happier.
   3. Subject of an Infinitive: I expect JOHN to be present. Let ME rest!
   4. Objective Complement: (See Predicate Nominative with Passive Verb) We elected him PRESIDENT. The Romans called Caesar FRIEND.
   5. Retained Object: (See 2a.) John was given our BOOKS.
   6. Adverbial Objective: I wanted to go HOME. The child is three YEARS old.
   7. Predicate Complement of Copulative Verbals:
      a. Referring back to the Subject of the Infinitive: I believed Allen to be the MAN.
      b. Referring back to the noun modified by a participle:
         Or lonely house,
         Long held the witches' HOME.
      c. Referring back to the Possessive with the Participial Noun: There is sense in your hoping to be SECRETARY. I was sure of John's being the AGGRESSOR.
   8. Noun in Apposition with a noun in the objective case: I gave the song, SOPHISTICATED LADY, to my friend to play.

II. Uses of the Pronoun
   A. Personal Pronouns: Similar to nouns in use, but, in addition, they must agree with the antecedent in <u>person</u>, <u>number,</u> and <u>gender</u>.
      1. Nominative Case:
         a. Subject of a verb: SHE bought a hat.
         b. Predicate Nominative with Copulative Verb: It is I
         c. Independent Construction:
            1. Nominative Absolute: SHE being ill, we decided to go.

3

2. Nominative of Direct Address: YOU, will you come!
3. Nominative of Exclamation: I! You cannot accuse me!
2. Possessive Case:
   a. To show ownership: HER hat is brown.
   b. To indicate relation of doer to an act or state expressed in a participial noun: HIS having a car saved the day.
3. Objective Case:
   a. Object of a
      1. Verb: The child ate IT.
      2. Verbal:
         a. Infinitive: At times it is a pleasure to eat IT.
         b. Participle: Having lost IT, we hunted for another.
         c. Participial Noun: Taking IT in large doses is bad.
      3. Preposition: She referred me to HIM for an answer.
   b. Indirect Object of a
      1. Verb: We gave HIM our books.
      2. Verbal:
         a. Infinitive: He asked us to give HER the money.
         b. Participle: Giving HIM the money I had borrowed, I heaved a sigh of relief.
         c. Participial Noun: Giving HIM money made him unhappy.
   c. Subject of the Infinitive: I expected HIM to be present.
   d. Retained Object: He was given IT for his own use.

B. Uses of "it":
1. Impersonal Pronoun, subject of a verb when no definite subject is expressed: IT rains.
2. Expletive, serving to introduce the verb "is" when the real subject is in the Predicate: IT may be true that he did not commit the crime.

C. Compound Personal Pronouns:
1. Intensively: I, MYSELF, will go.
2. Reflexively: I have harmed MYSELF. The neighbors left us severely to OURSELVES.

D. Interrogative Pronouns: Similar to personal pronouns in use, but, in addition, they assist in asking a question. WHO is that? WHOSE is that? WHOM do you expect? WHICH is the better student? WHAT is your aim in life? He asked me WHAT I had meant by that statement.(Indirect) WHO do you consider is the best agent the company has?

E. Adjective (Demonstrative) Pronouns: Similar to personal pronouns in use. THIS is a new hat. THESE are very interesting books. The mountains of Colorado are higher than THOSE. I bought ONE, too.

F. Relative Pronouns: Similar to personal pronouns in use, but, in addition, they con-nect the adjective clauses they introduce with the nouns or pronouns modified.

That is the girl WHO is going with me.
The men WHOM you see there are marines.
The men WHOSE lights are lit are seniors.
Ask her for the book WHICH I recommended.
Tell her WHAT you have told me. (That which)
That's WHAT I did it for.
The book THAT I gave her is lost.
This is the pillow THAT I asked for.

Who do you consider is the best agent (THAT) the company has? (Elliptical use)

Adjective clauses are also introduced by relative adverbs:
There was one time WHEN I almost caught you.
That is the house WHERE I was born.

    G. Compound relative pronouns:
I will go with WHOEVER is going my way. (Implies own antecedent: HIM WHO)

III. <u>Uses of the Adjective</u>
    A. Modifier of a noun (pronoun): That was an ORIENTAL rug. This dress is plainer than that PRETTY one. I must have the test-tube CLEAN. Of dark BROWN gardens and of PEEPING flowers.
    B. Predicate Adjective:
        1. With copulative verb: She was LAZY. This apple is RIPE.
        2. Passive Voice: This man was pronounced GUILTY.
    C. Objective Complement: I called the ship UNSEAWORTHY. I will make assurance doubly SURE. She wiped the plate DRY.

IV. <u>Uses of the Adverb</u>
    A. Modifier of a verb: She walked RAPIDLY. This matter must be acted UPON.
    B. Modifier of a verbal:
        1. Infinitive: She attempted to walk RAPIDLY.
        2. Participle: Having arrived SILENTLY, she overheard the conversation.
        3. Participial Noun: Passing COMMENDABLY is our aim.
    C. Modifier of an adjective: The ice was UNUSUALLY smooth this winter.
    D. Modifier of another adverb: The wheels revolved VERY swiftly.
    E. Modifier of a phrase or clause: He arrived JUST in time. That is EXACTLY what I expected of him.
    F. As a relative or conjunctive adverb, introducing a clause and modifying the verb in this clause: I passed the house WHERE he was born. AS he rose from his chair, the audience burst into wild applause.
    G. As an interrogative adverb, asking a direct or indirect question and modifying the verb: WHEN did you arrive? Tell us WHY he is always successful.

V. <u>Uses of Verbals</u>: Verbals take adverbial modifiers and complements.
    A. The Infinitive.
        1. As a noun
            a. Nominative Case:
                1. Subject of Verb: TO EXIST is a hard job these days.
                2. Predicate Nominative: Copulative Verb: To work is TO EAT.
                3. Independent Constructions: Apposition: Our ambition, TO ACT, was never realized.
                4. Nominative Absolute: To ENJOY ourselves being impossible, we left the theatre.
                5. Exclamation: TO SOAR! TO SOAR above the earth with wings!
            b. Objective Case:
                1. Object of a verb: The child asked TO SING. They expect TO TAKE one.
                2. Object of a verbal:(Infinitive) It is never safe to ask TO GO. (Participle) Having asked TO LEAVE, he refused when the chance came. Bill Brown came asking
TO BE ADMITTED to the house. (Participial Noun) Learning TO FLY is amusing.

3. Object of a Preposition: There was nothing to do but TO GO.
4. Retained Object: He was told TO GO.
5. Apposition with noun in objective case: We never realized our ambition, TO ACT.
6. Special Use: With an object noun or pronoun as its subject: I wrote for him TO COME.(Such phrases introduced by "for" are used as nouns.) He felt the ground TREMBLE.

2. As an adjective
   a. Modifying a noun: Houses TO RENT are scarce this year.
   c. Predicate Adjective: Our plan seemed TO WORK each day.
3. As an adverb
   a. Modifying a verb: Folks would laugh TO SEE a cindermaid at a court ball.
   b. Modifying an adjective: The army was ready TO MARCH.
   c. Modifying a verbal: (Participle) Having gone out TO SHOP, he could not be found. (Participial Noun) Trying TO STUDY is impossible.
4. As part of the complement of a verb or preposition with a noun as subject: Let me GO!
5. As an Independent Expression: TO LIVE! To live in utter forgetfulness.

B. The Participle: The participial form of a verb used as an adjective: The men HAVING WORKED steadily, the company decided to give them a raise. (Predicate Adjective) He appeared PANTING. (Objective Complement) I must have the test-tube CLEANED. Special Case: (1) With a noun in the nominative absolute construction: The day HAVING DAWNED, we started on our trip. (2) In rare cases, as an adverb: He ran CRYING down the street.

C. The Participal Noun: The participial form of a verb used as a noun. (Subject) SEEING is believing. (Predicate Nominative)Seeing is BELIEVING. (Apposition) The sport, SKATING, is an exciting one. (Nominative Absolute) SKATING being over, the children went home. (With Possessive Pronoun) MARY'S swimming did not succeed very well. (Object of verb) I love SKATING. (Object of Verbal) He wanted to go SKATING. (Object of a Preposition) The pleasure lies in EATING. We went SKATING. (Retained Object) The children were given WEAVING to do. (Adverbial Objective) That is worth THINKING about. The water was BOILING hot.

VI. Uses of Phrases
   A. As nouns:
      1. The Infinitive Phrase: His aim is TO BE WELL.
      2. Participial Noun Phrase: His only pleasure is BEING WELL. MENDING BROKEN CHINA was his occupation.
   B. As adjectives:
   1. Prepositional Phrase:(Modifier of a Noun) The trees OF THE FOREST are fading. (Predicate Adjective) The sun is IN ITS SPLENDOR.
   2. Infinitive Phrase: (Modifier of a Noun) The house TO BE SOLD was burned. (Predicate Adjective) The house was TO BE SOLD.
   3. Participial Phrase: (Modifier of Noun) RUNNING AWAY, he was shot.
   C. As adverbs:
      1. Prepositional Phrase: Frank came A-RUNNING. Tom ran crying DOWN THE STREET. The room was full OF PEOPLE.
      2. Infinitive Phrase: Folks would laugh TO SEE a cindermaid at a ball.
   D. As Independent Elements: It is true, TO BE SURE. It is better, IN MY OPINION, to face the situation directly.

VII. <u>Uses of Subordinate Clauses</u>
   A. Noun Clauses: Introduced by subordinating conjunctions such as THAT, WHETHER; interrogative pronouns in indirect questions, such as WHO, WHICH, WHAT; interrogative adverbs in indirect questions, such as WHERE, WHEN, WHY, HOW; all illustrated below.
   1. Subject of a Verb: THAT WE HAVE SURVIVED THE ORDEAL is evident.
   2. Predicate Nominative: The truth is THAT HE FAILED TO PASS.
   3. Noun in Apposition: The fact THAT THE EARTH IS ROUND is never disputed.
   4. Object of a Verb or Verbal: Tell me WHERE IS FANCY BRED. I wish HE WOULD HELP ME, I begged him to tell me WHAT HE WANTED. I asked him just WHAT HE REPORTED.
   5. Object of a Preposition: I am going there no matter WHAT YOU SAY. We came to the conclusion from WHAT WE KNOW.
   6. Retained Object: He was asked just WHAT HE REPORTED. I was asked WHETHER I ENJOY READING.
   7. Special Construction: In apposition with the expletive IT: It is commonly known THAT HE CANNOT BE TRUSTED.
   B. Adjective Clauses: Introduced by relative pronoun, WHO, WHICH, WHAT, THAT; relative adverb, WHERE, WHEN, AFTER.
   1. Modifier of a Noun: Thrice is he armed WHO HATH HIS QUARREL JUST. There is society WHERE NONE INTRUDES. I remember the house WHERE I WAS BORN. Who do you consider is the best agent THE COMPANY HAS?
   C. Adverbial Clauses: Introduced by relative (or conjunctive) adverbs; subordinating conjunctions such as BECAUSE, IF, SINCE, THOUGH.
   1. Modifier of a Verb, Verbal, Adjective, Adverb: Try AS WE MAY, we cannot swim to that rock. I intend to leave WHEN YOU GO. We are glad THAT YOU ARE WITH US. WHERE THE BEE SUCKS, there suck I.
   D. Independent Clause Element: Who DO YOU CONSIDER is the best agent the company has? He is, I THINK, able to do the work well.

VIII. <u>Uses of the Verb</u>
   A. Types of verbs
   1. Transitive verbs
      a. These require direct objects to complete the meaning: John ATE the <u>apple</u>, (direct object)
   2. Intransitive verbs
      a. These do <u>not</u> require an object to complete the meaning: The boy RAN down the mountain. (Common causes of error are the misuse of the intransitive verbs RISE, LIE, and SIT and/or the transitive verbs RAISE, LAY, and SET: She LAID on the bed, for She LAY on the bed.
   3. Copulative verbs
      a. These verbs, especially forms of the verb TO BE, are used to express simply the relationship between the subject and the predicate (or complement): She LOOKS good; The meat SMELLS bad; I FEEL better. (The most common copulative verbs are: BE, SEEM, PROVE, FEEL, SOUND, LOOK, APPEAR, BECOME, TASTE.)
   4. Auxiliary verbs
      a. These verbs assist in forming the voices, modes, and tenses of other verbs: She SHOULD go; They HAVE BEEN gone a month; We WERE given the information. (The most common auxiliary verbs are: BE,

HAVE, DO, SHALL, WILL, MAY, CAN, MUST, OUGHT, with all their inflectional forms.)
- B. Tenses of verbs (Verbs appear in different forms to indicate the time of the action):
  1. Present tense: The boy CARRIES the book; She EATS cookies.
  2. Past tense: The men COMPLETED the job; We VISITED him at home.
  3. Future tense: We WILL DO the job tomorrow; I SHALL GO alone.
     a. In speech and in informal writing, WILL and WOULD are now commonly used for all three persons except for the use of SHOULD to express obligation.
     b. In formal writing and careful usage, the following distinctions are observed between SHALL and WILL:
        1. To express simple futurity, use SHALL (or SHOULD) with the first person, and WILL (or WOULD) with the second or third persons: I SHALL be glad to go; They WOULD like to go.
        2. To express determination, intention, etc., use WILL (or WOULD) with the first person, and SHALL (or SHOULD) with the second and third persons: I WILL do it; You SHALL not go; They SHALL not pass.
        3. In questions, use SHALL with the first person: SHALL we see you tonight? SHALL I do it now? With the second person, use the form that is expected in the answer: WILL you lend us the car? (The answer that is expected here is: I WILL or I WILL not.) With the third person, use WILL to express simple futurity: WILL there be someone to meet him at the train?
        4. In indirect discourse, use the auxiliary that would be used if the discourse were direct: The company asked him whether he WOULD pay the bill. (Direct discourse: WILL you pay the bill?) He stated that he WOULD undertake the mission. (Direct discourse: I WILL undertake the mission.) His wife asked him whether he SHOULD be late for supper. (Direct discourse: SHALL you be late for supper?)
  4. Present perfect tense: I HAVE BEEN LIVING here for three years.
  5. Past perfect tense: He HAD BEEN CONVICTED of a crime many years ago.
  6. Future perfect tense: Before you arrive, I SHALL HAVE BAKED the pie.
- C. Mood (Mode) (The forms of a verb that indiqate the manner of the action):
  1. Indicative Mood (used to state a fact or to ask a question): The man FELL; ARE you well?
  2. Imperative Mood (used to express a command or an urgent request): DO it at once; ANSWER the telephone.
  3. Subjective Mood (used to express a wish, a supposition, a doubt, an exhortation, a concession, a condition contrary to fact): Wish: If only I WERE able to run faster!
  Supposition: They will be married provided their parents CONSENT. Condition contrary to fact: If you HAD more experience, you would know how to handle the problem.

IX. Special Uses
- A. Common Words Used as Different Parts of Speech:
  1. But: as relative pronoun: There is none BUT will answer.
     as adverb: You are BUT half awake, (only)
     as a preposition: Every man BUT him may leave, (except)
     I cannot BUT feel cherful.(except to feel)

as a coordinating conjunction: He leaves BUT I stay.
2. Like: (Never used as a conjunction)
as a preposition: He talks LIKE his mother,
as a verb: I LIKE his manner of speech.
3. As: as a relative pronoun: You own the same AS I.
as an adverb: I am AS young as you are.
as a subordinating conjunction: I am as young AS you are.
as a preposition: He has frequently appeared AS Hamlet.
4. Than: as a preposition: He loves money more THAN learning.
as a subordinating conjunction: He knows more THAN I.

B. BASIC SYNTAX

(NOTE: Rules are numbered for reference.)

A <u>noun</u> is the name of a person, place, object, or Idea.

A <u>pronoun</u> is a word used in place of a noun.

Nouns and pronouns are called <u>substantives</u>.

1. The subject of a verb is in the <u>nominative</u> case.
The <u>boy</u> threw the ball.

Transitive verbs express action upon an object or product.

2. The direct object of a transitive verb is in the <u>objective (accusative)</u> case. <u>Whom</u> shall I fear?

Intransitive verbs are often followed by substantives which rename their subject. Such complements are called <u>predicate nominatives, predicate nouns, or attribute complements.</u>

3. A substantive used as attribute complement agrees in case with the subject to which it refers.
It is <u>I. Whom</u> do you take me to be?

A substantive which helps to complete a verb but renames the object of the verb is called an <u>objective complement.</u>

4. An <u>objective complement</u> is in the <u>objective</u> case.
The class elected him <u>president.</u>

5. The <u>object of a preposition</u> is in the <u>objective case.</u>
Give it to me. The cat is under the <u>stove.</u>

The receiver of an action may sometimes be thought of as the principal word in an adverbial phrase from which the preposition <u>to</u> or <u>for</u> is omitted. Such a complement is called an <u>indirect object.</u>

6. An <u>indirect object</u> is in the objective case (dative object). Bring <u>me</u> a chair.

<u>Infinitives</u> and <u>participles</u> do not really assert action or being, but they imply it, and in this sense may have subjects.

Verbs of wishing, desiring, commanding, believing, declaring, perceiving, etc., are likely to be followed by objects which are at the same time <u>subjects of verbals.</u> It is this objective relation which justifies Rule 7.

7. The subject of a verbal is in the objective case. (Except in independent phrases.)
She has <u>me</u> to protect her. We thought <u>him</u> to be honest.

8. Substantives used with verbals in independent phrases are in the nominative case. ("Absolute.")
His <u>friends</u> advising it, he resigned.

An appositive is a noun or pronoun used as explanatory of or equivalent to another noun or pronoun.

9. An appositive takes the case of the substantive to which it is attached.
The book was his, <u>Peter's.</u> (Possessive.)
'Tis I, Hamlet, the Dane. (Nominative.)

Give it to me your brother.(Objective.)

10. A noun or pronoun <u>independent by address</u> is in the <u>nominative</u> case. ("Vocative".)
<u>"Hens of Athens.</u> Him declare I unto you."
<u>Mr. President,</u> I rise to a point of order.

11. A noun or pronoun used <u>independently with a following adjective, adverb, or phrase</u> may best be regarded as in the objective case, since it is virtually the object in a prepositional phrase from which the preposition is omitted.
<u>Hat in hand,</u> he stood waiting
<u>Beard unkempt, clothes threadbare,</u> he looked down and out.
<u>Fences down, weeds everywhere,</u> the place was desolate.

12. Nouns or pronouns showing ownership are in the <u>possessive</u> case.
<u>John's</u> farm; <u>your</u> shoes.

13. When an inanimate thing is personified, the <u>gender</u> of its noun or pronoun is determied by custom.
<u>She's</u> a good old boat! (Feminine.)
The <u>sun</u> is hiding <u>his</u> head. (Masculine.)

14. <u>Collective nouns are plural</u> when their units act separately as individuals; <u>singular</u> when the units act together as one. <u>Plural</u> titles are in this sense singular nouns.
The class has had its picture taken. (All together.)
The class have had their pictures taken. (Each person by himself.)
"The Newcomes" is by Thackeray.

15. <u>Nouns used adverbially</u> to measure time or distance are in the <u>objective case. (Adverbial objective.)</u>
We walked an <u>hour,</u> travelled four <u>miles.</u>

16. A <u>substantive</u> used as an exclamation is commonly held to be <u>nominative.</u> But if the exclamation repeats an idea already used, it will take the case of the term repeated.
We shall be rich. We! think of that!
"We'll make you do it!" <u>Me!</u> I guess not!

17. A <u>pronoun</u> must agree with its antecedent in <u>number, gender.</u> and <u>person.</u> Collective nouns take singular pronouns when the units act separately
The Ship of State has refused to obey <u>her</u> rudder.
<u>That</u> is <u>he whom</u> you seek. (All three are in 3rd Person, Masculine Gender, Singular Number.)
The <u>case</u> of a pronoun does not depend upon its antecedent, but upon its use in the sentence.
A verb is a word which asserts. (Tells something of its subject.)

18. A verb agrees with its subject in person and number. *I* am: You <u>are;</u> He <u>is;</u> She goes; They <u>go</u> .

19. A compound subject with <u>and</u> takes a singular verb if the idea of the combined subject is of <u>one</u> thing; if the compound subject is made of parts acting separately, the verb is <u>plural.</u>
Roosevelt and Wilson <u>were</u> of opposing parties.
The sum and substance of the matter <u>is</u> this.

20. A <u>distributive</u> subject with each, <u>every, everyone, either, neither.</u> etc., requires a verb in the <u>singular;</u> a disjunctive subject with <u>either-or. neither-nor,</u> takes a verb in the <u>singular</u> if the substantives are singular.
<u>Either</u> the book or the teacher <u>is</u> wrong.
<u>Each</u> of us must use his own judgment.

21. <u>Nouns plural in form</u> but singular in meaning commonly take a verb in the <u>singular.</u>
Hydraulics <u>is</u> a practical study nowadays.

Mumps <u>is</u> contagious.

The news <u>is</u> discouraging.

22. When the subject acts upon an object, the verb is in the <u>active voice;</u> when the subject is a receiver or product of action, the verb is <u>passive.</u>

The hunter <u>shot</u> the door. (Active.)

The deer <u>was shot</u> by the hunter. (Passive.)

23. The <u>indicative mood</u> is used in questions and in simple assertions of factor matter thought of as possible fact.

<u>Were</u> you there?

You <u>were</u> there.

If you <u>were</u> there, I did not see you.(See subjunctive mood, Rule 24.)

24. The <u>subjunctive mood</u> expresses a wish, or a <u>condition contrary to fact.</u>

Would he <u>were</u> here!

If he <u>were</u> here, we would know about it.

(Implying denial. He has.not been here.)

25. The <u>imperative mood</u> states a command or request. Please_go at once.

The subject of an imperative verb is you understood; the <u>you</u> is seldom expressed, unless the mood is emphatic.

26. <u>Infinitives</u> may be used as <u>subject</u>, <u>object of verb</u>, <u>attribute complement</u>, <u>object of preposition</u>, <u>appositive</u>, <u>adjective modifier</u>, ad<u>verbial modifier</u>, or in an <u>independent phrase.</u>

For examples, see discussion of <u>Verbals</u> in this section.

27. <u>Gerunds</u> (Verbal nouns in ing) have the uses of <u>nouns</u> together with the power of implying action, being or condition.

Examples have been given under <u>uses</u> of Verbals.

28. <u>Participles</u> may be used as <u>adjectives</u>, <u>adverbs</u>, <u>subjective complements</u>, <u>objective complements</u>, <u>following a preposition</u>, or in <u>absolute phrases.</u>

See examples under Verbals.

29. The comparative degree of adjectives and adverbs, not the superlative degree, is used in comparing two persons or things.

He is the <u>taller</u> of the two; in fact, the <u>tallest</u> of the three.

30. A <u>coordinating conjunction</u> connects words, phrases, or clauses of like rank, grammatically independent of each other.

I will come if I can <u>and</u> if the weather is good.

31. A <u>subordinating conjunction</u> joins a dependent clause to a principal one.

Make hay <u>while</u> the sun shines.

32. <u>Interjections</u> commonly have no grammatical relation in the sentence. In certain constructions, however, the interjection seems to have a phrasal modifier.

"Ah! for the pirate's dream of fight!"

33. Verbs <u>become</u>, <u>feel</u>, <u>look,</u> see, <u>smell</u>, <u>taste</u>, <u>sound</u>, <u>grow</u> may take an <u>attribute complement</u> to describe the subject, or an adverb to modify the assertion of the verb.

He grew <u>tall</u>. Poisonous mushrooms taste <u>good.</u>

"He looks <u>well</u>" may describe his own condition, and so the word <u>well</u> may be a predicate adjective relating to the subject; or the sentence may mean that he <u>searches thoroughly,</u> in which sense <u>well</u> is an adverb modifying <u>looks.</u>

34. <u>Assertions of Simple Futurity</u> take the form

I, we   shall

You   will

He, they   will

<u>Assertions of Strong Purpose, Promise, Threat, Consent</u> take the form I, we will You shall He, they shall

35. Adjectives should not take the place of adverbs, nor adverbs the place of adjectives.

36. The six tenses of English verbs in the Active Voice, Indicative Mood, are built up from the "principal parts" as follows:

<u>Present Tense. Past Tense,</u> as in Principal Parts, <u>Future Tense, shall</u> or will (Rule 34) with Present Infinitive (less "to").

<u>Present Perfect, have</u> or has. with Past Participle Past Perfect, <u>had,</u> with Past Participle.

<u>Future Perfect, shall</u> or <u>will</u> (Rule 34), with Present Perfect, the "have" form.

37. The six tenses of English verbs in the Passive Voice, Indicative Mood, invariably use the past participle of the given verb, preceded by an appropriate form of the verb "be."

38. <u>Gerunds,</u> being verbal nouns, are modified by adjectives and <u>possessive pronouns.</u>

Now do it without <u>my</u> watching you.

C. COMMON ERRORS IN USAGE

(Numbers refer to rules in the preceding section. Correct forms are given first.)

	RULE
This is the <u>better</u> of the two. *NOT* this is the <u>best</u> of the two	(29)
<u>You</u> and I, did it. *NOT* <u>you</u> and <u>me</u> did it, *NOR* <u>me</u> and <u>you</u>.	(1)
<u>We</u> boys will be there. *NOT* <u>us</u> boys will be there.	(1)
It was <u>I, she, he, they</u>. *NOT* <u>me, her, him, them</u>.	(3)
We believed it to be <u>her, him, them</u>. *NOT* <u>she, he, they</u>.	(3)
Between you and <u>me</u>. *NOT* between you and <u>I.</u>	(5)
She is taller than <u>I,</u> (am). *NOT* she is taller than <u>me.</u>	(1)
It was known to be <u>he</u>. *NOT* <u>him</u>. He agrees with "It."	(3)
We were sure of its being <u>him</u>. (Usage divided.)	(3,5)
Let everybody bring <u>his own</u> lunch. *NOT* <u>their own</u>.	(14,17,24)
We should all bring <u>our</u> lunches. (Action concerted.)	(17)
Every boy and girl should do his best. <u>Their</u> would be incorrect.	
<u>His</u> or <u>her</u> is correct, for formal,	(17)
Each of us <u>has his</u> problems. *NOT* <u>have their.</u>	(20)
The actor <u>whom</u> you saw was Otis Skinner. *NOT* <u>who.</u>	(2)
<u>Whom</u> did you call for? *NOT* <u>who.</u>	(5)
<u>Whom</u> did you select? *NOT* <u>who.</u>	(2)
<u>Who</u> do you suppose it is? <u>Who</u> agrees with <u>it.</u>	(3)
<u>Who</u> do you think I am? *NOT* whom. Agrees with <u>I.</u>	(3)
<u>Whom</u> did you take me to be? <u>Whom</u> agrees with <u>me</u>.	(3)
The tree looks <u>beautiful</u>. *NOT* beautifully.	(33)
The apple tastes <u>good.</u> *NOT* <u>well.</u>	(33)
The tune sounds <u>harsh.</u>	(33)
Roses smell <u>sweet.</u> *NOT* <u>sweetly.</u>	(33)
She looks <u>charming</u>. *NOT* <u>charmingly.</u>	(33)
We <u>shall</u> be drowned if we go there. NOT <u>we will be</u>	(34)
I <u>shall</u> be pleased to help you. *NOT* <u>will</u> be.	(34)
The senate has adjourned. *NOT* <u>have</u> adjourned.	(14)
There <u>are</u> all sorts of graft in town. *NOT* there <u>is</u> all sorts.	(18)
Here <u>are</u> wealth and beauty. *NOT* here <u>is</u>. (Unless taken separately.)	(18)
Neither of the men shows signs of giving in. *NOT* neither show.	(18)
In both cases, there <u>are</u> bad birth and misfortune. *NOT* there is. (Unless taken separately.)	(18)
Our class poet <u>believes</u> in symbolism. *NOT* <u>believe.</u>	(18)

He is one of the best actors that have ever been here. NOT has. (17,18)
Let him who will, come. NOT let he. (2)
The congregation were free to express their opinions, OR was free to
 express its opinions. (14)
I saw. NOT I seen. (36)
I did. NOT I done. (36)
We have gone. NOT have went. (36)
We were. NOT we was. (18)
You began it. NOT you begun it. (36)
The wind blew. NOT the wind blowed. (36)
The glass is broken. NOT broke. (37)
I caught, have caught. NOT catched, have catched. (36)
Have been chosen. NOT have been chose. (37)
We came along. NOT we come. (36)
We have come. NOT have came. (36)
The-baby crept. NOT creeped. (36)
You've done it. NOT you've did it. (36)
We drew. NOT we drawed. (36)
He has drunk a glassful. NOT has drank (36)
Have driven. NOT have drove. (36)
Have eaten. NOT have ate. (36)
I ate my dinner. NOT eat (36)
Eas fallen. NOT has fell. (36)
The boys fought. NOT fit. (36)
Has flown, NOT has flew. (36)
I've forgotten. NOT forgot. (36)
It grew. NOT it growed. (36)
You lie low. NOT lay low. (Lie, to recline; lay, to put down.) (36)
Have ridden. NOT have rode. (36)
We rang the bell. NOT we rung it. (36)
Had risen. NOT had rose. (36)
And then I ran away. NOT then I run away. (36)
Ve sang a song. NOT we sung it. (36)
Troubles sprang up. NOT troubles sprung up. (36)
Somebody has stolen my hat. NOT has stole. (36)
The place stunk. NOT stank. (36)
We swam a mile. NOT we swum. (36)
Who's taken my hat? NOT who's took? (36)
Have torn. .NOT have tore. (36)
Have written. NOT have wrote. (36)
Say it slowly. NOT slow. (35)
We can do that as easily as you please. NOT as easy. (35)
The horse threw my brother and me out. NOT my brother and I. (2)
We chose the foreman who we thought could handle the men. NOW whom. (1)
I never saw a taller man than he. NOT him. (1)
There isn't another girl in town so handsome as she. NOT her. (1)
MOSSES FROM AN OLD MANSE is a collection of essays and stories.
 NOT are a collection. (14)
Now skate without my helping you. NOT me helping. (38)
We ought to keep still about his being here. NOT him being. (38)

FIGURES OF SPEECH

Figures of speech are used to make language more effective. The common figures are *metaphor, simile, allegory, personification, apostrophe, metonymy, euphemism, hyperbole, antithesis, irony, climax, onomatopoeia,* and *alliteration.*

Metaphor and Simile are figures based on resemblance; metaphor implies the comparison, while simile expresses it, usually by either *like* or *as.*

Metaphor:

"Hearty and hale was he, an oak that is covered with snowflakes."

Simile:

"Lightsome as a locust leaf,
 Sir Launfal flashed forth in his unscarred mail."

"The gentlemen choristers have evidently been chosen, like old Cremona fiddles, more for tone than looks."

Allegory is a prolonged metaphor used to teach some abstract truth by the use of symbols. Examples: Bunyan's PILGRIM'S PROGRESS; Spenser's FAERIE QUEENE; Psalm lxxx., in which the "vine" stands for the people of Israel.

Personification attributes life to inanimate objects. When the object is directly addressed, the figure is called Apostrophe.

Personification:

"The little brook heard it and built a roof
'Neath which he could house him, winter proof."

Apostrophe:

"But, O Grief, where hast thou led me!"

Metonomy is the substitution of one name for another which it suggests. Examples:

"She keeps a good table."
"The pen is mightier than the sword."

Euphemism is a softened way of expressing an unpleasant thought.

Direct: He is a liar.
Euphemistic: He is purposely inaccurate in his statements.
Hyperbole is effective exaggeration.

"her eye in heaven
Would through the airy region stream so bright,
That birds would sing and think it were not night."

"her eye in heaven
Would through the airy region stream so bright,
That birds would sing and think it were not night."

Antithesis is a contrast of words or thoughts. Examples:

"Better be first, he said, in a little Iberian village
 Than be second in Rome."

"Fools rush in where angels fear to tread."

Irony is hidden satire.

"'Tis pretty, sure, and very probable,
 That eyes, that are the frail'st and softest things,
 Should be called tyrants, butchers, murderers."

Climax states a series of thoughts in the order of their importance, the most important last. A reversal of this order is sometimes used for humorous effect and is called Anti-climax.

Examples of Climax:

"It is an outrage to bind a Roman citizen; to scourge him is an atrocious crime; to put him to death is almost parricide; but to crucify him—what shall I call it?"

Onomatopœia emphasizes the meaning of adapting the sound to the sense. Example from CATARACT OF LODORE:

"And sounding and bounding and rounding,
 And bubbling and troubling and doubling,
 And grumbling and rumbling and tumbling,
 And clattering and battering and shattering."

Alliteration repeats the same sound in successive words. Examples:

"Silently out of the room there glided the glistening savage,
 Bearing the serpent's skin and seeming himself like a serpent,
  Winding his sinous way in the dark to the depths of the forest."

www.ingramcontent.com/pod-product-compliance
Lightning Source LLC
Chambersburg PA
CBHW082034300426
44117CB00015B/2479